WALKING THE WOLDS

Settrington Beck as it flows through Settrington village

WALKING THE WOLDS

by
Charlie Emett

CICERONE PRESS
MILNTHORPE, CUMBRIA

For
Bill Bamlett and Ron Dodsworth
because together, down the years, we have
walked the length and breadth of
Northern England and solved all the
problems in the world.

ACKNOWLEDGEMENTS

So many lovely people, whose names I never knew, opened their hearts and
stirred their memories in search of interesting snippets of material for the
book. I just hope the finished product lives up to their expectations of it.
Thank you, kind Wolds folk, you really are a smashing lot.

To Bill Bamlett, who navigated brilliantly, and Ron Dodsworth, who
drew the maps and line illustrations, my very special thanks. Having great
walking companions like Bill, Ron and Ruth is an awful lot of fun; so if I
sound replete with pleasure, well, I am.

The help received from Darlington and Beverley Public Libraries,
Durham County Library, York Minister Library and Nottingham University
Library is very much appreciated.

Unstinted help and encouragement from Mr G.Roberts, C.Eng. F.I.C.E.
F.I.H.T., Director, Technical Services Dept., Humberside County Council,
deserves and gets my sincere thanks. Many thanks also go to the East
Yorkshire Borough of Beverley Planning Dept, Hull Archaeological Museum,
Hull University History Dept, Humberside Archaeological Unit, York
Archaeological Trust, the Northern Shire Horse Centre and the vicar and
residents of Newbold.

Sincere thanks, also, to Sir Robert Storey, Settrington House and to Miss
M.Milner, Wharram-le-Street post office.

Many thanks, also, to my wife. She keeps letting me out, hopefully, yet
never complains when I come back and start writing. She deserves a medal.

Once again Barbara Barker has had the unenviable task of converting my
hand-writing into typescript and has made an excellent job of it: to her go
many thanks.

If I have omitted anyone it is unintentional and I apologise.

Charlie Emett 1993

CONTENTS

Advice to Readers

Readers are advised that whilst every effort is taken by the author to ensure the accuracy of this guidebook, changes can occur which may affect the contents. It is advisable to check locally on transport, accommodation, shops etc but even rights-of-way can be altered and, more especially overseas, paths can be eradicated by landslip, forest fires or changes of ownership.

The publisher would welcome notes of any such changes

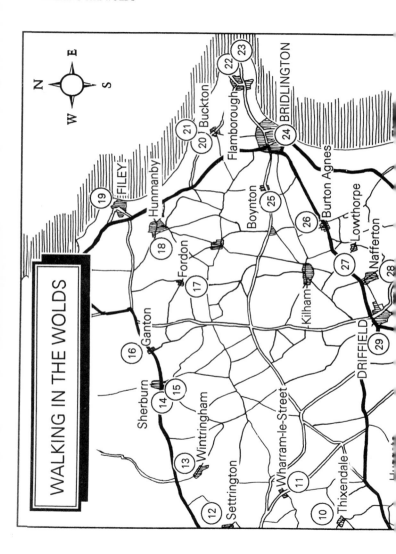

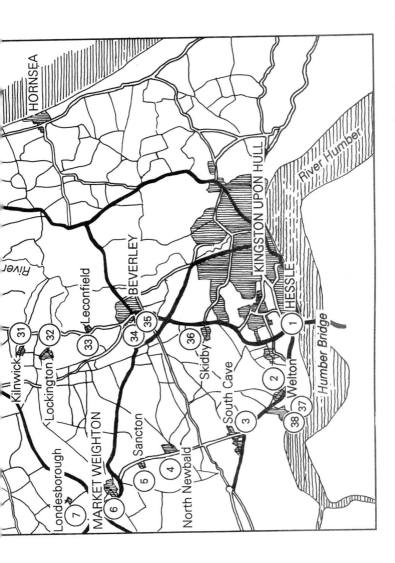

9

INTRODUCTION

The Yorkshire Wolds are not very high, averaging only 500 feet, the highest point being the top of Garrowby Hill which, at 807 feet, is just two feet higher than the highest point in Kent and not as high as the highest point in Sussex, which is 918 feet. The scenery is neither majestic nor specious. The strength of the Wolds lies in the underlying chalk, for from this bedrock stems its gentleness and boundless charm. Severe contrasts are rare in this peaceful landscape, where the great appeal is the subtleness of the harmonies. The whole of the Wolds is ideal walking country, a cornucopia of hidden delights. The hills are gentle, the dales tranquil, picturesque villages and attractive farmsteads abound, and there is a freshness about this uncluttered, open, sometimes windswept land that cheers, uplifts and makes you feel good just to be there.

Most of the 38 walks presented here are circular and collectively total 353 miles. Each is complete within itself and has much to offer; but when used as a link in a captivating chain that weaves over wold and dale, joining spectacular coastal scenery to the gentle, rolling, inland chalk downs, the whole evolves into something extra special.

Prehistoric man preferred the slightly higher ground of the Wolds to the swampy, forest clad surrounding lowlands, was quick to colonise the area, and left behind an abundance of ancient dykes and earthworks. Other remains - barrows, pottery and implements - found there stem from Iron Age and Bronze Age man. When the Romans arrived, they built forts and roads; and after them the Anglo-Saxons settled and brought about general agricultural improvements. Then came the Danes, initially to rape and pillage, but they took a liking to the climate and decided to stay. The Normans, during the "harrying to the north", were responsible for a reduction in the Wolds' population, a trend further influenced by the Black Death and, later, by the change in farming from arable to sheep production. The eighteenth century saw a gradual enclosure of the Wolds, transforming the vast, open sheep walks, with small settlements into an enclosed field system with hedgerows, wide lanes, scattered farmsteads, and the building of large houses with their "estate" villages, churches and woodland areas.

Today all that remains is a rich agricultural area in an attractive, peaceful setting, the distant past of the villages reflected in their names. Those ending in "ton", "ham" and "ing" mark various stages of Anglo-Saxon settlement, those ending in "by" and "thorpe" identify Danish settlement. Change in the

Wolds is more gradual these days, and certainly not as dramatic as in other parts of the country. Local gentry live in fine halls and some own complete villages and the odd pub; all of which means that the future of the Wolds is in good hands. For not only is the structure of local authority there, it is in the hands of people whose roots go deep into Wolds history and whose concern for the land is genuine. Sheep are still reared on the higher Wolds or in the steep dales and wheat and barley are the main crops.

Some of the most distinctive flora and fauna in Britain are found on chalk land and the well-drained, calcium-rich soils of the Yorkshire Wolds are rich in lime loving flowers like poppies, harebells, buttercups and cowslips, which, in turn, attract colourful butterflies. Chaffinches feeding on thistle seeds, wrens nestling among uncultivated grasses, kestrels hovering above a yellow field in a sky of blue, a silent owl on a twilight hunt, weasels, stoats, rabbits and hares, all common enough in themselves, breathe life into the rich tapestry of the Wolds countryside: a countryside made even more eximious because of its historic associations, making the Yorkshire Wolds a delight to explore, especially on foot. Gentle hills, hidden valleys, unspoilt villages await you; and the people who live there, the "Waudsmen", are the politest of people, thoroughly gentle and civilized. It is a pleasure just to be in their company. So walk the Wolds, take your fill of its joyous atmosphere and you will discover that, like the scents of a late summer night, the memory of it will be sweet and evocative.

The church at Wetton, seen across the stream

CHAPTER I
HESSLE TO SOUTH CAVE

Length of section:	linear 13¹/₄ miles (21.2km)
	Distance covered walking clockwise from Hessle: 13¹/₄ miles (21.2km)
Walk 1:	Hessle - North Ferriby - Welton - Brough linear 9¹/₄ miles (14.8km)
Walk 2:	Welton - Brantingham - South Cave linear 6³/₄ miles (10.8km)
Map Ref:	Landranger 106 and 107
Parking:	Humber Bridge car park, Hessle.
	Roadside parking in Welton but check with the residents first.

Handy hostelries: Ferry Boat Inn, County Park Inn, Hessle. The Green
                     Dragon, Welton. The Buccaneer, Brough. The Bear
                     Inn, The Fox And Coney, South Cave.

WALK 1. HESSLE - NORTH FERRIBY - WELTON - BROUGH.

From the Ferry Boat Inn at Hessle[1] cross the road and keep straight ahead,
edging Hessle Haven[2], to the River Humber where continue right, along the
river bank[3] on a very clear path towards the huge structure of the Humber
Bridge[4]. Soon a very useful parking area is passed close to the bridge which
is convenient if you are arriving by car to do the walk. Go underneath the
bridge and keep straight ahead soon to go through a wicket and past a Wolds
Way sign towards the Country Park Inn. Pass in front of the inn and continue
along the shore line on an unsurfaced track between trees in Hessle Wood.
It is very shady along here with lots of dog roses.

The tall chimneys ahead belong to Capper Pass Smelting Works.

As progress is made along the Humber's edge, the spire of North Ferriby
church can be seen straight ahead.

A lot of debris left by high tides is passed as you walk along the bank of
the Humber[5]. After a while a point is reached beyond which the foreshore
has been strengthened with huge boulders and it really is a superb job. The
pathway continues along the top of this strenghtened section and soon a fence
crosses your line of walk. Go through a gap in the middle of it and continue
straight ahead along a very broad, unsurfaced track. Soon bear left, away
from this track, along a clear path that hugs the edge of the river, eventually
becoming a grassy track. On approaching North Ferriby[6] a Disabled Riders
Association stable, complete with paddocks, is edged on the right. How good
it is to come across such establishments!

Once past it, do not turn right at a signpost. Instead, descend some
roughly hewn steps on your left to the foreshore[7] and turn right along it,
close to a boulder barrier on your right, passing a Wolds Way signpost. Just
past the boulder barrier turn right, up some wooden steps.

At the point where steps were descended to gain access to the foreshore
there is a car park on the right and this is the original start of the Wolds Way.
It is also the start of an alternative route to be used should the foreshore be
impassable because of high tides. Here are the route directions for this
alternative route. Turn right, go past the car park, along a road, over a railway
bridge and straight ahead, through North Ferriby, until High Street is
reached. Turn left, along High Street which continues as Walton Road to join

13

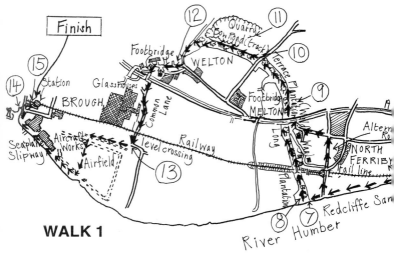

WALK 1

the A63 T, which is where the main route is rejoined.

Where the main route leaves the foreshore up the wooden steps just past the boulder barrier, turn left from the top of these steps, directed by a Wolds Way sign, along a path that goes through Long Plantation[8], at first edging the Humber briefly, then, at another footpath sign, turning right to cut through the middle of this long, thin wood, leaving the river behind. Soon the path crosses a railway on a bridge and keeps straight ahead, leaving the wood at the A63 T. Turn right, directed by a Wolds Way sign, edging this fast motorway until the far end of a rail barrier is reached at a point where the main route and alternative meet and embrace. Ah! At this point turn left to cross the road, taking great care because it is a busy one, and at the other side of it go left for a few yards to a Wolds Way sign where turn right, over a stile into a wood.

Prior to crossing the A63 T, should you find that it is really busy with traffic speeding past in both directions, go left, ignoring the Wolds Way direction to the right, to a nearby footbridge, cross the road on that and turn right along the verge to the above mentioned Wolds Way sign where turn left into the wood. It is better to be safe than sorry.

Once in the wood[9] which is long and slender like the one you have just left and is, in fact, a continuation of it, continue through it along a steadily climbing path. On reaching an unsurfaced, private road, cross it diagonally and continue along a clear path in the same direction, guided by a waymarker.

14

On reaching a waymarked stile, cross it and continue ahead along what has now become a broad track that leads to the end of the wood, which leave over a stile to the left of a gate. Cross a road diagonally right[10] and go through a kissing gate to the left of a large gate, directed by a Wolds Way sign. A large plant is on your right[11].

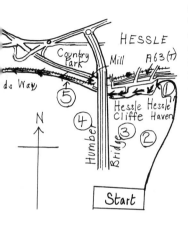

Follow a broad, unsurfaced, climbing track up the middle of a very wide lane with, over on the left, a good view of the Humber. As the ascent becomes less steep, turn left at a Wolds Way sign, over a stile, into woodland. Continue along a clear path that soon curves right and wanders very pleasantly just inside the wood's edge.

To the left the view of the curving Humber is really beautiful. The river dominates the whole of the middle distance and is absolutely superb.

The way ahead coincides with the Beverley 20s Walk and it is Beverley 20s waymarkers that are followed at this point. After some distance, where the path splits, take the right-hand one to join, in a few yards, a surfaced road at an angle and continue along it, descending to enter the village of Welton[12], which is an absolute delight. A beautiful stream flows through the middle of it and waddling along it was a proud female mallard fussing over thirteen - yes, a baker's dozen - little ducklings, when we passed. What a lovely, lovely sight! The stream widens alongside the church into a pond with a tree on a small island in the middle of it. The pond is edged with willows and spangled with mallard.

The next section begins in Welton but this linear continues for a further 3¼ miles to Brough. The distance so far walked along the Wolds Way is 6 miles.

Continue through the village, past the pond, soon to pass the Green Dragon on the left and when the road curves right, go straight ahead to cross the A63 T on a footbridge. Continue along a surfaced path, parallel to the motorway on your left and turn right at the end of it, passing Humber Growers on the left. Continue straight ahead along a pavement, down

Common Lane.

This is a land of greenhouses wherein plants are counted by the thousand. the land they cover is measured by the acre.

Cross the railway at a level crossing and continue along the road between fields of corn polka-dotted with poppies.

Everyone smiles around here, even passing motorists. The area has that effect on people.

Where the road curves left, turn right, along a clear farm track, edging a field of wheat. The path crosses the concrete entrance to Brough airfield[13] and continues as a green track, straight ahead, passing a wartime pill box on the left. The airfield is on the left and ahead are the airfield buildings. On reaching the wind sleeve on the edge of the airfield turn left, over a bridleway stile, and go straight across the airfield towards the Humber, crossing the perimeter track and then the main runway.

With the likelihood of aircraft taking off and landing, do not dawdle on the runways and remember to amend your road drill to read "Look right, left, right again and up above".

Soon after crossing the main runway a grassy runway is reached just beyond a sign which says "Caution: Active Runway Ahead". So repeat the amended road drill and, if all is clear, hurry across and continue along a grassy track to exit over a bridleway stile. It is low set and wide enough for a horse to jump over. Climb a little embankment to its flat top and immediately turn right, over a footbridge alongside a bed of reeds on the left which is filled with life. The Humber hereabouts is home to many sea birds and waders.

Continue along the embankment and soon the Brough aircraft works is passed on the right, while Brough Sand, a large sandbank in mid-Humber, is passed on the left. On reaching an inlet that contains a marina just beyond the aircraft factory, the riverside path turns right, along the inlet. Where the path ends, cross a stile onto a road[14] and continue along it. At the road end turn left along a road which almost at once curves right. Using a footpath, continue along it and when the footpath ends keep ahead. Just before the road bridges the railway, turn right along a road leading to Brough station. Just past a row of houses on the left, turn left at a sign directing to the station. On reaching it, cross the footbridge over the track and head for the booking office where this most interesting first section of a fabulous walk ends.

The return journey to Hessle, two stops away, will give you time to reflect on the pleasant scenery and the lovely, warm hearted people met on the way; and, perhaps, bring a deep, contented sigh.

Things Seen On The Way

(1) Hessle. An ancient town sited on the north bank of the River Humber and in imminent danger of being swallowed by Kingston-upon-Hull, Hessle dates from Anglo-Saxon times when it was the meeting place of the Saxon Hundred. Many of the old alleys leading from its main streets hold memories of an older township and recall its agricultural past. Ancient names like Southfield, Swinegate and Hesslewood live on in the modern centre. Originally the area where Hessle stands was a vast expanse of forest. The town developed between woods called Hesslewood and the salt marches which there spread eastwards to the River Hull.

The Romans destroyed most of the original woodland and when they left England circa AD 420 the area was occupied by various Saxon tribes, Ella being the last invader. He landed his troops along the Humber below Hessle in AD 560.

Dru de Beverver was given 100 acres of tillage at Hessle by William the Conqueror and a church was recorded there in the Domesday Book. When it was completely rebuilt during the King Stephen's reign, two Anglican coffins found near the church tower confirmed that this was the site of an earlier church, slightly further west, probably the Anglo-Saxon one mentioned in the Domesday Book. The present church was built between 1234 and 1240 by Joan de Wake in memory of her husband Hugh, who owned Hessle. Joan's seal was a woman on horseback riding side saddle and it was she, not Anne, Queen of Richard II, who started this custom which took some time to catch on.

In medieval times the ecclesiastical Parish of Hessle included the town and lands between Hessle Creek and the River Hull. All Saints Church in Hessle, therefore, was the mother church of Holy Trinity, Hull, for 350 years, until separated by Act of Parliament in 1661. Until 1301 the dead were brought from Hull via the Humber Bank to Hessle for burial. All Saints Church is the oldest surviving building in Hessle.

(2) Hessle Haven. The last remaining large shipyard on the Humber is at Hessle Haven, where many of the Humber's distinctive flat-bottomed keel-boats were built as recently as the early part of this century.

(3) Hessle Cliff. Here the Wolds' chalk ends; and here it was extensively quarried for the manufacture of whiting or whitewash, a traditional decoration. Five sailed Hessle windmill, which was used for grinding the chalk, was one of three mills in the area.

Shipbuilding was carried out at Hessle Cliff. In 1693, an eighty gun man-of-war was built here and shipbuilding is still alive today.

(4) The Humber Bridge. The northern access to the world famous Humber

17

Bridge is in Hessle. The bridge, one of the modern wonders of the world and the longest single span bridge on earth is Hessle's pride and joy.

The Humber which, with its tributaries, drains a fifth of England, is one of the largest estuaries in the country and a major commercial waterway. The Humber Bridge is the brightest jewel in its crown.

(5) The Humber's Northern Bank. Ever since it was opened on 2nd July 1840, the Hull to Selby railway line has kept close the northern bank of the Humber, on and off, almost to Broomfleet. An embankment carries it high enough above the foreshore to escape the severe south-westerly storms that sometimes make the riverside path impassable.

Red valerian grows in profusion along the embankment which, during spring and summer, houses a good number of shrews and voles, a fact not overlooked by hovering kestrels.

Freight, usually quarry materials, fertilizers and timbers, is carried on barges that still ply the estuary to and from the smaller wharfs of the Ouse and the Trent while larger, Goole bound vessels, usually car transporters, sail the Humber close to its northern bank. Before the building of the Humber Bridge, the river's navigable channel was on the southern side. Then a pier was built to take the south bank tower of the bridge and the bridge buttress diverted the water to the north side. This was an unexpected bonus to the seamen because the new, northern channel cut the distance between Hull and Goole by two kilometres, thus providing a saving in sailing time of six or seven minutes, time in which to sink an extra pint.

For many centuries the River Humber served as a boundary between tribal and political areas. During their invasions of Britain, the Romans used the Humber as a frontier against the northern tribes but subsequently established the *Transitus Maximus* of Great Ferry between Winteringham and Petuaria, today's Brough, linking the Roman roads from Lincoln and York.

A ferry boat ran across the Humber between Hull and New Holland until the opening of the Humber Bridge in 1981. The last steam-powered paddle boat, the Lincoln Castle, which first began to operate the route in 1940 was retired in March 1978, with boiler failure. The £10,000 required to make her ferry worthy again was considered to be a bad investment, especially with the new bridge's opening not far distant. She is now in honourable retirement, serving as a bar-restaurant for those romantic souls with sand in their shoes and distant, enchanted places in their heads.

The traditional means of conveying bulk goods cargoes like coal and grain up and down the river was by Humber Keel, a flat bottomed craft with square rig. Only one, *Comrade,* remains. The Humber sloop, like the

Humber Keel, is flat bottomed but its rig is fore-and-aft. Only one of these, *Amy Howson*, remains. Both are operated by the Humber Keel and Sloop Preservation Society.

(6) North Ferriby. Pleasantly sited where the wooded slopes of the Wolds slide gently into muddy waters, North Ferriby is the reputed northern landing place of the ferry the Romans used to cross the Humber, almost three miles wide at this point.

Circa AD 1200 Lord Eustace de Vesci founded a Priory of Knights of St John at North Ferriby. This Priory of Knights Templars, fighting monks, was taken over by the Canons of St Augustine until 1536, when they were suppressed.

Like North Ferriby, South Ferriby, on the river's south bank, has a smelting works. But it lies in South Humberside, once part of Lincolnshire, the land of the Yellow Bellies, and the burghers of North Ferriby are delighted that the Humber lies between them.

(7) North Ferriby foreshore. It was along this stretch of foreshore that, in 1937, two brothers saw some odd, wooden structures protruding from the mud. More similar waterlogged remains were found in 1940 and in 1946 excavations revealed that they were part of three of the earliest European plank-built boats ever discovered. The planks were of bevelled oak, sewn together with yew withies and caulked with moss. Carbon dating placed them in the late Bronze Age and this meant that as early as 890-590 BC the Humber was used as a navigable waterway.

Once in every four weeks, when there is a spring tide, the foreshore fronting North Ferriby is liable to flooding; when this happens, the alternative route through the village should be used.

(8) Long Plantation. This long, narrow wood, mainly of sycamore, shelters North Ferriby from the prevailing westerly wind and screens Capper Pass Chimney.

(9) Terrace Plantation. The path climbing through Terrace Plantation provides a gentle introduction to the Wolds hillside.

(10) Swanland. Despite recent development, Swanland retains its old world charm. Its pond is said to be the largest of its kind in Yorkshire.

(11) Melton Bottom Quarry. This is the largest chalk quarry in the Wolds.

(12) Welton. Picturesque Welton includes the townships of Welton, Melton and Wauldby and behind its fine houses, quaint cottages, village green and delightful millpond lies a fascinating past.

In the late eighteenth and early nineteenth centuries Welton and Melton villages were very popular residential areas for Hull's wealthy merchant classes and several handsome houses were built there at this time. The coming of the railways, which after 1830 gradually began to change the aspect of many East Riding villages, had no affect on these two villages. This was because Robert Raikes, the principal local landowner in the 1830s, objected to the Hull to Selby railway line passing through his estate.

Without a railway station Welton and Melton remained off the beaten track until the late 1920s when the Boothferry Bridge was constructed and the road system between Hull and the Bridge was improved.

There has been a church in the middle of Welton since Saxon times. In the eleventh century its south side was partially destroyed during a quarrel between the Bishop of Durham and King William II, William Rufus. Bishop Flambard began restoration work shortly afterwards and further rebuilding took place during the thirteenth and fifteenth centuries. In 1862-3, Miss Sophia Broadley, a local landowner, paid for the church to be restored by Sir George Gilbert Scott. She is commemorated by a cross inside the church.

The notorious Dick Turpin settled at Welton posing as a gentleman horse dealer, selling horses which he stole from neighbouring farmers. His evil temper got the better of him one day when, on returning from a shoot, drunk, he shot a neighbour's prize cockerel. When apprehended he called himself John Palmer, put the blame on a fellow fellon and threatened to murder him. Subsequently he was arrested at the Green Dragon, then called the Green Man. He tried to escape by leaping from a window but was unsuccessful. During the course of their enquiries, the police gained evidence of his horse stealing, his smuggling, poaching and other felonious activities. He was transferred, under guard, to York Castle where, on Saturday 7th April 1739, he was hanged.

(13) British Aerospace. In 1916 the Blackburn Aeroplane and Motor Company built a base at Brough for testing seaplanes. During World War II, warplanes like the Blackburn Skua were built there and, more recently, the Buccaneer. The factory is now part of British Aerospace and very much involved with the development and production of our latest fighters including vertical take-off Harriers.

(14) Brough. This road is part of Brough, which is part of the parish of Elloughton, the sleepy centre of which belies the importance of Brough in today's high tech world.

In 1887 workmen digging in a gravel pit on Mill Hill, to the north of Elloughton, found a mammoth's tusk measuring eight feet in length and eighteen inches around its thickest part. Unfortunately the tusk was broken in the attempt to remove it from the pit. Later, another tusk was found, more than five feet long, and this time the workmen successfully lifted it from the pit intact. The tusk is now in a museum in Scarborough. Five skeletons were also found in the pit in later years.

The castellated Gothic style dwelling on the slopes of Mill Hill, Castle House, was built in 1886 by W.D.Lyon.

An older house, Elloughton, was built in 1790 of stone and hand-made bricks.

Probably the oldest house in the village is Church Farmhouse, originally known as Glebe House. It dates from the sixteenth century and has eighteenth-century alterations.

WALK 2. WELTON - BRANTINGHAM - SOUTH CAVE.

From the front of Welton Hall[1] turn left, along Dale Road, between beautiful properties[2]. On leaving the village go past a public footpath sign and through a kissing gate to the left of the main gate. Here a notice informs: "Welton Dale[3]. Forestry, Game and Conservation: Please keep to the Footpath. Dogs on a Leash". Continue along this typical Wolds valley, the steep left side of which is wooded while a sprinkle of scrub covers the other one. Soon a waymarked stile at a gate is reached, which cross. Continue, now with forestry on both sides[4], along a path that cuts through the trees and exits the wood at a stile onto a concrete lane, which cross to a facing stile. Climb it and turn right along the edge of a field, directed by a Wolds Way sign. The path edges woodland for a while to another Wolds Way sign where turn left. The wood is a thin one and you soon leave it along the left-hand side of a large field of barley.

There is now a plantation on the left, shortly beyond which Wauldby Manor Farm[5] is passed, also on the left. As a pond is passed on the left, leave the field and turn left, directed by a Wolds Way sign. In a short distance, on approaching a farm house a little ahead on the right, turn right at another Wolds Way sign. Continue straight ahead along a broad, green track which meanders a bit, then turns right at a yellow waymarker. You simply cannot go wrong here.

On reaching a crossing of tracks, take the left-hand one, guided by a Wolds Way sign, and after about 3/4 mile, at the end of a pleasant lane, cross a minor road and continue along another minor road met end on[6]. When this road turns left continue ahead, along an unsurfaced lane, guided by a Wolds Way sign. The lane is very broad and may have been a drove road. There is a wood, Long Plantation, on your left and a field which when I did the walk was planted with peas on the right that must be half a mile square. Continue, crossing Brantingham Wold, with the Vale of York spread out in front of you and distant Drax power station seen ahead.

21

WALK 2

Eventually the broad lane meets a surfaced road and South Wold Farm is passed on the left. Continue down hill towards Brantingham village[7] and turn right at a signpost partly hidden by tall beech trees. Cross a waymarked stile and descend the field ahead diagonally left along a clear, green track which descends to another stile near the field's right-hand corner.

Further to the right is isolated Brantingham church[8].

Once over the stile, turn right at a Wolds Way sign, continue towards the church and join a surfaced road that passes to the left of it. The road goes along the bottom of a very pretty, wooded dale and when it curves right turn left, directed by a Wolds Way sign, cross a stile and continue along an unsurfaced lane, through woods. The way ahead soon becomes a smooth, green path that climbs gently along the valley bottom. Soon the path begins to climb steeper to leave the wood over a stile into a field.

Go straight ahead and descend to Woodale Farm, soon seen below. On approaching the gate to the farm buildings bear right, directed by a Wolds Way sign, and cross a stile to the right of the gate ahead. Keep straight ahead, through a wooded area on a clear path which descends into a dry valley.

Immediately, climb the valley's far side, guided by a yellow arrow on a tree, bearing diagonally right, up the steep hillside, to be further guided by another yellow arrow, this one on a telegraph pole half way up it. Cross a waymarked stile in the fence on your right close to the crown of the hill and keep on, through wooded undergrowth, on a clear path, contouring at first, then climbing steadily. Cross a facing stile and continue on this clear path, which soon levels out, along the left-hand edge of a long, narrow wood, soon to reach a house on the left. Here the path turns sharp right, directed by a public footpath sign, and goes straight through a very slim wood before turning left, along the left-hand edge of a field of peas and edging a long wood on the left.

Just beyond where the path passes some houses on the left, turn left, directed by a Wolds Way sign and continue past a Dutch barn on the right and some farm buildings on the left, going down hill on a surfaced farm road. Where it curves to the right, do likewise, directed by a yellow arrow. It is a lofty thoroughfare[9] and as it escapes from the wooded area South Cave is spread out below, on the left.

On reaching a public footpath sign to South Cave, ignore it and keep straight ahead, along the road. As it descends quite steeply and curves left, a Wolds Way sign directs downhill. On reaching a minor road, turn left along it, using a footpath on its left-hand side, soon to reach a crossroads with the A1074, where turn right to the Fox And Coney, smack in the middle of South Cave[10].

Because of the inordinate lengths of the alternative return routes to Welton and since the outward leg passes through one of the prettiest dry valleys in the Wolds, is lavishly endowed with broad arable fields and mixed woodland and offers fine views across the Humber estuary, I have no hesitation in simply retracing my steps. Even so, the mileage covered on this there-and-back section totals $13^{1}/_{2}$ miles (21.6km) which is just about the right distance for a good day's walking in good weather. Fully deserving, in fact, of a sup of the brown stuff at each end.

Things Seen On The Way

(1) Welton. Meaning "farm near the springs", it was so named because of the large number of springs thereabouts. Adjacent to Melton, Middle Farm was so named because it is midway between Welton and Ferriby.

The earliest archaeological finds in the parish date from the Bronze Age, 2000 BC to 600 BC, and include a triangular knife, scrapers, a plano-convex knife and a barbed arrowhead. An Iron Age settlement site dating from the first century BC was found to underlie the Romana-British Welton Wold

Villa, excavated to the north of Melton Quarry circa 1970.

Some land adjacent to both Welton and Melton was enclosed, by agreement, before the eighteenth century. Parliamentary enclosure of the remaining open fields in the parish took place in Welton in 1752 and 1772 and in Melton in 1771. The Awards enabled several roads to be diverted and provided the framework within which new building and future planting could proceed. New lanes were created and others became public highways. Lanes which had frequently been flooded by the Humber at high tide were protected by the construction of proper banks and drains.

Welton's larger houses tend to be discreetly hidden behind high walls or fences. Their size reflects the prosperity of the Hull merchants who bought estates in and around the village in the eighteenth and early nineteenth centuries. Most of the houses are of brick, an exception being Welton Grange which is brown limestone.

(2) Welton High Mill. One of the beautiful properties on your right as you walk along Dale Road is Welton High Mill. In the Domesday Book three mills are mentioned in the composite entry for Welton, Ellerker, Walkington, Hunsley and Yokefleet. Despite confusion over the location of the Domesday mills, Welton has possessed three water mills and at least one windmill in the past. Welton Low Mill, a water mill situated close to the church on Pool Beck, milled corn from the early nineteenth century until it was demolished soon after 1900. Welton High Mill survives largely intact. It is an imposing five-storey brick building housing a large water wheel almost thirty-five feet in diameter. The wheel's gearing design is a radical departure from other more traditional patterns. In 1904 a paraffin engine was installed to help supplement the water power. This was replaced at the outbreak of World War I by a gas engine. The mill ceased to operate in the 1960s.

(3) Welton Dale. This is a typical Wolds dry valley. The woodland planting was started in the early nineteenth century by Thomas Williamson who, along with his brothers Joseph and William, did so much to stamp on the landscape its pleasing, sylvan character we see today. The Williamsons were Hull merchants, very much involved with the then prosperous iron trade with Sweden. Joseph married the Squire of Welton's daughter, Ann Shaw, and built Melton Hill in 1780. Thomas, who owned Welton House, was the principal landowner. Between them, Joseph and Thomas planted extensively in what had previously been a somewhat barren landscape.

(4) The Mausoleum. Towards the north end of the wood, Welton Wold Plantation, on the left but on private land with no public access, is a domed mausoleum which was built in 1818 by the Raikes family, the last owners of Welton House.

24

(5) Wauldby Manor Farm. A fair sized hamlet once stood on this site but its old pre-enclosure houses and farm buildings were poorly made and have not survived. Today, only a little church, hidden by trees, and Wauldby Manor Farm remain.

(6) Typical wolds scenery. Here neat fields of bronzing barley, pale green wheat and darker pigmented peas, all sewn together with dark green hedgerows, dappled brown, spread like a pretty patchwork coverlet beneath a pure, cerulean sky.

(7) Brantingham village. Set in the slope of the Wolds this delightful village with its red roofs, neat gardens and trim hedges looks up a lovely Wolds valley and down to the Humber estuary. From Thorpe Hall, in the park, both Lincoln Cathedral and York Minster can be seen. It is an estate village with a pub which is not close to the church as you would expect. Almost a mile separates the two buildings.

(8) Brantingham Church. The medieval tower has Norman foundations and two of its bells were cast around the end of the fifteenth century. The south doorway is twelfth century and the font, which looks like an egg cup with four supporting shafts, is almost as old. There are some mice in the churchyard on two of the crosses. Thompson, the mouse man, put them there.

Hedge woundwort is prominent on the broad verge edging the churchyard. Its dull, purple flowers are the colour of an open wound and traditionally the plant was sometimes used as a poultice because the leaves contain an antiseptic which stops bleeding.

(9) The approach to South Cave. This is the very best cucumber growing area in the whole of Britain. On dark, winter evenings the sky hereabouts is lit with an orange glow from the cucumber greenhouses. There is a very strong link between the cucumber growers of South Cave and the Dutch growers with much interchange of information. The straight cucumbers are first class quality, those which curve slightly are seconds and those that are almost horse shoe shaped end up canned along with 56 other varieties.

(10) South Cave. Cave was an Anglian settlement named after the "swift" stream flowing from the Wolds, lengths of which are still open through the village. Traces of an Iron Age settlement have been found on the higher northern outskirts, near Love Lane.

South Cave, or South Cove as it was probably called in the old days, has been well served with road links since Roman times when it straddled Humber Street, the main road from Lincoln to York and Malton through Brough. Parts of this important link to the south are still visible. Having edged the wooded slopes of the Wolds to the north of the village it descends through it along Market Place and continues, sadly now only as a route on a map, true as the flight of an arrow. It's prosaic successor, the A1074, which bends right having crossed South Cave Beck, cannot match Humber Street for directness.

Cave is referred to several times in the Domesday survey, at which time the principal landowner was the Archbishop of York, who was succeeded by Robert Malet, Roger de Mowbray and Peter d'Eyville.

The first reference to a market at Cave was in 1156 at which time the village was known as Marcacave. In 1291 King Edward I granted it a charter, giving it town status, and further charters allowing fairs and markets were granted.

During medieval times the original market place was probably confined to the compact area between the stream and the junction of Beverley Road and Market Place, which in those days would not have been built up. It was considered important enough in 1668 for one of its tradesmen to issue his own halfpenny token. But perhaps the best guide to the growing importance of this market town, for that is what South Cave had become, was the number of inns it could support. In the mid eighteenth century there were eight or nine, a goodly number for the size of the place. In 1796 the Town Hall was built, as if to underline the town's role as an important commercial centre.

The arrival of the railway in the 1840s began to undermine South Cave's importance. The last of the corn markets ceased trading in the 1860s but the fairs survived for much longer. Within living memory it was common for the streets around the Market Place to be filled with cattle and sheep.

There were stocks in the Market Place until the late nineteenth century and a gallows once stood on Gallows Flat, to the west of the A1074 as it climbs Whiteclaypit Hill. To dwell at length on such grim associations is enough to parch the throat. But not to worry: the remedy is at hand, in the Market Place itself, in either the Fox And Coney, which was built in 1739, or The Bear Inn.

CHAPTER II
SOUTH CAVE TO SANCTON

Length of section: linear 10½ miles (16.8km)

Distance covered walking clockwise from Hessle: 23¾ miles (38km)

Walk 3:	Circular: South Cave - North Newbald - Hotham - North Cave - South Cave 12½ miles (20km)
Walk 4:	Circular: North Newbald - Houghton Moor - Sancton - Hessleskew - North Newbald 8½ miles (13.6km)
Map Ref:	Landranger 106
Parking:	Market Place, South Cave. Roadside, North Newbald but check with locals first.
Handy hostelries:	Fox And Coney and Bear Inn, South Cave. The Tiger And The Gnu, North Newbald. The Star, Sancton. The Hotham Arms, Hotham.

WALK 3. SOUTH CAVE - NORTH NEWBALD - SOUTH NEWBALD - HOTHAM - NORTH CAVE - SOUTH CAVE

From the Fox And Coney, South Cave, turn left, along the road, and take the first turning on the left, along Beverley Road. On reaching Littlewood Lane[1], turn left along it, between dwellings. It is a surfaced road through a residential area. A continuation of the road leads along The Stray. Go along it, now a surfaced lane which, with no confining hedge on the right, offers fine views across the countryside. The lane turns right, uphill, at a bridleway sign and where it curves left into a private drive, continue straight ahead, now on an unsurfaced lane from where the retrospective view down the valley to the Humber and beyond is very spectacular. Soon a Wolds Way sign[2] is passed, a short distance beyond which, where the path bifurcates, continue straight ahead along the right-hand path through Little Wold Plantation[3], which is mainly deciduous trees. At the end of the wood turn right, along an unsurfaced lane, and where it dips, turn left, guided by a Wolds Way sign and cross a stile. Continue down the side of the field ahead, close to a wire fence on your left. Where the fence ends, keep ahead, curving right[4], down hill. Soon the path continues parallel to a fence on the left for a short distance to turn left, over a stile onto the disused Hull and Barnsley Railway[5].

   Turn right along the line which curves to the left, along the dry bottom

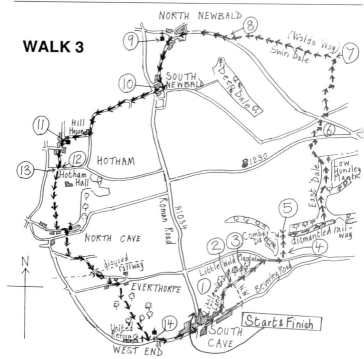

WALK 3

of a typical Wold valley. When the disused track begins to curve to the right, either go straight ahead, along a climbing track with a band of green along its middle, or continue along the track bed for a very short distance to a Wolds Way sign, where turn left, up steps to join the track you could have taken. At this point the track turns left, so do likewise, directed by a blue waymarker, straight into Low Hunsley Plantation. The way ahead is very clear and follows the bottom of a wooded, dry valley. Where it bifurcates take the left-hand track, marked Wolds Way.

After passing an area of small trees, three gigantic beech trees are passed on the right. They tower above the rest of the trees like triplet Gullivers in Lilliput.

Beyond these massive trees the track deteriorates into a path that remains very easy to follow as it continues along the bottom of wooded East Dale. Going along the dale the path climbs very gently but as the dale's head is

28

approached the ascent becomes much steeper. Where, at the head of the valley, you climb out of the wood, turn left, directed by a Wolds Way sign, edging a field of wheat.

The tall masts seen on the left, beyond the Warrens, are part of the police radio system.

The path crosses a Wold close to the remains of a hedge on the left, soon to reach a yellow waymarker on a post that confirms your route. The path curves right and is a doddle to follow. The way passes close to a trig point which gives your height as 162 metres above sea level. Soon two more yellow arrows on posts point the way. Leave the field through a gap in a facing hedge at its left-hand corner and turn right, along the B1230 directed by a Wolds Way sign. After 180 yards leave the road, left, directed by another Wolds Way sign[6] and continue down the edge of a field of wheat close to a wooden fence on your right. Exit the field and turn right, directed by a Wolds Way sign, along a quiet road. On reaching a crossroads, go straight across it, again directed by a Wolds Way sign. Continue along another quiet road and on reaching yet another Wolds Way sign, turn left along the left-hand side of a field of barley, close to a hedge on your left. At the field's end, turn right, directed by a yellow marker, still with a hedge on your left, edging the field. At the end of the field cross a stile, close to the left-hand corner and descend into a little valley, directed by a Wolds Way sign. Turn left at the valley bottom, like so many in the Wolds dry and a sheep walk, and as you descend the valley, turn left and soon, at a facing fence, cross a stile, following Wolds Way signs throughout. Immediately turn left, edging a wheat field, soon to curve right, keeping along the extent of the wheat on the valley side[7]. Ahead, another Wolds Way sign can be seen. Aim for this and, on reaching it, turn right, along a broad track that soon curves left and goes along the valley bottom. Soon a concrete dew pond is passed, beyond which a yellow waymarker confirms your route. Continue along the valley bottom, still on the broad, farm track.

Some distance before this farm road curves to the right, go diagonally left, along a clear track through wheat, aiming for a clearly seen footpath sign. Pass it and continue up the valley side, through an area of recently planted trees. The way is clear and quite steep: still, nil desperandum! Cross a waymarked stile in the right-hand corner of this vast field and continue straight ahead, close to a hedge on your right, and at the end of the field, at a footpath sign, turn right, along the road, going downhill, with North Newbald seen in front.

As the road descends, another lovely dry valley, wooded Deep Dale, stretches invitingly on the left.

The road enters North Newbald[8] along Burgate. Continue along it to the centre of the village where, facing the pleasant village green are two pubs, The Tiger and The Gnu. Bear left, between them and where the road bifurcates turn left along South Newbald Road, passing the church[9] on the right. Where the road splits again[10], go right, rounding a sharp bend, and on reaching the A1034, cross it and continue along a quiet lane to Hotham.

On the approach to the village the left-hand side of the road is edged with aspen whose windblown leaves quiver like the spangled skirts of jazz-age hoofers. What an evocative sight it is!

The road turns sharp right at Hill House and continues for a little way before skirting Hotham church[11] on the left and going through the village as Main Street.

Keep straight ahead at the road junction where the war memorial stands, ignoring the North Cave sign. At the south end of Main Street, where the road curves left at a chapel, go right, along a short lane, directed by a footpath sign. The lane leads past houses and gardens on the left to a stile. Cross this then over a field, close to a fence on your right, leaving through a kissing gate. Immediately, go over the facing road and continue, straight ahead, directed by a public footpath sign, along a surfaced road. The tower of North Cave church can be seen directly in front of you.

Where the surfaced road ends, continue forward, edging the left-hand side of a field, directed by a yellow waymarker on a post. There is some fine parkland to the left and the trees are absolutely superb! The path is clear and follows a line of trees between fields of wheat. Hotham Hall can now be seen through the trees, on the left.

Soon a plank bridge is crossed, beyond which another waymarker is passed. When the path reaches a kissing gate, go through it, into North Cave and turn left, along the road, which soon turns sharp right to pass the lodge-gate of Hotham Hall[12]. The road bridges a stream that flows from a lake on the left and reaches a T-junction just past the church on the left.

At the T-junction cross the road and go over a stile to the left of a row of houses[13]. Go straight ahead along a broad, concrete path and on reaching a cricket field turn left and edge it to the field corner where turn right and continue close to a tall hedge on your left. On reaching a facing waymarked stile in the left-hand corner of the cricket field, cross it and continue straight ahead along a lane. At the end of the lane cross a stile in a facing hedge onto a road, along which turn left, then curve right. Do not go straight ahead, along an unsurfaced lane. The road makes a long, straight climb to bridge the dismantled Hull and Barnsley railway.

As the road enters Everthorpe, turn right at the first turning down a minor road towards some buildings ahead. On reaching a facing road in front of them turn left, passing some nice dwellings on the left, soon to turn right at a footpath sign, through a kissing gate into a short field, which cross. Exit over a stile and keep straight ahead. As you go along, a waymarker confirms your route. On reaching a facing stile cross it and immediately cross a ditch on a wooden footbridge. Continue, edging a field close to a fence on the left. At the end of the field turn right, directed by a yellow marker. In a few yards turn left at a waymaker on a post, cross a plank bridge and keep straight ahead, over a field. Cross a waymarked stile in a facing hedge some 35 yards to the left of the right-hand corner. Edge the next field, close to a wooden fence on your right, exiting over a stile on your right, close to the right-hand corner. Go forward for a couple of paces and turn left, down a tarmac lane, between dwellings, entering South Cave[(14)].

At the lane end turn left and in a few yards turn right at a public footpath sign, along a little lane between houses. Cross a road and go down another lane. Keep straight ahead, along a surfaced road, passing a United Reform Church on the right. On reaching a main road turn left, along it and follow it to the crossroads in the middle of South Cave where the walk began.

Things Seen On The Way

(1) Littlewood Lane End. During the eighteenth century this was the site of a pinfold.

(2) Wolds Way sign. Little Wold Side. South Cave with its good accommodation and two pubs, is a very good stopping place for Wolds Way walkers. But for those wishing to by-pass it, the Wolds Way sign on Little Wold Side directs along its main route.

(3) Little Wold Plantation. From here the view down the valley, over the russet roofs and grey gables of South Cave, across the Humber Estuary with its shipping, to the dwarf steelworks of Scunthrope on the southern horizon is heart warming.

(4) Weedley Springs. Among the trees, a little to the left of where hidden Comber Dale meets Weedley Dale and your route curves right before reaching the disused Hull to Barnsley railway line, is Weedley Springs where the stream that flows into North Cave is born. This is as fine an example of a natural spring as you are likely to find in the Wolds; and that is a high rating, for there are a great many natural springs throughout this chalky landscape.

(5) Hull and Barnsley Railway. Of the three tunnels built to carry the Hull and Barnsley railway through the Wolds the largest was the 2,116 yards long Drewton Tunnel, now sealed. Trains going westwards through it emerged

31

into a short cutting, then went into a short tunnel; and it is just short of this one that the Wolds Way and the disused railway part company.

If, on reaching this disused line, the Wolds Way had turned left, it would have very quickly reached the third of these tunnels.

(6) High Hunsley. Just beyond the mast about ¹⁄₂ mile east of where the Wolds Way leaves the road is the site of the village of Hunsley, "the clearing belonging to the hundred", which was marked by distinct earthworks in 1852. Little of it remains today. A beacon stood on the highest ground, west of Hunsley House. In 1588 it took light from Bainton and passed it to Holme upon Spalding Moor. In the Domesday Book the Bishop of Durham was recorded as a major landowner in Hunsley village.

BBC radio programmes are transmitted to the area through the mast at High Hunsley.

(7) Swin Dale. Sheep farming and the growing of crops have been practised on the Wolds for thousands of years. For much of the Middle Ages sheep farming was its principal industry. Historically, therefore, sheep are an integral part of the Newbald scene. But it was the rabbits that, until myxomatosis knocked them for six, kept the grass land close cut. No amount of grazing by sheep is likely to eliminate the tall grasses so rampant there today, because sheep simply do not care for them. They much prefer the finer grasses and herbs.

Traditionally sowing was done with a fiddle. The arm was moved rhythmically across the body in time with the fiddler's stride and a string attached to a "bow" spun a disc which scattered the seed.

For centuries a reaping hook was used to cut the crops at haytime and harvest. One man using one of these curved bladed tools could cut a quarter of an acre of grass or barley in a day.

Ploughing or harrowing with a horse was a familiar sight in the Newbald area from the Middle Ages but especially from the eighteenth century until the tractor replaced the horse after World War II.

In the heat of a midsummer day the tall grasses on the higher sides of upper Swin Dale are sprinkled with a colourful display of wild flowers, the tall, nodding heads of field scabious, scarlet flowered bloody cranesbill and the common greater knapweed providing contrast to the yellow-wort, whose yellow flowers close like tired eyes in the early afternoon, and the Common St John's Wort, which is also yellow flowered. As its name implies, St John's Wort is associated with the Knights of St John and the Crusades and is hung around houses on St John's Eve to ward off evil spirits.

(8) Newbald. Two Danish settlements, North and South, make up Newbald, which, like other villages at the foot of the western edge of the Wolds was

Brantingham church and the Wolds Way (Walk 2) *(Bill Bamlett)*
Welton Dale, a typical Wolds valley (Walk 2) *(Ron Dodsworth)*

Entrance to South Cave castle (Walk 3) *(Ron Dodsworth)*
Huggate Wold and Dry Valley (Walk 8) *(C.L.Emett)*

established because of the presence of a water supply on the spring line where the Wolds and the Vale of York meet.

Ulph, son-in-law of King Cnut, dedicated his vast lands in Deira, which included Newbald, to the church at York in the eleventh century. His famous horn, made from an elephant's tusk and carved in Southern Italy, is kept in that city.

(9) St Nicolas's Church. North Newbald church is the most complete Norman building in the East Riding and one of the finest unspoilt Norman parish churches in England, it replaces a pre-Conquest Saxon church on the site and was built mostly in the second half of the twelfth century. It shows similarity with contemporary churches in Normandy. Built of an attractive pale grey stone taken from the same local quarry at Newbald that provided some of the stone used on Beverley Minster, St Nicholas remains primarily a rare and unspoiled example of Norman architecture. Its four lavishly carved original Norman doorways, in particular the one on the south wall of the nave, and the nave itself are exquisite. There is also a carving of the "Hound of Heaven" which is said to be the only example in the country.

(10) South Newbald Hall. Mid way along South Newbald Road, on the left, is the site of South Newbald Hall. The Hall and its estate became the new name for what had been the medieval Manor and its land. The property had always been let by the church, and in 1664 the lease was acquired by Sir Philip Monkton, whose family already had connections with the village through his grandfather. The house had been newly built earlier that century, replacing the medieval manor house; and during the seventeenth century the estate had a corn mill and a paper mill. The Monkton family had left the village by 1727 although the estate remained in their hands until the early 20th century. The Hall was demolished by the time of the Enclosure in 1783.

(11) Hotham. A plaque on a wall outside the church was placed there "to celebrate 900 years of Norman heritage. This community is recorded in the Domesday Book of 1086." What it doesn't impart is that Hotham, with its long, neat Main Street, is a traditional estate village, that it is sited on the north side of a fine park that links it to North Cave and that, rare in Humberside, many of its buildings are of local limestone. Its church has a sturdy tower and its pub, the Hotham Arms should have been named the Hotham Open Arms because of the genuine warmth of its welcome, on both sides of the bar.

(12) Hotham Hall Lodge. The following thought-provoking facts are displayed on a wall of the lodge, placed there by the late T.C.Clitherow D.S.O.

"Ypres 347 miles, In defending the salient our casualties
were 90,000 killed, 71,000 missing and 110,000 wounded."

From the lodge a long, peaceful stretch of water edges woodland, all but part of the lake's northern shore shaded by trees, among them tall chestnuts, ash and weeping willows. It is a splendid place, a haven for water fowl and other wild life, a world away from the mud of Flanders.

(13) North Cave. The Romans had a camp near North Cave and three miles to the east of it, where St Austin's Stone stands by the road to Beverley on a hillside, is a meeting place of Druids. Like its twin, South Cave, it snuggles into the Wolds foot hills. Once it was an important village on the road between Beverley and Howden, providing power for three mills, the last of which closed in the 1920s. There are many fine eighteenth- and nineteenth-century houses and cottages in North Cave and the lively stream that flows from the lake in adjoining Hotham park runs between the two main streets.

(14) South Cave: West End. Eight centuries ago a castle stood where now a Gothic style house with corner turrets and tall chimneys lords it over a lovely park with lovely grounds and a fish pond. Today it is a hotel and restaurant of local repute and it has a slender link with world history. It is thought that George Washington's great grandfather lived there for a while.

A smaller building in the south-west corner of West End was home to Teavil Leason who was the Officer In Charge of Napoleon during his captivity on St Helena.

Outside the entrance to Cave Castle, on the war memorial, beneath the names of those who made the ultimate sacrifice is carved this stinging question:

"Is it nothing to you, ye that pass by?"

Well, is it nothing to you? Because if it isn't, it should be.

WALK 4. NORTH NEWBALD - HOUGHTON MOOR - SANCTON - HESSLESKEW - NORTH NEWBALD.

From North Newbald[1] village green take the road signposted Market Weighton and at a T-junction turn right, up Galegate. Where the road curves left along Westgate, do likewise.

At a crossroads with the busy A1034, the old Roman Road, keep straight ahead, directed by a footpath sign. Continue along a quiet country road[2], passing first a small industrial estate on the right, then, after about ³/₄ mile, the entrance to Moor Farm, also on the right, beyond which there are high hedges on both sides.

As you continue along this now unsurfaced lane, another footpath sign confirms your route. Ahead is a large wood and the lane leads into it and

WALK 4

N

Houghton Hall

Beverley Lane

SANCTON

Castle Farm

Houghton Moor

The Cott

Moor Farm

minor road

Unsurfaced lane

NORTH NEWBALD

Sancton Hill

Hesslekew Gare

(Wolds Way)

Trig Point

Sober Hill

A1034

Start & Finish

continues through it, soon to pass a cottage called The Cott, on the right. The cottage is fronted by a huge copper beech. On reaching a crossing of tracks, turn right, directed by a footpath sign, along a broad, clear track, going roughly north easterly, through the middle of the wood, which is called Houghton Moor[3]. Stay on this track for about 1½ miles, ignoring any turnings left and right.

There are lots of rhododendrons and birch hereabouts, the ground cover is predominantly bracken and tall Scots Pine tower above them all.

As you walk along, a post with a yellow arrow confirms your route. After a while other prominent tracks go right but "Keep Out" signs prevent their use. Simply continue along the easy-to-follow track that curves left, soon to exit the wood over a stile. Continue straight ahead, through a field, edging a ditch on your right.

Sancton village and the church can now be seen on the right. The farm on the left is called Castle Farm. Just ahead, but hidden behind trees, is Houghton Hall.

Cross a facing stile in the right-hand corner of the field. Cross a very narrow field, leaving over another facing stile, waymarked. Continue close to the hedge on the right for a short distance and go through a gateway in a step of this hedge. Keep ahead, bearing slightly right, pulling away from what is now a fence on your left, aiming for a waymarked stile alongside a signpost. Once over the stile turn right, along a surfaced road into Sancton[4].

35

North Newbold from the village green

As the road enters the village it splits. Take the right-hand one, signposted High Street, with a roadside footpath. At a T-junction with the A1034, turn right, along it, passing a green area with trees on the left, fronted by a King Street sign. Turn left along Beverley Lane, a minor road which climbs steadily. After a mile Sancton Hall Farm[5], a clay-shooting centre, is passed on the left.

Almost a mile beyond it, where the road turns sharp left, soon to pass Hessleskew Farm[6], turn right at a Wolds Way sign, rejoining this famous walk. Continue along an unsurfaced lane, soon to pass another waymarker.

Hessleskew Gare is passed on the right; and before the lane begins to descend, a trig point, 144 metres above sea level, is passed on the left.

The lane[7] descends into a patchwork of neat, well managed fields. On reaching a minor road, turn right along it, guided by a Wolds Way sign. In a short distance ignore another Wolds Way sign directing left, down hill, and keep straight ahead, leaving the Wolds Way. The road descends quite steeply, through typical Wolds scenery, neat, tidy, clean and as fresh looking as though recently showered. It is very pleasing, indeed.

On reaching a T-junction at a slant, turn right, into North Newbald where, on reaching the pretty village green the walk is complete.

Things Seen On The Way
(1) Newbald. Today's road pattern in Newbald is almost certainly that of the Middle Ages but the only building remaining from that time is the church. The Green was probably the site of the weekly market, held every Thursday, which was granted by Royal Charter in 1348.

During the Civil War, 1643-45, Newbald was midway between a Royalist York and a Parliamentary Hull. At one point during the fighting the village was the scene of a skirmish and thirty soldiers are buried in the churchyard.

By the end of the eighteenth century new stone houses with pantiled roofs were being built both in the village and, for the first time, in the countryside. Ploughed and hedged fields were being developed in place of grassland and scrubland. So, whereas the Anglo-Scandinavian period gave Newbald its plan form, the late eighteenth century gave it its present appearance and character.

During the nineteenth century Newbald's population grew only from 661 to 731, but with the advances made in agriculture and the protection of the Corn Laws farming prospered in the middle of the nineteenth century. Newbald vicarage was built in the 1840s, other buildings in the village followed and in 1871 Manor Farm was re-built.

Pubs also flourished. At one period there were five of them in Newbald: the Rose And Crown, The Tiger, the New Inn, now called The Gnu, The Angel and the Fox And Rabbit.

The famous Wolds Waggon was introduced during the second half of the nineteenth century. It was made by Levitt's, a family business, of timber from nearby Houghton Woods. The last waggon was made circa 1923.

(2) The Stone Quarries. After agriculture, quarrying has been the longest living industry in Newbald, spanning a period of almost 1900 years. The quarries were sited on both sides of Cliffe Road, to the west of the A1034. For there lies a limestone ridge, close to the northern end of the great limestone belt that curves north-east from the Cotswolds. Quarrying first took place to the north of Cliffe Road in an area now known as The Grass Pits and was at its most prosperous during the twelfth and thirteenth centuries when many local churches, like the one at Newbald, were being built. The stone, which had hard wearing qualities, was used at Hull docks and for the sea wall at Hornsea. By the end of the seventeenth century The Grass Pits was being used to pasture sick animals and the quarrying had moved to the south side of Cliffe Road, where it ended in the 1960s.

(3) Houghton Moor. Better known as Houghton Wood, the moor is famed for its lovely rhododendrons which during the summer months bring a flush of warm colour to hidden bowers. With public rights of way running east to west and north to south through it, Houghton Wood is very popular with walkers. However, other tracks are private and out of bounds.

(4) Sancton. This small village, lying in a hollow of the steep western slope of the Wolds, has a church with an unusual octagonal tower, about the only part of the church that has not been rebuilt. The tower is fifteenth century and is one of the most beautiful on the Wolds. There are some Norman stones in its arch.

One of the largest known pagan Anglian cemeteries was excavated at Sancton in the 1950s. The surrounding fields are rich with relics of Ancient Britons, Romans, Angles and Saxons. In one grave were found the remains of an Ancient Briton with his sword and spear, his wife with her work basket and a child with its toys.

(5) Sancton Hill Farm. Sited on the south-west edge of the Wolds where they drop steeply to the Humber Estuary, Sancton Hill Farm enjoys a warmer climate than is found on the higher and more northerly parts of these chalk uplands.

Throughout the Wolds the soil is of good quality: on these south-facing slopes it is particularly good. The loam is medium to heavy with large numbers of pebbles and chalk stones giving good drainage, helped by the good drying winds that blow across the gentle hills.

(6) Hessleskew Farm. The area around Hessleskew was the site of a monastic grange.

(7) The lane on Newbald Wold. This $2^{1/4}$ miles long, straight lane was host to a rare mix of butterflies and bees when we walked it that hot, summer afternoon. Tortoiseshell were plentiful, fluttering from nettle to nettle, flower to flower, sharing erratic flight paths with green veined whites, common blues, brown arguses and orange tips. Red admirals were fewer but a no less welcome sight.

The Wolds Inn at Huggate

CHAPTER III
SANCTON TO LONDESBOROUGH

Length of section: linear 9¹/₄ miles (14.8km)

Distance covered walking clockwise from Hessle: 33 miles (52.8km)

Walk 5:	Circular: Sancton - Arras - Market Weighton - Sancton 9¹/₂ miles (15.2km)
Walk 6:	Circular: Market Weighton - Londesborough - Goodmanham - Market Weighton 8 miles (12.8km)
Map Ref:	Landranger 106
Parking:	Side street, Sancton, but check with locals first. Side street, Market Weighton, but check with locals first.
Handy hostelries:	The Star, Sancton. Hotels and pubs, Market Weighton.

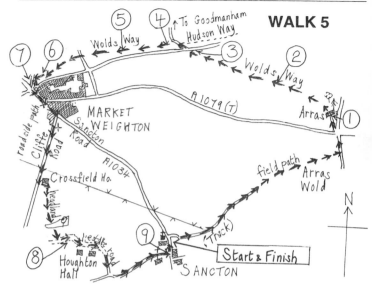

WALK 5. SANCTON - ARRAS - MARKET WEIGHTON - SANCTON.

From The Star in Sancton turn left, along the A1034, and take the first turning right, directed by a bridleway sign. Continue along a lane, which at first climbs steadily before levelling out, soon to pass another bridleway sign. Keep straight ahead, along the lane, which runs along the bottom of a dale that pushes into Sancton Wold. The right side of it, as you walk along, has been developed into a motorbike scramble circuit.

At the lane end, go through a facing gate where a yellow waymarker confirms your route. Continue along a green track until it begins to curve right, up the valley side, where stay in the valley bottom, following the line of a fence interspersed with hawthorn, on the left, soon to cross a waymarked stile in it. Immediately turn right, along a path that cuts through a patch of thistles to become a broad, very clear track which continues up the dale, climbing steadily towards Arras Wold, ahead.

As you walk along, another side valley shoots off to the left; and barley, when we passed, was bronzing the lower ground.

The chalky track separates barley and wheat on its way to the head of the dale and onto Arras Wold; and from it the all-round views are superb. It leads

40

through a broad gateway at a public footpath sign onto a minor road, where the Wolds Way is joined. Turn left, along the road and, on reaching the A1079, cross it, directed by a Wolds Way sign. Go along a surfaced road, which soon bifurcates. Take the left-hand fork, directed by a yellow waymarker, and continue along an avenue of trees to Arras Farm[1], which is also a bed and breakfast place. Keep ahead, between buildings, directed by another waymarker and beyond them turn left, directed by yet another yellow waymarker, into open country.

Bear left and continue parallel to a wood on the left. The track continues past the wood, develops a kink and zig-zags to the right to a yellow waymarker and continues alongside a hedge on the right.

Over on the right, on the horizon, towering high above the landscape, is the spire of South Dalton church.

To our right, as we passed, was a huge field of peas with, beyond that, a field of flax.

The hedge, an awfully long one, coincides with a line of telegraph poles that edges, for part of the way, a field of peas, reddened with poppies. What a wonderful sight it is! Yellow waymarkers, fixed to some of the poles, confirm the route.

At the end of the field continue along a path that edges another huge field, now with a hedge on the left. This field[2] slants away to a small dale which is called - wait for it - Small Dale. Like so many Wolds fields, this one is vast. Two crops are grown in it, wheat and peas and there are lots and lots of poppies. Continue along the edge of this field, soon to dip into Spring Dale that makes a rather dramatic entrance from the right. The disused line from Beverley to Market Weighton runs along the bottom of the dale.

At the end of the field cross a facing stile in its bottom left-hand corner and descend on the left-hand side of the next field into the dale bottom[3], leaving the field over a waymarked stile at a Wolds Way sign, onto a road. Continue down the road leading to Goodmanham, directed by a Wolds Way sign, soon to turn left, directed by a footpath sign, along the disused railway line, which here is part of the Hudson Way[4]. Climb a bank, cross a facing stile and continue along the trackbed, using the Wolds Way alternative route into Market Weighton, until the site of Market Weighton station is reached.

The route is along first a cutting, then an embankment, both of which are heavily wooded, with good ground cover, making it a good area for a rich variety of wild life[5].

At Market Weighton[6] railway station site take the footpath that leads, briefly, to a road at Aspen Close, from where go straight ahead, leaving a cul-de-sac along Hall Road. Turn left at a T-junction, along Londesborough

Road, passing The Griffin on the right and aiming for All Saints Church[7], just ahead. At the road end turn left, along York Road, going through the middle of Market Weighton. On reaching a roundabout, where stands The Red Lion, turn right, along the A1034, the York to Hull road, and on reaching Cliffe Road, where a Roman Catholic church and a fire station face each other at its end, turn right along it. Where the road reaches a dead end on reaching the town's bypass at a wooden fence, the path continues round the left of the fence and crosses the bypass at footpath signs. Continue along a footpath that turns right, briefly, then left, along a minor road.

Where the path ends, continue along this quiet road and just past a farm on the left, turn left, directed by a footpath sign. Go along an unsurfaced track until just past the farm buildings, where turn right, just beyond a prominent ash tree, into a field of peas, which edge, close to a hedge on the right. Soon the path bears left as the hedge does. On reaching a field corner, do not turn left. Keep straight ahead, directed by a yellow arrow, for 40 yards and turn right, over a ditch. Immediately turn left, edging a field of corn, and at its left-hand corner, turn right, briefly, to a yellow arrow on a post from where edge the field ahead, close to a hedge on the right. At the field corner turn right, directed by a yellow arrow, edging a wood on the right, soon to join a green track. Turn right, directed by a yellow arrow, going through the wood. On exiting, keep straight ahead, through a corn field, still on a clear track, to reach a surfaced road.

Turn left, crossing a white cattle grid and curve right, towards Houghton Hall[8], in front of which, at a junction of roads, turn left, along an unsurfaced road to a T-junction, where turn right, still on an unsurfaced road, directed by a footpath sign and a yellow arrow. At the road end turn left, along a surfaced, minor road, to return to Sancton[9] where at least one Star will be shining.

Things Seen On The Way

(1) Arras Farm. A charioteer, complete with his chariot and horses was discovered in a nearby long barrow.

(2) Pea harvest. It was in this huge field that we watched the pea crop being harvested. Huge, specialised pea harvesters, like the ones we saw, operate throughout the pea fields from June for about four or five weeks, depending on the weather and the conditions. Inside these monster machines there are double rollers between which the complete plants are pressed to separate the peas from the shells without damage to the peas. The removed shell and the stalks are spewed out of the machine; but the peas remain inside it, to be

removed by the operator at the right time. It is a 24 hours a day operation and worked to a carefully arranged tight schedule.

The time for picking the pea crop is determined literally by the man from the purchasing firm who, prior to making his vital decision makes various checks which include taking the soil temperature. The order to lift the crop can come at any time, day or night, and it is imperative that work starts at that time.

The shelled peas are loaded onto lorries and the driver has to ensure that they arrive at the factory at the time shown on his working schedule. It is all planned to the minute. The time the driver leaves the pea field is shown on the timetable and he or she must not leave before then, because to do so would be to upset the complex movement of other lorries of peas from other fields spread over a broad canvass. So he leaves at the appointed time, and has to be at the factory at the time shown on his document.

(3) Pea harvest transfer point. The shelled peas are taken to a valley bottom road side point by a tractor-pulled trailer working a shuttle service. Once the trailer is backed alongside the awaiting lorry it is hydraulically raised, then tipped to allow the peas, millions of them, to pour into the back of the vehicle for onward transportation to the Birds Eye factory at Grimsby.

The time allowed for this operation, from the picking of the peas to their arrival at the factory, is two hours. Once there, they are graded. Those late in arriving are not wasted. They reach the market place, neatly packaged, as mushy peas.

(4) Hudson Way walk. As the last Ice Age ended water from the melting ice cap formed a lake between it and the eastern side of the Wolds. The overflow from this lake wore away a valley along which water flowed, spilling into Lake Humber on what is now the Vale of York. Today this valley, one of a number of hanging valleys in the area, is, for the most part, dry, the only stream being a tiny one, Mill Beck, which starts at Springwells and flows towards Market Weighton. The valley cuts through the Wolds from east to west and the Hudson Way follows it.

(5) Nature reserve. This length of disused railway line is a nature reserve managed by the staff and pupils of Market Weighton Secondary School on behalf of Yorkshire Wild Life Trust. Here school parties are encouraged to explore and become involved with interesting projects. Trees and plants are identified, plaster casts of animal footprints are made, bird song is taped and insects living within a given area are classified. The school children are taught to observe the Country Code and to "take nothing but photographs and leave nothing but footprints".

(6) Market Weighton. The little town of Market Weighton sits in a gap of the

Wolds at a meeting point of roads from York, Selby, Beverley and Driffield. It also stood at the junction of four railway lines until Dr Beeching gave them the chop. It is thought to have been the site of the Roman Delgovitia, itself set between roads running east and west of it.

(7) All Saints Church. Standing close to the Londesborough Arms, just off the Beverley to York road, All Saints occupies the site of a Saxon church, although no part of the present building is pre-Norman. Traces of its eleventh century origins can be seen in the lower part of the tower and in the adjacent walls. The tower, which houses a peal of six bells, formerly had a wooden spire, which was removed in 1785 when the brick top was added. The tower houses a large, plain, circular font, which is Norman.

The north aisle is of Gothic Decorated style, which prevailed until the end of the fourteenth century; and when the clerestory and the south aisle were built, it was widened in the Perpendicular style. At that time the chancel was widened, putting it out of line with the nave. The chancel roof is blue and decorated with gold stars and crosses. There is a priest's doorway with a low arch in the south wall of the chancel and the arcade which separates it from the north chapel has two pointed arches.

A fine Madonna in blue glass is depicted in the lancet window in the sanctuary. Other, more modern, stained glass in the north wall of the north aisle shows St Christopher and the Archangel Michael. The son of a nineteenth-century vicar of All Saints, the Rev. Joseph Foxley, M.A., was responsible for the lovely, ebony inlaid, oak pulpit.

Sarah Andrews, wife of Francisco de Miranda, the famous South American freedom fighter, was baptised in All Saints church on 24th July 1774. She was the daughter of a Market Weighton shoemaker. Her husband later became Venezuela's first dictator; but he ended his life in a Spanish prison cell. Sarah returned to their London home where she died in 1847. She was buried in a pauper's grave. On 26th September 1981, a polished slate plaque in her memory was unveiled at All Saints church by the Venezuelan Ambassador. It is located just below the tablet to William Bradley the "Yorkshire giant".

(8) Houghton Hall. This attractive, old house is set behind a large lake.

(9) Sancton. Although the ancient sport of cock fighting was stopped under an Act of the Lord Protector in 1654, it continued to attract a strong following at sub-rosa meetings, where bets were placed on the outcome of a "main", where several birds fought until there was only one survivor. Sancton became famous for the sport because the fights were conducted under the special patronage of the local vicar.

During one of his services the vicar fell asleep while a long psalm was being read. On being wakened, he exclaimed: "All right, a guinea on the black cock! Black cock a guinea".

Thereafter, Sancton people, especially the worst ones, were known as "Sancton Cockins".

WALK 6. MARKET WEIGHTON - LONDESBOROUGH - GOODMANHAM - MARKET WEIGHTON.

From All Saints church at the end of Londesborough Road turn left, along York Road[1], leading out of Market Weighton. Just past the very last house along this road turn right at a public footpath sign and continue across the field ahead[2] on a clear path, following the line of electricity poles, one of which has a yellow waymarker on it. Leave the field and continue straight ahead[3], directed by another yellow waymarker on a post, soon to cross a ditch on a plank bridge. Continue, close to a hedge on your right, which gradually curves to the left. Cross a facing waymarked plank bridge and continue, still with the hedge on your right, soon to cross another plank bridge with two waymarkers on it. Edge the next field and at the end of it cross another waymarked plank bridge, also with two yellow waymarkers on it. Keep straight ahead, still close to the hedge on your right and, on reaching a facing hedge, go through a very clear gap in it, close to the left-hand corner. Immediately cross a

45

waymarked plank bridge and cross the next field close to the hedge on your right, leaving it at public footpath sign close to its right-hand corner. Immediately cross the A163 and continue straight ahead, along a surfaced lane, directed by another public footpath sign. Go through a gate with Towthorpe Grange on it. On passing a Dutch barn on the left, go through a gate, into a field[4], which cross, bearing slightly right, along a rather muddy track that goes through a broad gap between trees. It is very easy to follow.

On going through this gap, cross a little bridge over a stream, East Beck. Keep straight ahead to cross a facing waymarked stile to the left of a gate and continue in the same direction, edging a field of wheat, close to the stream on your right.

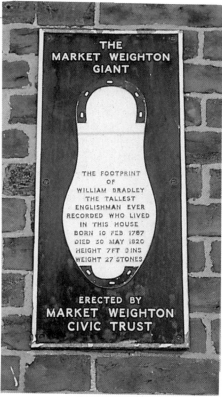

Imprint of giant William Bradley's foot, Market Weighton

Go through a broad gap to the right of a facing hedge and continue along what has now become a green track. Soon, at a very broad gap in the hedge on your right, go through a wide, gateless gateway onto a road and turn left for a short distance, to turn right, through imposing gates, into Londesborough Hall grounds[5], guided by both a public footpath sign and a yellow waymarker.

Just past a lodge on the left, cross a facing stile, alongside a gate, where a sign says: "Please keep to the road. Lake and park are strictly private." Follow a broad track, which has a stripe along its middle, like fluoride toothpaste, only green.

46

Entrance to Londesborough Park

You are now in Hudson territory.

Continue along this track, through parkland, soon to pass a walnut tree[6], laden with fruit when we passed. The track climbs steadily to pass close to the foundations of the original old hall[7], and where it bifurcates, take the left-hand fork, soon to go through a waymarked gate, into a wooded area. Go forward, briefly, and, just past a Wolds Way sign, bear left where the way splits, directed by a yellow arrow. Soon the eastern end of Londesborough village is reached[8].

Turn left, through this estate village, passing the church on the left, and having looked in vain for the expected pub, turn right, along the road near its western end. As it climbs, take the first turning right, along a road that contours parallel to and above the one you have just used. At the end of the road, turn right, down hill, back to the point of entry into the village[5], directed by a Wolds Way sign.

From here, retrace your steps through the wooded area used to reach the village, exiting through the same waymarked gate, beyond which ignore the stile on the left and descend the parkland track to where it splits at a public footpath sign. Turn left and go along a clear track that curves right, then bears left, up a hillside[10]. Where it bifurcates, take the right-hand fork, directed by a yellow waymarker. The track becomes green and descends along an avenue of elms to a waymarked stile, which cross. Continue over a short, flat, marshy area[11] that divides two lakes. Cross a footbridge above a little weir and go forward briefly, to cross a waymarked stile.

Go forward, up the field ahead, bearing left and aiming for the left-hand corner of a wood that lies to your right and, on climbing the hill, spreads across your line of walk near its brow. As you climb the hill a green track can now be seen on your left. Simply join it and continue climbing to the top of the field, exiting at a facing stile to the left of a gate with a footpath sign. Continue forward, briefly, to turn right along a surfaced farm road, directed by a footpath sign.

Where the farm road turns right, keep straight ahead, directed by a yellow waymarker, close to a hedge on your right, on an unsurfaced track, part of the Wolds Way. Where the track ends, at another Wolds Way sign, go diagonally left, across the A163 to Towthorpe Corner picnic site. Here go right, along a road, for a few yards, then left along an unsurfaced farm track that curves to the right at a Wolds Way sign. At the end of the field, where the track turns left, do likewise, directed by another Wolds Way sign[12].

As the track descends gently, it passes a yellow arrow on a post. A little further on it goes under a railway bridge that carries a disused line and continues straight ahead, climbing quite steeply. Where it bifurcates, take the left-hand route which continues uphill, into the middle of Goodmanham[13].

Pass beautiful Goodmanham church, set on raised ground to your right, and turn left, directed by a Wolds Way sign, climbing steadily out of the village. On leaving it, turn right at a Wolds Way sign, along a minor road, where it makes a sharp turn to the right and, almost at once curves left, cross a stile onto a disused railway track and walk along it all the way into Market Weighton.

On reaching the site of the old railway station, continue along quiet Hull Road leaving a cul-de-sac, and turn left at a T-junction along Londesborough Road at the end of which lies All Saints, which should, collectively, be thanked for providing such a super circular.

Things Seen On The Way.

(1) William Bradley Esq. 1792-1820. Where a road coming from the south-east joins York Road, opposite the Bay Horse, one of the buildings carries a plaque showing the imprint of a huge boot. It was put there by Market Weighton Civic Trust to identify the home of England's tallest man, the celebrated Yorkshire giant, William Bradley. Weighing fourteen pounds when he was born, he eventually reached the impressive weight of 27 stone and stood 7 feet 9 inches tall. His shoes were 15 inches long and $5^1/_2$ inches wide, his stockings were 3 feet 9 inches from top to toe and his walking stick measured 5 feet 10 inches. The house in which he lived was specially built and had extra large doorways. He made a fortune as a fairground freak (it cost

a shilling to see him) and appeared in most towns in England. He was presented to King George IV, who gave him a massive gold chain as a souvenir. A moderate eater, who drank nothing stronger than tea, William Bradley was only 37 years old when he died of consumption.

It is said that he was buried secretly, then re-buried inside the church at a later date in order to foil the resurrectionists, or body-snatchers, who would have obtained a good price for so large a corpse. In fact it was 52 years after his death that he was re-buried inside All Saints. There is a commemorative plaque over his grave on the west wall of the church.

Edwin Calvert was born at nearby Shiptonthorpe in 1842. He never grew higher than 36 inches, drank like a fish and died aged 17 years.

There is a moral somewhere within this cautionary tale.

(2) Market Weighton to York Railway Line. This field has been reclaimed from the Market Weighton to York railway line, which once crossed it on an embankment. Both this line and the one from Market Weighton to Beverley were closed on the same day in 1965.

(3) Weighton Clay Field. The five, flattish fields between Market Weighton and the A163 are collectively called the Weighton Clay Field because of the clayey nature of the soil.

(4) Towthorpe Village. To the left, as you cross this field, on the east bank of East Beck, is the site of medieval Towthorpe village. The only identifiable remains are the fish ponds, the site of a moated house and the line of the former streets, all cocooned in wondrous mystery that stirs the imagination.

(5) Londesborough Park. Comprising 400 acres of woodland and pasture, the park is delightful. It was Richard Boyle, the third Earl of Burlington, an architect as well as a statesman and the builder of Burlington House in Piccadilly, London, who laid out Londesborough Park with lakes, a terrace and a waterfall. He also planted an avenue of elms in memory of David Garrick, the actor, who used to stay with him.

(6) Walnut Tree. The timber of this tree is highly prized for veneers and furniture. The fruit is harvested for pickling or for eating raw. The more an English walnut tree is walloped, so the saying goes, the bigger the crop it produces. Hence the rhyme:

> A woman, a boy and a walnut tree,
> The more you beat them the better they be.

(7) The original Londesborough Hall. It was supposedly built on the site of the summer palace of the Kings of Northumbria and where the Saxon King Edwin was converted to Christianity in the year 626.

The original mansion was built in the sixteenth century and the third Earl of Burlington made considerable additions to it.

From the Burlington family the mansion passed to the Cavendish family; and it was a Cavendish, the sixth Duke of Devonshire, who demolished it in 1819 and used much of the material to build new buildings at Chatsworth House.

The story behind the demolition is unusual! When his Duchess gave the 5th Duke of Devonshire a daughter, his mistress, at the same time, presented him with a son. So the Duke switched babies in order to have an heir. This was discovered but the boy was allowed to succeed the title and estate on condition that he never married. The bastard sixth Duke, having no heir and therefore no interest in his successor, pulled down his Londesborough mansion because he was tired of paying for repairs.

When the Duke re-visited the site, following the demolition, he burst into tears, but consoled himself by selling the 12,000 acres of Londesborough to George Hudson, the "railway king", in 1845 for £470,000.

Today a stepped terrace and some urns on pedestals are about all that remain: that and the beauty of the place which even the pulling down of the original Hall could not destroy.

(8) Londesborough village. Neat, attractive Londesborough village stands on the line of the Roman road from Lincoln to Malton. Remains of the road were found in 1740 in the form of 24 foot wide wheel tracks and more evidence was unearthed in 1865 when the lake in Londesborough Park was cleaned out. Its re-roofed cottages and quaint seventeenth-century almshouses snuggle under shading trees and one of the houses, stone built and overlooking the church, carries a plaque that gives its date as 1750. Two brick built cottages next to it were built at the same time.

(9) The new Londesborough Hall. As you descend to your point of entry into the village, the entrance to the present hall, set deep in private grounds, is passed on your left.

Built in Tudor style in 1839, it replaced the former hall, which stood $1/4$ mile to the west, demolished in 1819 after years of neglect. Its most famous owner was George Hudson, the famous "railway king", who purchased it in 1845 at a time when he was planning the York to Market Weighton railway line, which opened in 1847. This was at the height of Hudson's power; and he had a private station built from which a two-mile carriage way was built through an avenue of trees, Londesborough Avenue, to the hall. The station buildings have gone now, but part of the avenue remains.

Hudson was three times Lord Mayor of York, a city he made the railway capital of England. At the height of his success he controlled more than 1,000 miles of railway. He lived in grand style; but not for very long because, accused of fraudulently operating the Eastern Counties Railway, his business collapsed in 1849.

Following Hudson's downfall, the estate was sold to the trustees of Lord Albert Conyngham who was given a peerage and he used Londesborough as his title. Keen on racing, he had a stud at Grimston, near Tadcaster. He died in 1860. His son, who attained an earldom and married a daughter of the Earl of Westmorland, lived at Londesborough Hall and managed the estate for over 40 years. Royalty often attended his shooting parties; and the game on the estate was particularly well looked after because of the affection in which he was held by his tenants because he never dismissed a farmer or raised a rent.

(10) Easthorpe medieval village. The northwards view from this hillside includes Londesborough Hall which, from this distance is a confusion of red brick, chimneys and round, point turrets. Eastwards, near Easthorpe Farm, which was mentioned in the Domesday Book of 1086, is the site of Easthorpe medieval village, which was "depopulated" when Lord Burlington expanded Londesborough deer park, the last five cottages being demolished in 1738.

(11) Greylag geese. On crossing this marshy area, we spotted a flock of greylag geese just ahead and to the left. They were easily recognised by their yellow bills and white under-tail feathers. Identification was made much easier because we were able to use a telescope thoughtfully provided by the present owners of the estate "to help you to enjoy your walk through the Londesborough Estate. Please keep to the path, especially during the breeding season."

(12) Ermine Street. From Towthorpe Corner to this Wolds Way sign you have walked along the route of Ermine Street, which continues southwards from this point to Sancton.

(13) Goodmanham. There has been a settlement here since the Stone Age and it was the scene of one of the most dramatic and significant episodes in English history.

Goodmundingham, as it was then called, formerly housed the pagan temple of Delgovine, and was the main centre of Woden worship in the north of England. The temple's high priest, Coifi, was a frequent visitor to the court of King Edwin of Northumbria.

King Edwin's beautiful second wife, Ethelburga, was a Christian, and when she came to Londesborough from Kent, she brought the apostle Paulinus with her, hoping that he could persuade her husband to embrace Christianity. At the Great Council of Northumbria, AD 627, held in Edwin's summer palace at Londesborough, Paulinus tried to convert all the assembled company to Christianity. Oddly enough, it was the temple's high priest, Coifi, who was the first to be persuaded by the teaching of Paulinus. He advised that the old pagan temple be destroyed.

"But who shall desecrate the great temple?" asked the King. Coifi promptly said that he would. "So I can set a public example and destroy the idols that I worshipped in ignorance."

He rode into the temple and hurled his spear at the pagan images. The onlookers expected some terrible manifestation of the wrath of Woden to appear; but when nothing happened they followed Coifi's example, flung themselves on the idols and set fire to the temple.

This marked the end of the old pagan religion. Edwin was baptised on Easter Day, 12th April 627, at a well in York. The hastily built wooden church of St Peter which Edwin built on the site was the humble origin of York's magnificent Minster. Some years later the wooden church was replaced by a stone one and York Minster was eventually built on the same site.

Once the temple of Delgovine at Goodmanham had been destroyed, a Christian church was allegedly erected on the same site, some say by Paulinus himself. Some stained glass in the chancel of the present, mainly Norman church, All Hallows, commemorates this celebrated episode in Goodmanham's history.

CHAPTER IV
LONDESBOROUGH TO HUGGATE

Length of section: linear 10¾ miles (17.2km)

Distance covered walking clockwise from Hessle: 43¾ miles (70km)

Walk 7:   Circular: Londesborough - Warren Farm - Londesborough: 14 miles (22.4km)

Walk 8:   Circular: Huggate - Warren Farm - Huggate: 9½ miles (15.2km)

Map Ref: Landranger 106

Parking: Wayside in Londesborough and Huggate.

Handy hostelries: The Wolds Inn, Huggate

WALK 7. LONDESBOROUGH - WARREN FARM - LONDESBOROUGH.

From Londesborough church[1] go left, through the village, along a road that curves right, uphill, to a crossroads where go straight ahead along a minor road signposted Wolds Way for a good mile to a T-junction[2]. Turn right, briefly, then left to nearby Partridge Hall Farm. Continue through the farmyard, turning left between farm buildings, then right, through a facing gate with a yellow waymarker. Cross the field ahead on a clear track, through a gate and across the next one, aiming for the right-hand corner of a wood, seen ahead[3]. Cross a waymarked stile at a gate and go straight on, close to the edge of the wood on your left and past it, now with a hedge on your left, to a corner stile, which cross. Keeping close to the hedge on your right and with no defined path, cross the sloping field ahead then turn left, following a waymarker, go downhill, cross a beck on a footbridge and continue over a pasture to cross a stile on the edge of Nunburnholme village[4].

Turn left, directed by a Wolds Way signpost, along the road, passing a church on your left[5], and turn right at a signpost on your right, cross a field close to a hedge on your left, then right, along its top, still with a hedge on your left, to join a road through a gap in the hedge at another signpost. Turn left along the road for 300 yards, then turn right, uphill, on a clear track, through Bratt Wood[6], beyond which go straight ahead along a waymarked path. Where the path fades away continue in the same direction, close to a hedge on your right, as directed by an arrow on a post. Leave the field at a gated stile and continue close to a hedge on the right to join a track to Wold Farm[7] just ahead.

Immediately before the buildings turn left, following markers, along a track that curves right, around outhouses, into a farmyard, which leave going half left, then right, onto a farm road to a gate where turn right at a cottage, following a sign, along a climbing field path to another signpost clearly seen on the horizon. Turn left at the signpost and, keeping close to a fence on your left, go to the stile ahead, beyond which cross a minor road. Continue in the same direction on a clearly defined way to the right of a wood where, at a signpost, turn right on a clear track to Warrendale House Farm[8], reaching it round the back.

From Warrendale House Farm go along a surfaced road, downhill, bending round the side of a wood to where another minor road is reached, where turn right at a waymarked signpost, uphill, on a clearly defined track across unfenced, arable land, continuing along the edge of a wooded dale on your right.

At the valley head, where the wood has been felled, turn left at a signpost and go straight across a cornfield along a clear track where, following markers, go first left, briefly, then right and, almost at once, right again to continue along the rim of an escarpment with Millington village[9] spread below on your left.

Stay on this waymarked path for two miles to Warren Farm.

Walkers doing the linear walk to Huggate should turn left just beyond Warren Farm as indicated by Wolds Way and Minster Way signs and continue following yellow markers. Full and clear directions are given in the second half of Walk 8.

To complete circular Walk 7 turn right just beyond Warren Farm and go along a farm road for $1/4$ mile to minor road where turn right. After a mile, at as trig point with three beech trees, turn left along a green lane leading past Newcote Farm and curving right to join the B1246.

Turn right along it, through parkland for $1/2$ mile[10], at first on the level, then climbing, and where the trees end on your left, turn left at a signpost and continue just inside a beech wood along a delightful path, first descending, then climbing and descending again[11] leaving the wood just short of its far end, going right, through a wide gap into a lane.

Go left along this lane, which soon turns right and exit into a field where turn left as signposted.

You have now reached that part of the walk used on the outward journey. Retrace your steps through Bratt Wood, turn left when a minor road is reached and stay on it into Nunburnholme where turn left through the village and bear right along another minor road which climbs steeply for one mile before levelling out[12]. At a crossroads just beyond the summit go straight ahead and gently downhill for a further mile back into Londesborough.

Things Seen On The Way

(1) Londesborough church. Inside the south porch of Londesborough church there is an ancient Norman doorway above which are an equally ancient sundial and a Saxon cross. There are two more sundials on the outer wall together with some old inscriptions, one dated 1735. There are two yew trees in the large churchyard, which is not surprising; but the village has no pub, because Londesborough is an estate village. Locals seeking a pint must travel at least as far as Shiptonthorpe, $1 1/2$ miles away.

(2) Cleaving. Prehistoric man much preferred the chalk hills of the Wolds to the surrounding carrs, flatlands, which were subjected to seasonal flooding. Clearing vegetation presented few problems and the light soil was easy to bring into cultivation without the need for complicated tools. Above all, he felt safer on the higher ground. So he settled there in long vanished villages and began producing his own food. One such vanished village is Cleaving, which is sited close to cleaving Grange, a highly mechanised farm.

(3) Shiptonthorpe. From the outset the views are good as the route hereabouts edges the Wolds: to the west and south towards Shiptonthorpe and, further

back still towards Market Weighton are particularly fine.

(4) Nunburnholme. Much of Nunburnholme village, which takes its name from a long vanished, 12th century priory of Benedictine nuns once sited there, is strung along a quiet country road. Its cottages are red roofed and white walled, its surroundings lush and green, its hedgerows and fields home to a rich assortment of bird life.

(5) Nunburnholme Church. As church towers go, the one at Nunburnholme is a poor specimen: it just doesn't look right. But don't let that put you off because the rest of the building is very attractive, especially a blocked Norman door in the north wall and an eyecatching Norman window. Inside, a splendid Norman tower arch, richly decorated in an elaborate zigzag design, has, as its pièce de résistance, a row of fantastic faces, their multiform expressions reminiscent of a gurning contest. If you look at them long enough you will recognise somebody.

Hanging inside that same tower, which looks so disappointing from outside, there is a bell which is inscribed "I will imitate your birds by singing". This is apt for the rector of Nunburnholme from 1854 until he died in 1893 at the ripe old age of 83, was Rev. Francis Orpen Morris, who was also an ornithologist of note and a prolific writer.

A magnificent eleventh-century Anglo-Saxon shaft once stood in the churchyard. More than four feet tall, it was once part of a cross. Now it stands inside the church where it attracts more people than it did when it was outside. It dates from the tenth century and is smothered in carvings of humans and animals, including the Mother and Child, a lamb, dragons and a centaur.

The nearby old rectory is Georgian, cream painted and looks lovely.

(6) Bratt Wood. A steep climb through Bratt Wood and, less steeply, over fields to Wold Farm will bring you out of the valley that houses Nunburnholme, back onto the shoulder of the Wolds, there the landscape is uncluttered with fine views all round.

(7) Pocklington. West of Wold Farm lies the township of Pocklington. It is a busy place and some 4,000 people live there. Its church boasts a fine fifteenth-century tower. William Wilberforce was educated at Pocklington Grammar School.

(8) Warrendale House Farm. From several places along the approach track to the farm, coming from the south, the bulk of York Minster can be seen, given reasonable conditions, some $15^1/_2$ miles (24.8km) west, across the Vale of York.

(9) Millington. Nicely sited at the foot of the western escarpment, Millington village contains a little pub, The Gate Inn, a fact worthy of note by anyone

with a tendency to dehydration en route. For no public house lies actually on the Wolds Way between Goodman Farm and Fridaythorpe; and there are not many close to it.

The south door of the village church is Norman. Millington Beck flows southwards between the village and the scarp separated from it by a lot of little, fenced fields.

(10) Warter Priory. The Manor and Soke of Warter was granted in the twelfth century to Warter Priory.

(11) Warter. Seen on your left as you go through the wood and neatly tucked into a dale of Warter Wold is Warter village where the Kiplingcotes Derby takes place. It is the most economically organised horse race in the land, held on the third Thursday in March every year, and is the oldest and strangest horse race in England.

Traditionally the race was first run in 1519, the date shown on the winning post by the side of the lane leading from the A163 to Warter; but this is disputed. The first authentic record of the race puts it at 1555 and at that time it was called Kibling Cotes. In 1618 it was founded as the Kiplingcotes Derby and endowed by Lord Burlington and "five noble men, 19 baronets and 25 gentlemen of the county of Yorkshire". Between them these 50 men contributed 360 shillings, the interest from which was the prize money.

The race is open to horses of all ages and they must carry ten stones, not including the saddle. The weigh-in takes place near the winning post and flints are added and hung around the waist of any underweight rider.

All competitors must enter before 11 o'clock on the morning of the race, which must be run before 2pm. It is about four miles long, for the most part, along a rough track across fields, ending in a metalled lane near Warter.

The winner receives the interest on the original endowment, about £15 to £20 these days. The second frequently fares much better, receiving £4 out of each entry fee of £4.25. Since there may be a dozen or more entries he or she can expect to pick up about £40 to £50. The few pounds remaining are used by the committee to cover any expenses.

(12) Kilnwick Percy and Burnby Hall. Stately Kilnwick Percy Hall can be seen westward peeping over protecting trees and looking completely unspoiled. Jousting knights would not be out of place in such a setting, yet it dates only from the eighteenth century.

When Major P.M.Stewart died in 1962 he left Burnby Hall gardens and museum to Pocklington. The garden has a famous collection of water lilies and, the hall houses a unique display of sporting trophies. But it is the Major's collection of items collected during his extensive travels that stimulates most interest.

WALK 8. HUGGATE - WARREN FARM - HUGGATE.

Leave Wolds Inn, Huggate, going right and turn left, south at the crossroads. Continue along the road towards Warter and after ³/₄ mile, where it dips slightly on a gentle bend, turn right along a green lane[1] for just over a mile where turn left along a minor road for a further mile, passing Cobdale Farm on your right. When a road junction is reached turn right along another minor road for ³/₄ mile, passing Coldwood Farm on your left and take the farm road on your right to Warren Farm.

The linear walk from Londesborough to Huggate is joined here.

Short of the farmhouse turn right along a clear signposted route, shared with the Wolds Way and the Minster Way, following yellow markers along the brow of a hill, and the line of an earthworks[2] to reach a dry valley called Rabbit Warren[3].

Descend into the valley, at first close to a fence on your left and where it turns left ignore the obvious track following the fence and continue straight ahead, downhill, aiming for a signpost clearly seen in the valley bottom. From the signpost the way is straight up the steep dale side, close to a line of trees on your left, to a stile at the top, which cross.

Go straight ahead, on level ground, close to a hedge on your left, to drop into Nettle Dale[4] and straight up the other side, turning right near the top along a clear track to Jessops Plantation, which enter over a stile.

At the end of the wood

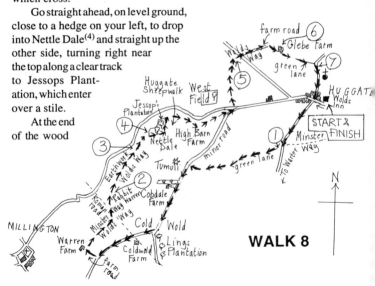

WALK 8

58

urn left, as indicated, for ¼ mile, then go sharp right along the rim of another ale called Huggate Sheepwalk, passing along the edge of a larch wood on our right to reach a minor road at a tangent. Continue along this road for 200 ards to where another road joins it from the left where turn left to cross a stile etween two white gates and take the clear track close to a hedge on your left, climbing gently to cross the 197 metre contour, one of the highest points on he Wolds Way[5].

Turn right with the path, as indicated by a waymarker, to a nearby road, which cross. Continue along a farm road to Glebe Farm[6], passing in front f it and continuing along a green lane for ½ mile to join a surfaced road to he north of Huggate. Here leave the Wolds Way, turning right, uphill, along he road into Huggate[7].

Things Seen On The Way.

1) The Minster Way. The Minster Way, which coincides with the Wolds Way between Warren Farm and Rabbit Warren, where it shoots off, eastwards, along the dale bottom is rejoined along the full length of this green ane. It meanders delightfully for 51 miles between the Minsters of York and Beverley. The walk is mainly flat, the only hills encountered being when it climbs to cross the Wolds.

2) La Tene Earthworks. Earthworks run along the eastern rim of Millington Dale, which lies between Rabbit Warren and Millington Pasture. They were built by the La Tene people from northern France, who began arriving 300 BC, and continued to do so for the next few hundred years.

Several warlike tribes, led by powerful chieftains made up the La Tene people. The tribe that invaded the Wolds and other parts of Yorkshire was the Parisii and this tribe is responsible for the earth works along the rim of Millington Dale.

The tribal chieftains were all powerful people, much feared by the Parisii warriors. When a chieftain died he was buried in a square barrow on the lower slopes of the Wolds.

As the Romans settled in the Wolds the Parisii were incorporated into the Roman way of life and adapted to Roman ways of farming, preferring the arable kind to predominantly livestock farming.

3) Rabbit Warren. About ½ mile north of Warren Farm both Wolds Way and Minster Way cross a steep sided dale called Rabbit Warren. The name stems from the seventeenth century when local farmers were encouraged to breed rabbits for their meat and fur. In those days the place lived up to its name but few rabbits remain today.

4) Nettle Dale. More often than not places have been given names appropriate to a particular characteristic of that place and, no doubt, when Nettle Dale was so named it was probably thick with nettles; but not any more. Today few nettles remain in Nettle Dale but, in season, there are lots of cowslips.

(5) While making few claims to superlatives either of landscape or history, the Wolds can make many to sustained excellence of scenery and interest. The attractions are many and varied, the changes from wide, arable acres to woodland and from valleys to ridges and broad, flattish uplands being frequent and often sudden and dramatic. The hills never rise much above 200 metres but, since they are the only ones for miles around, the views from their tops are very fine indeed.

On a wide stretch of open country to the south-west of Glebe Farm the Wolds Way reaches one of its highest points at 246 metres (807ft) above sea level. No dramatic climbing is involved, yet from this moderate elevation the views, given clear conditions, are almost beyond belief. A local farmer once placed a trailer loaded with hay on this spot and stood on it to see how far his view stretched. He saw Hull and Sheffield, the towers of Lincoln Cathedral and York Minster and, at night, looking towards the coast, he could see the beam of Flamborough lighthouse.

(6) Diamond Wood. To the north-north-west of Glebe Farm is a diamond-shaped wood, Horsedale Plantation, which was planted with larches in 1887, the year of Queen Victoria's Diamond Jubilee. The larches were cut down for pit props during World War II and a mixture of trees, bushes and weeds grew in their place, still forming the same diamond shape on the landscape.

(7) Huggate is tucked away in the very heart of the Wolds. Sited just below the famous Huggate Dykes, a line of entrenchments probably made by the Ancient Britons, it is one of the highest villages in the Wolds and is frequently blocked by deep snowdrifts in winter. Its houses and cottages are gathered around a spacious green with a well, at 339 feet the second deepest in England.

In 1726 Mrs Francis Barker of York left £50 for poor relief and the education of poor children of Huggate. However, between 1730 and 1764 the village had no school-master. By 1819, Huggate had three private schools and a national school was opened there in 1892.

The chancel arch and nave of Huggate church, St Mary's, are thirteenth century. The perpendicular clerestories are fifteenth century and above the chancel arch are two small Norman windows. The mediaeval tower, with its traceried battlements, strange gargoyles and weird faces, is topped with a stone spire, which has short buttresses on four sides. In 1830 the spire was repaired by Mr T.Filey without the use of scaffolding - that's what I call really putting your trust in God!

The village has a post office/shop and a friendly pub called The Wolds.

The interior of the ruined church at Wharram Percy

CHAPTER V
HUGGATE TO WHARRAM-LE-STREET

Length of section: linear 12¾ miles (20.4km)

Distance covered walking clockwise from Hessle: 56½ miles (90.4km)

Walk 9: Circular: Huggate - Fridaythorpe - Thixendale - Huggate
9¾ miles (15.6km) plus 1½ miles each way extension.
(4.8km) Total mileage: 12¾ miles (20.4km)

Walk 10:	Circular: Thixendale - Wharram-Le-Street - Thixendale 10 miles (16km)
Map Ref:	Landranger 100 and 106
Parking:	Wayside parking in Huggate and Wharram-Le-Street.
Handy hostelries:	The Wolds Inn, Huggate. The Cross Keys, The Manor House, Fridaythorpe. The Cross Keys, Thixendale.

WALK 9. HUGGATE - FRIDAYTHORPE - THIXENDALE - HUGGATE.

From Huggate go northwards along a tarmac road, soon to pass, on your left, the road end to Glebe Farm, where the Wolds Way is joined. Continue downhill, then uphill and along an avenue of young trees, beyond which the road curves gently right towards Northfield House. On the curve turn left along a signposted field edge close to a hedge on your left to a stile, which cross.

Descend diagonally right, into a dry valley, along a clear track and at the bottom of it ignore two facing stiles and cross a signposted one on your left. Continue along a steep sided valley, climbing steadily[1] and where it splits bear right to cross a stile.

Ignoring paths going left and right keep straight ahead to Fridaythorpe[2] and bear right through the village, to facing Manor House Inn. Now go left, passing a lovely duck pond on your left and, a few yards further on, a lovely Norman church. At the end of the village, just before Northern Nutrition Ltd., turn left, as signposted, along a broad, chalky farm track close to a hedge on your left passing on your right, a bank of poplars which, in time, will camouflage Northern Nutrition's large buildings.

Where the track ends at a fence cross a stile on your right and follow a clear path diagonally down into a facing dry valley which has Ings Plantation on its far side, reaching the valley bottom at the right side of the plantation, cross the narrow valley bottom, cross a signposted stile and begin the gradual ascent of a side valley, at first close to the plantation on your left, then continuing past it, guided by clear markers. On reaching the head of the valley cross some level ground to a stile near a metal gate, which cross.

Continue straight ahead along a clear track to pass between the outbuildings of Gills Farm[3] with its protecting trees to reach a tarmac road. Then right, along the road, for a short distance towards a clearly seen solitary house, close to which turn left as signposted. Go along a track near a hedge on your left, descending gently, then turning left and continuing to drop.

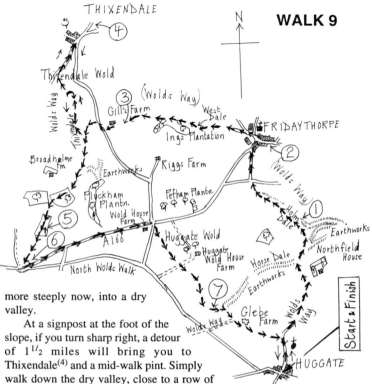

WALK 9

more steeply now, into a dry valley.

At a signpost at the foot of the slope, if you turn sharp right, a detour of 1½ miles will bring you to Thixendale[4] and a mid-walk pint. Simply walk down the dry valley, close to a row of trees on your left, cross a stile and continue along a track and over another stile to reach a minor road. Go right, along it, for about ½ mile and, where five roads meet almost at the same spot, turn left into Thixendale, through which the Wolds Way continues.

Retrace your steps to the signpost in the valley bottom where you turned right for the detour and continue up the valley bottom to a facing fence with two stiles. Here turn left to enter a side valley over a stile in a fence.

Go up this side valley and where it splits turn right towards a wood, which skirt, close to its edge on your right. A marker on a tree confirms your route. Where the wood spreads across your line of walk enter it over a stile and walk through it on rising ground along a pleasant, meandering path[5]. On leaving the wood continue ahead, climbing out of the valley, to reach the A166[6]

Bell shaped Roman field boundary stone alongside the A166

Go left, along its broad verge, for about 1^1/$_2$ miles to Wold House Farm where turn right, immediately cross a side road diagonally right, to a signposted path and continue along a field edge, close to a hedge on your left, soon to cross a farm road which leads to Huggate Wold House. The way is straight ahead, still close to a hedge on your left, eventually turning right to reach a stile near a gate, which cross. Keep on, now with a fence on your left, and where it turns left continue ahead, descending steeply to the bottom of a dry valley, where go through a gate and diagonally left up the far side.

Continue along the rim of the valley to a facing fence[7] where turn right through a signposted gate and along a field-edge path to Glebe Farm, where the Wolds Way is rejoined. Turn left on reaching the farm road, go in front of the farmhouse and bear right through a gate and along a clear track, first downhill, then uphill to reach the road along which you left Huggate. Here leave the Wolds Way, turning right and uphill, briefly, into the village.

Things Seen On The Way
(1) Holm Dale and Holm Village. Orange tip butterflies seem to have taken a liking to Holm Dale and its surroundings, for large numbers of them can be seen fluttering in and around this lovely, little valley whenever the mid-summer weather is warm and sunny.

Typical Wolds country - the descent to the edge of Ings Plantation,
west of Fridaythorpe (Walk 9) *(C.L.Emett)*
Ford over Settrington Beck, Settrington village (Walk 11) *(Ron Dodsworth)*

Holm village once stood close to the eastern rim of Holm Dale where today orange tips flap and grasses shake in the wind. It was one of a network of Wolds' settlements that had already experienced a century of gradual decline when the Black Death, a form of bubonic plague, struck Yorkshire in March 1346, and accelerated the process. It was one of the smallest and poorest villages in the area - one in six of which had been deserted, for a variety of reasons, since Saxon times.

No medieval peasant houses survive today because until the early thirteenth century most were built of timber, turf, clay or cob, which is clay mixed with straw and chalk; and these materials continued to be used in areas where building stone was not available.

The houses at Holm were probably built with walls of cob or wattle and daub, supported by vertical posts. Peasant houses were frequently repaired and often rebuilt, sometimes on different alignments or in different positions. The medieval peasant had little security of tenure or incentive to build for the future. Moreover, he was hampered by a shortage of long-lasting building materials. Once the surrounding forests had been cleared little good timber would have been available and he would have been dependent largely on the scrub timber of the valley sides. The chalk walls or footings would weather badly unless carefully protected and probably needed regular repair and replacement. Rebuilding every fifty years or so was common in medieval towns and villages.

The ordinary peasant of Holm probably lived in a single or two-roomed cottage while a villein, who had land and animals, might have lived in a long house with a two-roomed domestic section, the other part being used for housing stock or as an agricultural store.

Holm has changed out of all recognition and all that remains is its site. *(2) Fridaythrope.* Sited above the 500 feet contour, which for a Wolds' village is high, Fridaythrope has a green where ducks swim on two large ponds, houses that look over distant hills and, half hidden behind a farm and a row of beeches, a little church with a squat tower.

The church is quaint, simple and mostly Norman, the magnificent Norman doorway in its fine porch being richly adorned with zigzag; and its capitals are all differently carved. The zigzag is repeated on the chancel arch.

At the restoration the north aisle was built on an earlier site and the thirteenth century arcade was opened out from the wall in which it had been built up. The font is Norman. Part of a coffin lid is built into the porch and there is a fragment of an old cross set into the outside of the aisle wall. An unusual feature is the screenwork separating the aisle from the nave and the pews from the west end. One of the column capitals holds a mystery. Inscribed on it is a legend which says THIS 713 FOUND HERE. No one knows what it was and when it was found.

(3) Gill's Farm. Gill's Farm, surrounded by protecting trees, is a typical Wolds' farmhouse. Scattered throughout these broad acres stand many similar farmhouses, all with warm kitchens which are the real centres of home life on farms. From them both the domestic economy and the general management of the surrounding countryside are controlled.

Modernisation has transformed the farmhouse kitchen, removing much of the toil of yesteryear.

(4) Thixendale. Thixendale is shown as Sixtedale in the Domesday survey of 1086, perhaps because six dales meet there. The village is superbly sited in a lonely valley, ten miles from the nearest town, in the middle of a complicated dry valley network comprised of the following sixteen dales: Bowdale, Breckondale, Broadholmedale, Brubberdale, Buckdale, Courtdale, Fairydale, Fotherdale, Honeydale, Longdale, Middledale, Pluckhamdale, Warrendale, Waterdale, Williedale and Thixendale. Therein lies another reason for its name.

(5) Waytham Farm. The path which climbs easily to the dale head near Waytham Farm spends part of its course meandering through woodland which in springtime is carpeted with a rich pattern of wild flowers, of which snowdrops are the earliest. Although well established throughout the country their real home is central Europe from where they were introduced to Britain in the Middle Ages.

Sharing the same shaded dale-side is the lesser celandine, which unfolds its glossy star-like flowers while many of the other plants are still dormant. More prominently displayed, nodding, fragrant bluebells bloom a little later, between April and June, as does the garlic mustard, so called because it smells of garlic when crushed. Peeping shyly from hidden corners, violets add balance; but it is the primroses that steal the show. Maybe this is because of the way they are grouped beneath the trees, or perhaps because their pale, yellow flowers are seen to advantage in shade, or, again, it may be because they exude a delicate perfume, which has to be savoured at close quarters to be fully appreciated. Whatever the reason, they are delightful. When the wood ends, short of where the A166 crosses the head of the dale, primroses continue adorning the now grassy bank, adding colour and cheer.

(6) A166. At various points along the A166 and other side roads the entrances to various fields of a "Roman" farm are marked with large, bell-shaped concrete blocks. Built circa 1960, they all carry different inscriptions, mostly in Latin, like VALLUS, VALLIS, ALIO and HUGGATE ADITIUS. Others

read VALLIS WATERMANHOLE MAGNA and VALLIS LINGUA.

(7) Huggate Wold. Scenes like the herd of cattle we observed slowly wending up the dry valley bottom that edges Huggate Wold and the grazing sheep occupying flat and steep areas alike are common in this part of the world. This is because so many of the valleys share the same geological characteristics. Their sides are usually too steep for cultivation so sheep are grazed on them. An estimated 200,000 ewes and lambs, in a variety of cross breeds are being reared on the Wolds at any one time, making sheep the most numerous livestock found there.

Both beef and dairy cattle are reared there, the most common breeds being Friesian and Holstein with fairly recently introduced breeds like Charolais and Limousin becoming more widespread. Yet, despite the various cross breeds of sheep and the presence of oddly assorted beef and dairy cattle Huggate Wold and its side valley simply ooze Englishness.

WALK 10. THIXENDALE - WHARRAM-LE-STREET - THIXENDALE.

Leave Thixendale by the west end of the village, turning right briefly, then left, through a gate and uphill along a broad track to a ladder stile just beyond a barn on the right. Cross the stile and continue, following yellow markers, to a signpost stile, which cross, and immediately go left, close to a hedge on your left as far as the field corner. Now turn right, keeping close to another hedge on your left and cross the field to a stile, in so doing traversing Cow Wold. Go over the stile and continue straight ahead, descending into a dry valley[1], and half way down the hillside go left, over a stile in a hedge, then right to cross the bottom of the valley. Climb the far side of it, close to a fence on your right, and cross a stile at the top.

Continue straight ahead, close to an ancient earthworks on your right, to a crossing of paths where turn right, along a grass track, for two miles, contouring the side of the Wold, gradually curving left, using stiled gates and keeping close to a wall on your right, beyond which are two distinct plantations - both called North Plantation.

Along the outward section to Wharram-le-Street use Wolds Way signs only. En route, along this Wold edge, an excellent guide is Wharram Percy Farm[2], magnificently sited beyond the prairie-like farmland over to your left.

Cross a stile near a gate at the eastern corner of the second of the North Plantations and continue along a clear, broad track that edges a wood on your left and crosses Burdale Tunnel[3] to reach a tarmac road.

Go left along this quiet road for a mile, passing Bella Farm on your left after half a mile. From here the red roofs of Malton are clearly seen to the north-west.

Where the road turns sharp right go straight ahead along a field path to enter Wharram-le-Street[4], seen ahead, at its western end.

Turn left, along

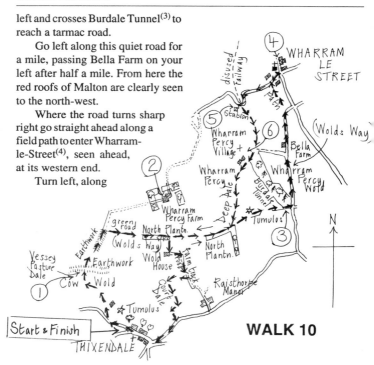

WALK 10

a minor road, for half a mile and where, at the foot of a steep bank the road bends sharp right, go left, along a signposted path past Wharram Station[5], now a private dwelling, and continue along the course of the disused Malton to Driffield railway line to where, opposite a footbridge on your left, turn right, through a gate, and climb a broad path to Wharram Percy[6] medieval village and church.

Leave Wharram Percy through a kissing gate to the west of the church yard, bear left past the bottom end of a fish pond on your right and cross a stile signposted "Footpath to Thixendale".

Climb the bank immediately beyond it, using a track which eventually fades, and keep straight ahead to a facing fence where turn right as indicated by two closely spaced yellow markers. Keeping close to the hedge on your left contour the north of the valley on your right, aiming for the two North Plantations, seen ahead. On reaching the eastern end of the nearest one,

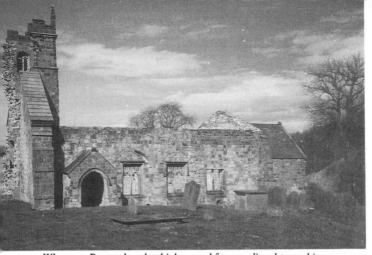

Wharram Percy church which served four medieval townships

where the Wolds Way is rejoined, at the signposted stile used on the outward journey, turn right and retrace your steps to the eastern corner of the second plantation where, at a Centenary Way signpost, turn left and cross arable land on a clear track.

At ruinous Wolds House continue along a clear farm track, which curves left then turns right, along the head of a valley. Ignore the first clear path leading away on your right and continue to where the track curves left and where, on that corner, a hedge goes from it on the right. Here turn right along a path close to this hedge on your right and continue to a facing stile, which cross. Immediately turn left, along the rim of a dry valley to its end where descend and go through a gate in a fence. Cross the field ahead, parallel to the road on your left, to another stile, which cross. Keeping on the same contour continue towards Thixendale cricket field, then descend, passing it on your left, to enter the village close to the strategically placed pub.

Things Seen On The Way

(1) Vessey Pasture Dale and Back Dale. The dry valley immediately to the north of Low Wold, where Vessey Pasture Dale and Back Dale meet, is the site of a long earthwork running east to west along the dale bottom and curving northwards to Birdsall Brow. On climbing out of the dale, passing close to a former chalk pit on the hillside, there is another earthwork, this one running roughly north to south. For a little while your route is close to and parallel to it. Ancient dykes, earthworks and tumuli like these are scattered throughout the Wolds, clear evidence of early settlement in these parts. They

were built by the warlike Parisii, who came from the Seine and Marne valleys and established themselves throughout east Yorkshire, including the Wolds, and Lincolnshire.

(2) Wharram Percy Farm. Wharram Percy Farm, surrounded on three sides by protecting trees, overlooks the head of Deep Dale. From its broad, hilltop site some 700 feet above sea level, one of the highest points in the Wolds, it overlooks very wide fields, examples of how intensive farming can change the face of the Wolds.

In the late fourteenth and fifteenth centuries there was a great shift of emphasis in Wolds farming from crop production to sheep rearing and many villages, like nearby Wharram Percy, were abandoned as the Wolds became a vast sheep walk. For more than 300 years sheep farming on a vast scale was carried out on the chalk uplands.

But by 1850 permanent grassland was rare, the sheep walks and the common fields having largely gone owing to the arable policies of Sir Christopher Sykes and others. Enclosures continued well into this century and today virtually the only traditional chalk pastures remaining in the Wolds are the steep sided banks of the dry valleys.

(3) Burdale Tunnel. Because of the steep gradients involved and the one mile long Burdale tunnel needed to lift the Malton and Driffield line out of the Vale of Pickering onto the Wolds the line's construction was something of an engineering triumph. The tunnel itself took almost six years to cut through the Wolds chalk at a time when mechanical aids were few.

The navvies lived in a nearby wooden encampment and were generally well behaved. But when work on the tunnel was stopped for a time in 1849 because of a cash flow problem, fifty discharged workers ran riot "killing game and whatever came their way".

From the car park at Bella Farm a winding track leads to the disused line and from it the old tunnel entrance, long blocked up, can be seen. The only trace of the tunnel in the wood is an air vent.

(4) Wharram-le-Street. Five beeches shade one side of Wharram-le-Street which, as its name implies, is sited on the line of a Roman road. The tower of its church is Saxon and its nave is also Saxon but was later altered by the Normans. The aisle is medieval and the chancel is nineteenth century. The plain doorway, set inside a tiny porch, is Norman and the tub font is probably Norman as well. From the churchyard there is a good view over the Vale of Pickering to the North Yorkshire Moors.

(5) Wharram Station. Now a private dwelling, this wayside station was part of the Malton and Driffield, an independently built line with the prime purpose of serving the chalk quarries at Burdale and Wharram-le-Street. The

line, known locally as the "Malton Dodger", was opened on 19th May 1853 and closed for passenger traffic on 5th June 1950. Goods traffic continued to be carried along it until 20th October 1958, when it closed completely. Traffic was never very heavy, but the line was a Godsend to Wolds farmers, especially in winter.

South of Wharram station, but before Burdale tunnel is reached, a branch to the left leads off to Wharram chalk quarry, which was worked until the 1940s. The quarry is now a nature reserve released from the Birdsall Estate Co. Ltd. to the Yorkshire Naturalist Club. Members have free access but unaccompanied non-members require a permit.

Burdale quarry, at the southern end of the tunnel, supplied 99% pure chalk to the Redcar steel mills. The chalk left Burdale in train loads of nine wagons which were doubled to eighteen at Wharram.

From Burdale tunnel, the summit of the line, the way via Garton-On-The-Wolds to Driffield is through unspectacular but satisfying scenery.

(6) Wharram Percy. Perhaps the most famous of all 'lost villages'. The name is derived from a combination of the Old Scandinavian HWERHAMM, meaning "at the bends", and the family name of the Percies who were the lords of the manor from the twelfth to the fourteenth centuries. The village covers 33 acres and its associated field systems another 1,250. The main earthworks of the village are on the chalk plateau, some 450 feet (150m) above sea level: the church of St Martin and the site of the medieval fishpond are in the valley.

The broad, climbing path from the disused railway line to St Martin's church passes a row of nineteenth-century labourer's cottages which are built on the foundations of an eighteenth-century farm. On the chalk plateau a sunken road runs north to south through the village between the outlines of peasants' houses and their property boundaries. The site of a twelfth-century manor house to the north of the village has been brought into view during excavations. The earthworks of the the twelfth/thirteenth-century manor house are to the south of the village, concealed by the same humps and bumps that cover the remains of demolished medieval houses and even earlier boundary features.

It was not by chance that a village came into being at Wharram Percy. It was the existence of seven springs, all within a distance of 1,800 feet (600m) of one another. That was what first attracted settlers for they provided a constant supply of water, on the mainly dry chalk Wolds.

The forests of oak and alder which once surrounded Wharram Percy have long since been cleared for farming but the remains of medieval "ridge and furrow" farming strips are visible to this day in the different growths of crops, even after modern ploughing.

Wharram Percy was part of a network of settlements and it depended on good communications to sell its products in the local markets and buy from them other necessary items. So trade routes became established and many of our present day roads follow those ancient trade routes.

It was Neolithic farmers who, circa 3500 BC, cleared the forests around Wharram Percy, using stone axes, some of which came from the Lake District. Where they settled is not known for certain but they would have made regular visits to the great Neolithic ceremonial enclosure some two miles distant from Wharram Percy at Duggleby Howe. At that time it was a major centre of life and ritual for the inhabitants of the Yorkshire Wolds.

During the Bronze Age, circa 2300-700 BC, and the Early Iron Age, circa 700-500 BC, a series of substantial boundary banks was built to divide the land and these remained in use until the Middle Ages.

The earliest known houses at Wharram Percy date from the Iron Age, circa 100 BC. Close to the junction of three pre-historic earthworks stood the home of a local chief. It was defended by a large ditch and there was easy access from the plateau to the water supply in the valley below by means of a *hollow* way. Scattered over a wide area along the valley bottom was another settlement.

During the Roman occupation the wealthiest homestead, which may have been a villa (a farm built in Roman style), was built over the remains of the Iron Age Chief's homestead. Already this part of the settlement was becoming established as the residence of the most prosperous inhabitants.

Excavations on three of the four Romano-British sites on the plateau have produced Saxon finds suggesting that the Anglo-Saxons who settled at Wharram Percy may have continued to use parts of the existing farm system.

A number of small huts set into pits have been found near the site of the north medieval manor, which is where the wealthiest Roman had his villa. So the importance placed on this area of the settlement by the Iron Age people and the Romans seems to have continued into Anglo-Saxon times. The eighth-century owner of one of the huts was wealthy enough to have been able to use pottery from Northern France and also possessed a finely decorated bone comb.

During Anglo-Saxon times the neighbouring parishes of Wharram-le-Street and Wharram Percy may have formed part of a single Anglo-Saxon estate containing a number of farms. An eighth-century smithy found behind the twelfth-century manor house and the huts near the north medieval manor are the only Saxon structures to be found on the site.

No remains of a church of this period have been found, although it is possible that the lord of the estate had his own private chapel at his house.

From the eighth and ninth centuries a more centralised society was developing, bringing a greater stability in attitudes to property and settlement. This change came about partly as a consequence of the establishment of permanent churches and, in part, from the tenth century, as a result of Viking influence. The change was widespread throughout the land and two of the ways in which it showed itself were in the establishment of a compact layout of houses around a clear street pattern and the emergence of long-lasting property boundaries.

At Wharram Percy the old scatter of isolated settlements was replaced with a new village layout of two parallel rows of TOFTS (houses with rear yards) and CROFTS (enclosed paddocks behind houses) running north to south, a row to the north which ran east to west and a triangular green enclosed by rows of houses. It was a common type of plan and seems to have resulted from the unified scheme of one lord.

By the time of the Domesday Survey in 1086, Wharram Percy consisted of two manors and it is likely that the original village plan was modified to include the two manor enclosures. Settlements which had more than one lord appear to have been quite common in medieval England.

Although oxen were usually used for ploughing throughout England horses were also used around Wharram Percy. Evidence of this is the unusually high number of horses bones found here. Horses would have had no difficulty ploughing the light chalky soil of the Wolds. They could also pull a plough longer without turning as would have been needed to make those at Wharram Percy as long as they were.

All the available flatland on the plateau being brought into cultivation implies a large population and the subsequent increased demand for food. This may have been connected with the arrival of the Vikings whose influence is seen in the almost complete replacement of English by Scandinavian place names around Wharram Percy.

The settlement's first church was a wooden structure that was rebuilt in stone during the tenth to eleventh centuries. The lords of the manor would have worshipped inside the building while the rest of the village did so outside.

In 1254 the two manors were combined and in the twelfth century the south manor house was demolished, the site being used for a while as a chalk quarry. From the fourteenth century a series of peasant houses was built on it. Later some of the original peasant houses were pulled down to make way for a fourteenth- to fifteenth-century courtyard farm next to the site of the now abandoned manor house.

From circa 1300 the Percies did not actually live at Wharram Percy, which was administered by a bailiff, who almost certainly lived in the courtyard farm. In 1402 the Percies exchanged the manor with the Hilton family from near Sutherland. They, in turn, sold the property in 1573 to Matthew Hutton, later archbishop of York. Throughout its history from the mid twelfth century to present day, only six families have owned Wharram Percy.

Village life centred around the lord of the manor and the church.

The medieval lord owned all the land, nominally through the King. He controlled the life of his tenants, who both farmed for him and undertook other duties when required. These included the annual maintenance of the fish pond and doing land improvements like building the extension of the terrace around the south end of the church in the fourteenth century. They were also obliged to have their corn ground at the lord's mill at whatever cost he chose to make. The lord of the manor, in contrast, was a law unto himself, evicting villagers as and when he fancied and without fear of retribution.

The medieval church at Wharram also served four other townships in the newly formed parish: Thixendale, Raisthrope, Burdale and Towthorpe. This placed Wharram Percy as the focal point for a number of secondary settlements.

In common with many medieval villages, Wharram Percy was based on farming. Barley was the most important crop but wheat and oats were also grown. Sheep provided wool for clothing and milk as well as meat. Cattle, though not as numerous as sheep, were probably the most important meat providing animals. The villagers wasted nothing. Animal bone provided handles for tools and was made into a wide variety of implements and dress fittings. Hide from cattle, sheep and goats provided leather for jerkins and shoes. Yarn, made from locally produced wool, was spun using bone and stone spindle-whorls.

Not all the villagers were farm labourers. Iron working was widely practised and most of the iron tools were probably made by the local blacksmith. The roasting of local ores and iron smelting were probably also carried out there during the thirteenth and fourteenth centuries.

The stream running through Wharram Percy was an important .esource and the landscape of the south part of the village is dominated by the pond. Originally developed as a small mill pond serving a string of small mills, it became a good source of fish and fragments of basketwork traps for fish or eel have been found there. Cattle were also watered there. During the twelfth century the mills became derelict and the pond silted up. In the fourteenth century it was dug out again and enlarged to create a fish pond. By this time the corn was being milled at another mill, referred to in a document dated 1368, which was sited close to the village's north manorial complex.

From circa 1300 an increasing proportion of pottery was brought to Wharram Percy from York, Scarborough, the Humber, the Netherlands, France and Germany. This supplemented locally made pots from Staxton, some 14 miles (22.4km) away.

In Wharram Percy, as elsewhere in England, the size and quality of the house depended upon the wealth of the occupant. The earlier dwellings were built of cob or wattle and daub supported by vertical posts. Later ones, which came into being when the climate began to worsen, were either built on stone footings or had stone walls reaching up to eaves level. Some of the fifteenth-century houses at Wharram Percy were built with wooden posts set on individual stone pads to prevent the bottoms rotting.

The size and quality of the house depended mainly on the wealth of the occupant and to modern eyes would have appeared ramshackle, dark, dirty and overcrowded. Usually single storied, their heating was provided by an open hearth in the centre of the main room. Oxen were usually kept at one end of a long house and here the medieval equivalent of turning down the central heating would have been to put the oxen out to grass.

The lord of the manor lived in much more splendid style. The manor house had a stone built range with a cellar which had probably originally been attached to a timber hall, with other buildings around it. The cellared range had a fireplace and two light windows closed by internal shutters. A large pit nearby was probably used as a cold meat and dairy store.

Wharram Percy's medieval villagers ate mutton and beef but not much pork and they ate bread made from wheat and barley. The limited supply of fish from the fish pond was supplemented by dried haddock and cod. They also ate snails, but very few vegetables.

The standard of living, by modern standards, was squalid with little sign of luxury. But the villagers were houseproud and kept their earth floors so carefully swept that they were worn into a U shape. Rubbish was slung onto a midden from where it was taken periodically and spread on the fields as a valuable source of fertilizer.

Door locks and keys and smaller locks for chests, found at Wharram Percy, suggest that not only were there some items of value around but also some thieves.

Following a general period of expansion in the twelfth and thirteenth centuries during which much marginal land was settled there came a period of economic contraction coupled with climatic deterioration in the fourteenth century; and it was then that the decline of Wharram Percy began, long before the arrival of the Black Death in the mid-fourteenth century. In 1323 two thirds of the lord of the manor's lands were uncultivated and his corn mills were derelict.

The slight increase in prosperity for those who survived the plague was short lived. For although labour was at a premium for a while, the once large population had shrunk and with it the demand for arable products. Landlords and wealthier tenants got some relief through converting fields to sheep pastures. This change of policy meant that fewer labourers were needed to do the shepherding, and those no longer needed were evicted.

From its peak of 30 houses in 1368, Wharram Percy dropped to only 16 in 1435 and by circa 1500 there were none: all had been deserted.

Wintringham

CHAPTER VI
WHARRAM-LE-STREET TO WINTRINGHAM

Length of section: linear 10¾ miles (18.2km)

Distance covered walking clockwise from Hessle: 67¼ miles (107.6km)

Walk 11:   Circular: Wharram-le-Street - Settrington - North
            Grimston: Wharram-le-Street. 11 miles (17.6km)

Walk 12:   Circular: Settrington - High Bellmaneor - Wintringham
            - Thorpe Bassett - Settrington: 9 miles (14.4km)

Map Ref: Landranger 100 and 101

Parking: Wayside parking in Wharram-Le-Street and at the north
            end of Settrington.

Handy hostelries: The Red House, Wharram-le-Steet. The Middleton
                   Arms, North Grimston.

WALK 11. WHARRAM-LE-STREET - SETTRINGTON - NORTH GRIMSTON - WHARRAM-LE-STREET.

From the church[1] at Wharram-le-Street[2] go left to the crossroads where turn left as indicated by a Wolds Way sign and on leaving the village take the signposted path on the right. After about 3/4 mile of exhilarating, uphill walking along a broad, chalky way through an expansive landscape the B1253 is reached. Cross it, as signposted, to begin a gradual descent down Duggleby Wold. Just past a Dutch barn on your right, turn left at a Wolds Way sign and continue down the field on your left, keeping close to a hedge on your right. At its bottom corner turn left, following a yellow marker.

The countryside hereabouts is enchanting and in Maytime the valley on your right is a froth of white hawthorn blossom and alive with birdsong.

When a signposted stile is reached turn right, across it, and go left close to an electrified fence on your left to another clearly seen Wolds Way signpost where turn right, downhill as indicated. Cross a stile in the valley bottom, go over a field and cross a stream using a footbridge. Continue straight ahead, steeply at first, uphill to a signpost which soon comes into view halfway up the hillside. On reaching a surfaced farm road turn right along it to Wood House Farm, going through the farmyard. The farm road ahead is now unsurfaced but is broad and easy to follow. Keep going, curving uphill and then continue northwards, following markers. Where it splits on approaching Settrington Wood[3] go right, as directed by a Wolds Way sign. Where the farm road enters the wood turn right, as signposted and continue along its edge, keeping close to the fence on your left. On reaching some farm buildings, turn left, as signposted, go through the narrow wood and turn right along a broad, unsurfaced track, keeping close to the wood, which is now on your right. After almost 1/2 mile turn left at a footpath sign and cross an arable field that slopes away from you, keeping close to a hedge on your left, to exit at a stile at the corner of a wood.

From where this circular walk turns left at the signposted field path the linear section, which coincides with the Wolds Way to its northern limit, continues northwards, alongside the wood on the right. Circular walk No. 12, which starts at Settrington, rejoins the Wolds Way where this one leaves it.

Continue straight ahead, keeping close to the wood on your left to reach a signposted gate, which go through. The way forward is to the right and descends the scarp in an indistinct curve to reach Low Bellmanear Farm, seen on your left as you come down the hillside. There are yellow markers on posts as the farm is approached. On reaching it, turn right, along a winding farm road, for almost a mile to reach a surfaced country road, where turn left.

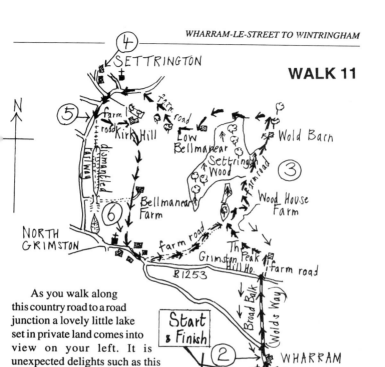

WALK 11

As you walk along this country road to a road junction a lovely little lake set in private land comes into view on your left. It is unexpected delights such as this that add sparkle to a country walk.

From the road junction ahead a detour to see lovely Settrington village[4] and All Saints Church is well worth the effort. To do so, turn right at the road junction, briefly, then turn right again into the village to cross the stream along which it lies, using a footbridge near a ford. Go left as far as the first turning right, where turn right between houses and right again to visit the lovely church seen ahead.

Retrace your steps to the junction and turn right, along the road, climbing over a shoulder of land and passing a road junction to Malton on your right. After a quarter of a mile turn left at a cottage on a disused railway line[5] and follow the farm road to Kirk Hill Farm, crossing a stream just before it as waymarked. When close to the farm buildings turn right, through a gate, into a field, which cross on a clear track to another gate, which go through. Continue along a clear track which curves right, then ends abruptly. At this point go right to a nearby stream and cross it. The way is now left, close to the stream on your left, to pass Bellmanear Farm on your left. Cross the farm

79

road and, using the stiled fields ahead, continue to North Grimston[6], seen ahead, entering the village using a stone step stile.

Go left into the village and if your timing is right, enter an oasis called the Middleton Arms where a warm welcome is assured. From the pub continue through the village and turn left along a gated farm road which leads to the same Wood House Farm passed on the outward leg. Where the farm road curves left, turn right to climb a steep valley in the hillside to Grimston Hill Farm and a minor road. Turn left, along it, over the brow of a hill and, as it begins to descend, turn right at a familiar signpost and retrace your steps to Wharram-le-Street now seen ahead.

Things Seen On The Way

(1) Wharram-le-Street Church. Its tower is Saxon and the middle shafts of its belfry window are topped with long stones. A window set into its west doorway is lofty and horseshoe shaped and its arch has a stringcourse. The Saxon nave was modified by the Normans who built the doorway inside the tiny porch and probably built the tub font as well. The aisle is medieval and the chancel, originally medieval, was rebuilt in 1860.

(2) Wharram-le-Street. The village hall, the hub of village social life, was built in 1871 as a school. Today there is no school in the village.

From the crossroads the road going north-east leads to Duggleby and adjacent Duggleby Howe, the largest known Neolithic barrow in Britain. The howe is round, 120 feet in diameter and was originally about 30 feet high. It now has a height of 20 feet.

From the village, the public bridleway that leads so pleasantly up Duggleby Wold is broad and firm and, during the summer months, edged with flowers that seem to glow in the warming sunshine as if they were lit from within.

(3) Settrington Wood. That part of Settrington Wood the route edges and cuts through is really a long, thin extension of it called Screed Plantation. It is mainly sycamore with some beech and ash.

During the months of spring and summer Screed Plantation is suffused with pink campion.

(4) Settrington village. Trim, red roofed cottages backed by long gardens, a former rectory, Glebe House, surrounded by a high brick wall that adds a touch of class, Greystones, another fine house, originally built as a water mill in 1790, beautiful All Saints church and splendid Settrington House, built in English classical style, all gathered around a long village green itself cleaved by gently flowing Settrington Beck. This is an estate village of great charm set in a broad, wooded valley. Unfortunately the village has no pub; but the shop is also an off licence.

The old rectory, Settrington House and the church all stand at the same end of the village where, in the park in which the fine house stands, magnificent beeches, yews and other trees lend enchantment.

All Saints' Church is mainly fifteenth century but some parts are much older. The south doorway, decorated with zigzag and floral carvings, dates from the thirteenth century. Buttresses with seven steps support the fifteenth century tower and the shields of the Bogods adorn its battlements, below which there is a gallery of quaint heads. More heads can be found beside the windows, which are also fifteenth century. In one corner the carved figure of a man stands behind another that is kneeling. A fragment of old stained glass includes part of what is thought to be St Christopher. There are two little mice in the white painted church, one on the Litany desk and another on the organ seat. They are the work of Mr Thompson, the mouse man of Kilburn. The church also contains a memorial to Isaac Taylor (1829-1901), who pioneered the study of names and alphabets. Known as the Darwin of Philology, he was rector of Settrington from 1875 until he died. This beautiful church exudes harmony, warmth and interest which collectively provide an atmosphere conducive to worship.

The village's most outstanding feature is Settrington House, a fine eighteenth-century country house in yellow stone consisting of a main block with seven bays and two lower wings with grand round arched windows. Storks carrying little bundles of joy greatly enhance its magnificent gateway. It is home to the Hon. Sir Richard Storey.

(5) Station House. The cottage on the disused railway line where the route leaves the North Grimston road is a former Malton to Driffield Railway station house. The trains which once worked this line were affectionately referred to as either the Malton or the Driffield Flier, depending on the direction in which they were going.

(6) North Grimston. Where the road through the village turns left a strange sight presents itself. For on this corner stand two very large round pillars built entirely of thousands of horseshoes with, set back between them, a third one, half completed. With horseshoes, those nailed to walls with the open end at the top to prevent luck running out denote a pagan household while those with the open end downwards, allowing the luck to run out, belong to Christian households where luck is not important because faith is stronger. On the completed columns, all the horseshoes except the pinnacle ones, which are fixed open end up, are placed horizontally, indicating, perhaps, that these structures were built by someone who was not sure that he believed in but was taking no chances of his luck running out.

The long, low, mainly Norman church is approached along a lime tree shaded path. A small statue on its slim, thirteenth-century tower is thought to be of its patron, St Nicholas. There are carvings of two small dragons above the now blocked round doorway in the north wall and there is an old gable cross in the porch that shelters the south doorway. Inside, the walls slope, the arches lean and the carved heads of men and animals stare from under the roofs. One of the coffin lids in the back chancel is richly carved with a sword and a shield. The huge, lop-sided Norman font is decorated with scenes of the last supper and of Christ descending from the cross.

The Middleton Arms offers a warm welcome with good food and beer.

WALK 12. SETTRINGTON - HIGH BELLMANEAR - WINTRINGHAM - THORPE BASSETT - SETTRINGTON.

From the south end of Settrington village take the North Grimston road and turn left at the T-junction, soon to pass Settrington House on the left and a lake on the right. As the road begins to climb a hill, go right along a farm road, to Low Bellmanear.

On reaching the farm, turn left as indicated by waymarkers and follow a track, indistinct in parts, that curves right, uphill, to a waymarked gate at the near edge of a wood. Go through the gate and continue close to the wood on your right. Where the wood ends, cross a facing hedge at a stile and go straight ahead, along the left-hand side of a hedge, over arable land, to a broad farm road that crosses your line of walk and

WALK 12

edges a shallow wood.

It is at this point that the Wolds Way is rejoined. Turn left along it. Soon the unsurfaced road swings right, through the wood, then past some outbuildings; and it is signposted. Go ahead, to a large wood, beyond which a mast[1] is easily seen. Cross a road to enter the wood over a stile and continue along a broad, waymarked, unsurfaced road to a junction, where turn right, as directed[2]. This part of the wood is beautiful beech and where the road through it turns right and ends, take the green lane left, as indicated, to exit over a stile into a sloping field[3].

Go diagonally left, down a sunken, green lane[4], towards Rowgate Farm ahead through an area of polka dot mole hills, a common feature in the Wolds. At the bottom of the hill, where the path curves right, go through the metal gate ahead as directed by a signpost. Continue along a pleasant, surfaced lane for about a mile where, at a signposted stile, go right, along the bottom of a field, close to a hedge on your left, leaving through a gate on your left. Cross the field ahead diagonally right to a metal gate, which go through. Continue ahead to cross a stream on a footbridge near a ford. Go along a path, briefly, and on entering Wintringham[5] turn left for 300 yards and, past the last house on your right, turn right, as signposted, and follow a clear, unsurfaced track parallel to the village to Wintringham's mellow fourteenth-century church, where turn right along the road. This soon turns sharp right into the village, passing on the outside of the corner the classical styled estate gates of Place Newton.

Continue through the long village with its white cottages and pleasant gardens and, almost at its far end, turn left, along the same signposted path you used to enter the village.

Retrace your steps over the footbridge, through the metal gate, diagonally over the arable field and right, close to the hedge on your right, to regain the surfaced lane left earlier. Cross it and continue along a field's edge, close at first to a hedge on your right and, further on, with it on your left. The path becomes a farm road which, keeping in the same direction, goes first through a metal gate, then, further on, through a red gate with a footpath sign onto a metal road where turn left, along it into Thorpe Bassett[6].

Where Wintringham is long and thin, Thorpe Bassett is squat, showing that villages, like sweets, come in all sorts of flavours!

Where the road divides, take the left fork which in Maytime is awash with cow parsley and, soon after it bends right, leave it at a footpath sign on the right and follow a narrow path, which soon crosses a little stream, beyond which, cross a stile and immediately go left, edging a vast field, following the bank of the stream just crossed.

Where a wood straddles the stream, the path keeps to the edge of it as indicated by a marker on a post. At the far end of this field cross a waymarked stile in its corner and continue straight ahead, crossing the stream you have been following as it crosses your line of walk from the right.

Cross a waymarked stile ahead, go left briefly, to the field corner, then go right along the field's edge to a disused reservoir. Skirt it, first right, then left and go forward to a waymarker near an ash tree in a hedge ahead. Turn right as directed, and continue close to the hedge on your left and cross a stile in a facing hedge. Turn left, keeping close to the hedge on your left to another stile in a fence, which cross.

Continue straight ahead and climb the Wold's steep scarp, keeping close to the wood on your right, there being no path to follow. Where the top of the wood and the right-hand corner of the field meet, go through a waymarked gate and skirt a ruin ahead, going right, then left and left again.

From here the retrospective view across the Vale of Pickering to the North Yorkshire Moors is superb.

Having skirted the ruin, continue in the same direction, close to a fence on your left, to cross Thorpe Bassett Wold on arable land. On reaching a facing fence, cross a wobbly stile and continue over the next field, aiming for the top half of a telegraph pole a little to your right. Exit there, cross the facing road and, following a footpath sign's direction, take the farm road downhill to Wolds House Farm. On approaching the farmhouse turn right, beside an old nisson hut, cross to a fence without a stile and step over it. Yes, it is a right of way and we did it with the farmer's blessing.

Go right, diagonally, down the next field, towards a gate, hidden, at first, by the lie of the land, cross a double, waymarked stile beside it and continue diagonally left, uphill, towards a wood on your right. Soon a narrow path is reached, which follow, going roughly parallel to the wood. At the end of the field, which is also where the wood ends, go through a gateway and cross the field ahead, passing Wardale Farm on your right. Exit through a gate onto a farm lane, go left, along it to a road where turn left downhill. At a road end to Low Bellmanear, close to the foot of the hill, the circle is complete. Continue along the road, passing Settrington House on your right and at a road junction just past it turn right to return to the start of the walk.

Things Seen On The Way

(1) Settrington Beacon. The beacon stands at a point along the way close to where a trig column, through a gate on your left, gives your height above sea level: 198 metres. Nearby is a service reservoir for a bore hole into the chalk. It is at this point that the lovely, broad chalk road along which you have

walked to get here is exchanged for a delightful forest track.

2) South Wold Plantation. Conifers allow so little light to penetrate that about the only plants capable of establishing themselves between them are Dog Mercury and Wood Sorrel, both of which use underground food resources stored in their extensive root systems. But beeches, being deciduous and not so tightly packed, allow more light to stream through their thin, dormant branches before the new leaves unfurl. For this reason it is the springtime herb that is the woodland flower. Before new life stirs in the deciduous trees and a green canopy spreads, the woodland floor is alive with activity as the bulbs develop and vigorous foliage growth begins. From late April to early May white drifts of anemone carpet the wood, followed from mid-May by bluebells. Then the white returns as wild garlic flowers.

Throughout the summer months the path through this most attractive wood is overhung with lush, green boughs, sufficient enough to provide a cool, shaded way.

3) Stile Overlooking South Dale. Because it is so unexpected, the panoramic view seen on climbing the stile out of South Wold plantation is that much more attractive. You are overlooking South Dale and the next objective, Wintringham. The patchwork of fields beyond is the Vale of Pickering, behind which the North Yorkshire Moors spread across the northern horizon. To westwards, as the escarpment falls away to flat farmlands, Malton is seen some six miles away as the crow flies.

'3) Langton Wold. Langton Wold lies to the south-east of this racing town and is bounded by Settrington, North Grimston, Birdsall, Langton and Auburn Hill. It is a rather special Wold because of its long and prominent associations with the sport of Kings. Malton, on the north bank of the Derwent and Norton, across the bridge, on the south bank, lie just off the Wolds but because of their horse breeding and training associations cannot, in this context, be separated from Langton Wold. Today Malton's racing links are weaker than they were because, although the town still has strong turf connections, all the stables are in and around Norton.

During the second World War the local Agricultural Executive Committee decided, very reluctantly, that it could not leave Langton Wold untouched when so much good pasture nearby was going under the plough. So more of the "velvety turf" became arable and the training area was further restricted.

(4) The descent to Rowgate farm. There are as many irregular lumps of white chalk in the mole hills scattered about the northern edge of South Wold as there are currants in a fruit cake; and this phenomenon is common throughout the Wolds.

(5) Wintringham. Wintringham is long and slim and rather lovely. It lies in a cleft in the Wolds and from its red roofed, white cottages the view is over meadows to hillsides many of which are pine covered. At its eastern end

Place Newton stands in 180 acres of pleasant parkland. Nearby and set among majestic beeches, is attractive Wintringham church, but the village has no pub.

(6) Thorpe Bassett. Sited in trees below Thorpe Bassett Wold, the village is a small huddle of houses and farms. The south doorway of the church, with its shafts and zigzag carving is Norman, as is the font. The nave arcade is late Norman and the chancel is medieval. The aisle was built on the old foundations of the nave wall last century. Old stones built into the aisle wall include the head of a cross and a gravestone carved with a fine cross and a sword.

CHAPTER VII
WINTRINGHAM TO SHERBURN

Length of section: linear 15 miles (24km)

Distance covered walking clockwise from Hessle: 82$\frac{1}{4}$ miles (131.6km)

Walk 13:	Circular: Wintringham - Knapton Plantation - Manor Wold Farm - Whin Moor - Wold Farm - East Farm - Wintringham. 10 miles (16km)
Walk 14:	Circular: Sherburn - Weaverthrope - Helperthorpe - Manor Wold Farm - Sherburn. 11 miles (17.6km)
Map Ref:	Landranger 101
Parking:	Near Wintringham Church. Roadside in Sherburn.
Handy hostelries:	Pigeon Pie, Sherburn. Inn at Weaverthrope. East Riding, Sherburn.

WALK 13. WINTRINGHAM - KNAPTON PLANTATION - MANOR WOLD FARM - WHIN MOOR - WOLD FARM - EAST FARM - WINTRINGHAM.

From Wintringham Church[1] on the eastern edge of the village turn left along the road, briefly, and where it curves right turn left on to a signposted track. Immediately go right, as directed and edge a large field to enter vast Scardale Plantation, directly ahead, over a waymarked stile. Turn left, along a forest road signposted Wolds Way, which keeps just inside the plantation.

After $\frac{1}{2}$ mile, where the road goes downhill, bending left, go right, along a green track as indicated by markers, climbing between trees. The incline is steep and becomes steeper, levelling as another forest road crosses it. Go left, along this road, as indicated, to exit the plantation over a stile into a field.

Continue straight ahead, along its left hand side, as before you a panorama unfolds. On your left is Pickering, beautifully sited in lush farmland which carpets the Vale ahead. There is an earthwork, more than a hedge, on your left as the field is crossed to reach a broad, unsurfaced road. Go right, along it, as waymarked, climbing steadily towards two masts. After half a mile, just before reaching them, go left, as waymarked, still on a broad road.

Before the road forks, turn left, over a waymarked stile and cross the field ahead, close to a fence on your right, into Knapton Plantation where, following yellow markers, go right. Where the track begins to descend take a thin track

WALK 13

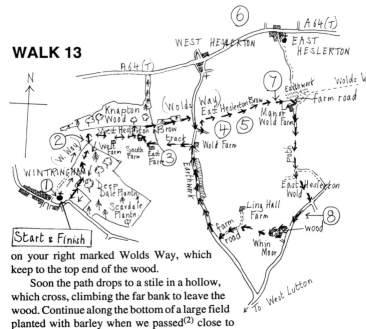

on your right marked Wolds Way, which keep to the top end of the wood.

Soon the path drops to a stile in a hollow, which cross, climbing the far bank to leave the wood. Continue along the bottom of a large field planted with barley when we passed[2] close to the wood on your left. The way is clear, grassy and a joy to walk. We found it redolent with new mown hay and rock rose abounded.

Cross another stile, still edging the wood, still on a clear path along a huge field of peas and continue to the field corner close, on your left, to a hedge which in May time is pink with blossom and glorious to see. Turn right at the corner as signposted, still with a hedge on your left, to a stile with a Wolds Way sign, which cross.

Cross the road ahead[3] and continue along an arrowed road close to a plantation on your left and turn left at the end of it as waymarked. Go ahead, alongside the plantation on your left, edging a barley field that must cover 200 acres. When a Wolds Way sign is reached turn right, as indicated, along a path dividing the barley field from one on your left which when we passed was growing 200 acres of peas. As progress is made an edging fence is reached.

You are on East Heslerton Brow[4] and below is East Heslerton with its beautiful spire. The Vale of Pickering[5] is spread out below and from this vantage point it can be seen that most of the villages tend to congregate along its northern and southern edges rather than along its middle.

88

Turn left for 100 yards at a waymarked stile, then right at another, and continue along the edge of a field, contouring the escarpment. From here, almost directly ahead, the distant sea can be seen.

Cross a waymarked stile, go down the escarpment as indicated, keeping close to a fence on your left and cross a stile in a facing fence. Turn right and, descending to a faint trod for ease of walking, continue parallel to the fence on your right. We had some Jacob's sheep for company hereabouts.

Cross a stile at the end of the field and continue close to a line of trees on a clear track to edge a wood on your right, curving right with it, following a marker, to a stile in the field corner, which cross[6].

Turn right, along a farm road, through the wood to Manor Wold Farm from where take the path southwards, straight as a die for the first mile, and on to join a minor road at a T-junction.

Turn right along the unfenced road, which goes to West Lutton[7], for $3/4$ mile to reach a wood on your right where turn right as signposted. The fields of barley around here go on for ever, stretching into infinity.

Keeping the wood on your left go to the end of it and turn left to a farm gate, seen ahead, where turn right and cross a field to a facing hedge. Go through a broad gap in it and continue down the next field close to a hedge on your left to join the farm road clearly seen below and ahead of you.

Go left, along it, uphill, to a facing surfaced road and turn right, along it for just over one mile, passing a long wood on your right. At Wold Farm on the right turn left along a broad, unsurfaced track to East Farm where turn right, along the left-hand side of a field.

Where the track bears left there is, on the left, a piggy township where Russian hybrid minimal disease breeding pigs and their offspring live in detached splendour, happy, by the look of them, as the proverbial...

Just past this delux piggery, the outward route is rejoined. At this point retrace your steps to Wintringham.

Things Seen On The Way

(1) Wintringham Church. Wintringham is dominated by its splendid church which is built of pleasing yellow stone and looks impressive both inside and out. Most of it was built from about 1400, although there is some twelfth century walling in the chancel. The tower buttresses look larger than necessary for the job they do and the high battlements are a bit much. Quarterfoils and heraldry enrich them and the corbels below are carved with faces and flowers. The magnificent nave roof, repaired in 1685, rests on more than 30 faces and the modern chancel roof has carved borders. Ten stone human heads are set like pinnacles on the plain parapets of the nave and the

aisle. Lovely medieval screens with lacelike tracery enclose the aisle chapels and a medieval screen leads to the chancel. Angels are carved on the 200 years old cover of the Norman font. There are some old, carved stones, an altar stone and a bracket with two faces in the chapels; but perhaps the most interesting features of the church are its seventeenth and eighteenth century inscribed tablets.

Some of the white, yellow stained glass is fifteenth century and rare outside the City of York.

(2) Barley. The Yorkshire Wolds are well suited to the growth of barley which lies at the very heart of all good beers. Hops add flavour and bitterness, pure water binds them together and yeast transforms them into an alcoholic brew.

Although beer can be made from sugar corn, rice, wheat and even potato starch, barley is the preferred grain because of the quality of its malt and its husk which acts as a natural filter bed during the brewing process. Brewing cannot begin until the barley is "malted" and its starches become fermentable sugars.

When barley is harvested it is taken to maltings where the grains are steeped in tanks of water and left to germinate. The wet grain is then spread on the floors of warm, dry rooms and within a few days shoots break through the husk. The cells of the barley are broken down by germination, making the conversion from starch to sugar possible.

The malt then goes into a kiln which is heated by hot air. The heat stops further germination. The greater the heat the darker the finished malt. Light malts are used to produce larger brews or pale ales. Crystal, amber, chocolate, black and roast maltings are made for different beers. The darkest malts have little fermentable sugar left but are used to add colour and flavour to special beers such as stouts and barley wines. What happens to the malt in the brewery depends on the stile of beer, whether ale or lager is being produced. The brewing of ale includes mild, pale ale, bitter, porter, stout, old ale and barley wine. Cheers!

(3) West Heslerton. Northwards, less than a mile away, along the road, and sheltered by the Wolds is tiny West Heslerton. Its hall is hidden behind trees and its church is hidden behind houses. Although most of the church was rebuilt last century, the original one was thirteenth century. The chancel, with its piscina, is thirteenth century. An inscription in the church is dedicated to Sir Christopher Sykes of Sledmere, who changed the sheep walks into arable land.

(4) East Heslerton Brow. Grass on the heavily grazed slopes of East Heslerton Brow, in common with other Wolds grasslands, sleeps late, often remaining dormant as late as June, as do the flowers; and with good reason. For once the winter cold has penetrated the soil it takes some shifting. So, the

flora slumbers on, until the sun's strengthening rays have warmed the ground.

Rock rose, salad burnet, common thyme and hairy violet are among the earliest plants to flower. The first two tend to dominate the steep slopes but all four have adapted morphologically to help them withstand the drought conditions which are the commonest stress factors plants have to endure when growing on a shallow soil on top of porous chalk. The leaves of the rock rose are evergreen and their thick cuticles resist water loss. Salad burnet has a long root system to tap any deep sources of moisture. Beneath the delicate aerial system of common thyme is an extensive root system up to 38cm deep. The hairy system and leaves of the hairy violet trap still air over their surfaces and all these features assist survival in dry habitats.

By late June the grassland is full of flowers, but for many, like mouse ear hawkweed, soft hawksbeard, lesser hawkbit and other dandelion like plants, liguates, their short life cycle is completed by the end of July. Only the deep rooted species like salad burnet keep their foliage throughout the entire summer.

In late summer the slopes of East Heslerton Brow are spangled yellow with common ragwort, the plants often sporting foliage that looks distinctly moth eaten. This is almost literally true because it is the caterpillar of the cinnabar moth that does the damage. Yellow, with black hoops, it chomps merrily away until the leaves have almost gone. The resulting moth is most active in the evening but often takes wing when disturbed during the day. It's flight is rather weak and its colouring rather dull. The front wings are marked with brilliant red, cinnabar, hence its name. Its hind wings are red with black margins.

(5) Vale of Pickering. At the outset of the last Ice Age ninety thousand years ago the Vale of Pickering was an inlet from the sea and the River Derwent flowed directly to the coast north of Scarborough. Afterwards, the effects of the ice, erosion of new channels and the accumulation of glacial deposits permanently deflected it inland, down Forge Valley, to join the Ouse near Selby. Today the rivers of the southern dales of the North Yorkshire Moors all leave the National Park separately before uniting at various points across the Vale of Pickering to form the main stream of the Derwent at Rye Mouth, three miles upstream of Malton.

(6) East Heslerton. Lying under the Wolds, to northwards, on the road from Malton to Filey, East Heslerton has a nice church which was given to the village by Sir Tatton Sykes. It was designed in the thirteenth century style by Mr G.E.Street and contains an iron screen which is a splendid piece of craftsmanship. The north tower has an octagonal belfry and spire.

(7) West Lutton. Another example of Mr G.E.Street's work is West Lutton church, which was re-built by him for Sir Tatton Sykes. It is set in a walled churchyard beside a stream which is crossed by a tiny bridge to reach a lychgate. The wooden belfry has a small, shingled spire and a weathercock. The lovely porch has a vaulted roof. The Madonna and Child are in a niche above the outer doorway. The chancel is vaulted and the other roofs are painted in medieval style. The church has a round traceried window. The vestry wall contains the oldest stones, part of an arch saved from the original Norman church.

Church and inn, houses and farms cluster round the village pond.

WALK 14. SHERBURN - WEAVERTHORPE - HELPERTHORPE - MANOR WOLD FARM - SHERBURN

From the south end of Sherburn[1] cross the A64 (T) and continue southwards, along the road, soon to reach a junction. Take the left fork, pass the lane end to High Mill Farm on the left and continue along the broad roadside verge for about $^{1}/_{2}$ mile to reach a second road junction. Here take the right-hand road which soon cuts through woodland[2] and climbs quite steeply up Sherburn Brow. Stay on this road which crosses Sherburn Wold between vast fields of barley, climbing to another junction. Take the right fork, passing the entrance to Duggleby Wold Farm on the right. This quiet road[3] soon descends to Weaverthrope slack at the bottom of the hill.

From here a footpath leads off, right. Where, after almost $^{1}/_{3}$ mile, a spur of East Heslerton Wold is reached, keep left, ignoring Sunning Dale, where there is no right of way, and continue along the shallow dale bottom to reach the Sherburn to West Luton road just south of East Heslerton Wold Farm. When we walked this right of way it was very overgrown. We informed the footpath officer at Pickering and he promised to look into it with a view to making it walkable again; and it may now be up to the required standard for public use. But just in case this right of way is still overgrown, use the longer but trouble free route given below which makes use of quiet country roads. We found it to be fine walking with good views in all directions and it touches two Wolds hamlets that otherwise have been missed. This short cut reduces the walk by just over a mile. On reaching the Sherburn to West Lutton road turn left along it for a short distance to a T-junction from where further directions are as given for the longer route.

From Weaverthorpe Slack the road climbs, passing the entrance to High Dale Farm on the right, then levels out, briefly, and soon after passing the

WALK 14

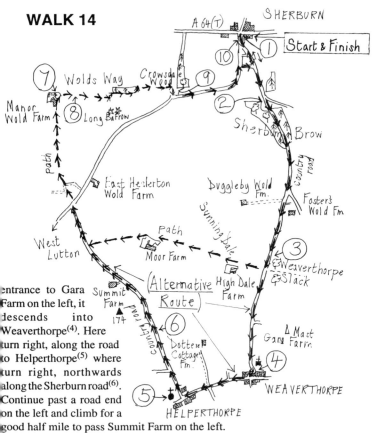

entrance to Gara Farm on the left, it descends into Weaverthorpe[4]. Here turn right, along the road to Helperthorpe[5] where turn right, northwards along the Sherburn road[6]. Continue past a road end on the left and climb for a good half mile to pass Summit Farm on the left.

A trig point just south of the farm gives a reading of 174m (571ft) above sea level.

The road now descends gradually, passing, on the right, the long drive to Moor Farm to reach a T-junction, from where leave the road and go roughly northwards to take a path northwards, straight as a die for a mile to reach Manor Wold Farm, from where take a farm road through a wood to join the Wolds Way, which comes from the left at the wood's end. The farm road goes straight ahead, briefly, then turns right into a field[7] and continues east

93

for just over half a mile. Eventually a signpost is reached which points left, down a faint track that divides two crops. At the bottom end of it turn right, along the side of a hill to reach the top, western corner of Crowsdale Wood[(8)]. Here turn right, uphill, and turn left on to a metalled lane. Continue along it, descending steeply. Soon after the lane curves left and levels out turn right, along a clear path that edges a field for 400 yards to join the road used out of Sherburn at the start of the walk. Turn left, along it into Sherburn.

Things Seen On The Way

(1) Sherburn. Sitting at the foot of the northern slope of the Wolds, the sizeable village of Sherburn overlooks the fertile Vale of Pickering. Here good food and accommodation are available at its two inns, the Pigeon Pie and the East Riding. There are several shops, a fine cross displaying a statue of St Hilda and eight scenes from her life, and an ancient church that has been beautifully restored. In Sherburn ancient and modern blend rather well.

The aisles in the church are modern restorations. A modern font stands underneath a thirteenth-century arch and a second font is Norman. The imposing Tower has battlements with tracery and shields and a corbel table of grotesques. A bird perched on the shoulder of a little man is shown on some Saxon stones in the tower. The great arch of the mainly fourteenth century chancel is one of the finest the Normans built in Yorkshire. The modern oak screen is also one of the most beautiful in the county. It is part of a fine array of modern woodwork decorating the church. The tops or poppyheads of the stalls are richly carved with animals and birds, including a ram, a lion, an eagle with a serpent, a pelican, a dragon and a dachshund. There are the four evangelists on the arm-rests. There are shields and faces on the pulpit and the altar is very elaborate. All in all a lovely church.

(2) Woodland On Sherburn Brow. Like many other woodlands scattered throughout the Wolds, the one growing on the northern slope of Sherburn Wold is more akin to primary than to natural woodland. A woodland is termed primary when the site has been continuously wooded since the return of the deciduous woodland after the last Ice Age.

(3) Quiet Road Crossing Sherburn Wold. The hedgerows alongside this (but by no means all the other roads crossing the Wolds) have become ecosystems in their own right, providing shelter, food and nesting sites for birds. When mature they provide a wider range of food than do most deciduous woodlands which makes them very attractive habitats, especially during autumn and winter when migrating fieldfares and redwings join blackbirds, thrushes and starlings, finches, buntings, sparrows and tits to feed on the seasonal

succession of berries and seeds. Having feasted on elderberries and blackberries in the autumn the birds turn to rose hips and haws, then sloes and later ivy berries.

Many of the autumn hedgerow fruits are merely pecked at by birds, exposing the juicy flesh underneath. The sweet smell released by this pecking invites a host of insects, most of which overwinter as eggs or dormant pupae or hibernate as larvae or adults. Shrews, blue-tits, wrens and other insect eating predators take their toll of these creatures, but many survive.

Woodland mammals like foxes and stoats use hedges as an extension of their hunting territory or as corridors when crossing from one copse to another in relative safety.

Fortunately, there is a growing concern among conservationists about the damage resulting from hedge removal. So perhaps the destruction of hedges in the Wolds and other places may be coming to an end.

(4) *Weaverthorpe*. Weaverthorpe's ancient church sits high on a hill-top to the north of the village, keeping spiritual guard. It is an ancient structure, the tower, nave and south doorway dating back to Norman times. The tower has a great turret stairway and deeply recessed belfry windows but no buttresses. The arch into the nave is narrow and very high. The chancel is fourteenth century but the plain arch is Norman, as is the font. A porch was added during the fourteenth century and some alterations were carried out. Since then the fabric of the church has remained much as it was. There is a Saxon sundial in the recess above the large lintel of the doorway. It carries an inscription which says that Herbert of Winchester built the church in honour of St Andrew circa 1110. This sundial is thought to be one of the most important of its kind in the land. There is a large statue of St Andrew inside the church and the fourteenth century porch has stone seats and pieces of old coffin lids in its walls.

The shallow mound in the field below the church is thought to be the site of an ancient settlement.

The Gypsy Race, a stream running beside the village high street is crossed by several little bridges.

Butterwick, the hamlet lying to the east of Weaverthorpe, is a scattering of farms and cottages, a forge, a church with a double bellcot and a pond. The church is small, it has no dividing arch between the nave and the chancel and it is lit by only three windows. The font is Norman, the rest, for the most part, medieval. There is a thriteenth century coffin lid on one side of the chancel and the figure of a Knight on the other. Thought to be Robert Fitz Ralph, he lies, his head supported by a cushion, with one foot on a dog and the other on a scaly dragon with the head of a woman. Could this half-human figure represent his wife?

(5) Helperthorpe. G.E.Street designed Helperthorpe church which Sir Tatton Sykes built in 1874. It stands on raised ground behind a farm; and the churchyard is entered through a stone lychgate.

A stream runs alongside the road in the village, swelling into a pond used by ducks and geese. It is a pretty sight, and the surrounding Wolds are beguiling.

(6) The Sherburn Road. The Sherburn road crosses East Heslerton Wold, an area of prairie farming where field sizes are measured by the square mile rather than the acre and crop spraying is carried out by light aircraft.

The sparsity of hedges and woodland on East Heslerton and other Wolds encourages the claim that the name comes from the Anglo-Saxon WEALD or WALD, signifying a treeless, bleak and unprotected land while others argue that the word is derived from the Danish VOLD, meaning a field, mound or rampart.

(7) Long Barrow. Set back from the line of walk are two long barrows; mounds of earth built to cover one or more bodies and the objects buried with them which were sometimes placed in an underground chamber and sometimes on or above the surface of the ground. Barrows, both round and long, are plentiful throughout Britain where they were built from 2500 BC to the Saxon period.

(8) Crowsdale Wood. From the approach to Crowsdale Wood it is possible to look along the full length of the Vale of Pickering.

Gateway to Hunmanby Hall (Walk 17) *(Ron Dodsworth)*
Bridlington - The Bayle Gate *(Ron Dodsworth)*

'The smallest church in the Wolds' - Fordon church

CHAPTER VIII
SHERBURN TO FORDON

Length of section: linear 9³⁄₄ miles (15.6km)

Distance covered walking clockwise from Hessle: 92 miles (147.2km)

Walk 15:	Circular: Sherburn - Potter Brompton - Ganton - Foxholes - Potter Brompton Wold - Sherburn. 10 miles (16km)
Walk 16:	Circular: Ganton - Staxton Wold - Lang Dale - Fordon - Willerby Wold Farm - Ganton. 10 miles (16km)
Map Ref:	Landranger 101
Parking:	Roadside parking in Sherburn and in Ganton where first check with residents to avoid obstructing any local access.
Handy hostelries:	Pigeon Pie and East Riding, Sherburn. Greyhound Inn, Ganton.

WALK 15: SHERBURN - POTTER BROMPTON - GANTON - FOXHOLES - POTTER BROMPTON WOLD - SHERBURN.

From the Pigeon Pie Inn, Sherburn, go left along the A64(T) to the nearby crossroads and turn right, southwards. Where the road forks, take the left-hand one signposted "Weaverthorpe"[1]. After about half a mile turn left at a Wolds Way sign and climb a minor surfaced road at a gradient of one in six. Just before the road curves right, go left, into a field, as directed by a Wolds Way sign.

The path goes along the bottom of a very large field of barley and continues as a broad lane, close to a plantation on your right. A good mix of trees lines this lane; crab-apple, sycamore, elderberry and hawthorn.

When a facing wood is reached turn right, climbing steeply, close to its boundary on your left, as far as a gate on your left. Here turn left, using the gate with its Wolds Way and Centenary Way signs and enter the wood. Contour through it, on a clearly defined way that becomes even clearer the deeper it penetrates. On approaching, on your left, the wood's edge, turn left to a clearly seen waymarked gate leading into a cornfield. Continue straight ahead, close to a hedge on your right, descending into the Vale of Pickering with great, white drifts of bladder campion for company, easily recognised by its bladder like calyx.

On reaching a facing electric fence turn right, as signposted, and continue along a track with a fence on your right and a small plantation on your left, beyond which there is a huge field[2]. On the far side of it are lots of multi-coloured detached buildings which, we discovered, are sites for free range pigs.

As you walk along this clear track another Wolds Way sign confirms your route. On approaching some farm buildings, continue between them and a farm house on your left. This is Manor Farm and at the tarmac road beyond it turn right for a few yards, then left, as indicated by the Wolds Way sign.

Continue along a good track close to a tall blackthorn hedgerow which, when we passed, was laden with sloes. It is on the left, there is a field of barley on your right and, to walk on, a pink and white bindweed carpet.

On nearing a T-junction with a minor tarmac road, Ganton village church[3] spire peeps through the trees and Ganton Hall[4] comes into view on your right. Here, instead of following the signposted direction to the village, turn right, along a quiet road, southwards for almost 3½ miles of very pleasant walking across Ganton Wold[5] to the village of Foxholes[6]. Throughout, the views are excellent, the skyscapes being particularly dramatic. When close enough to Foxholes to see its church tower, turn right, along a surfaced lane for the final four miles back to Sherburn, wending a

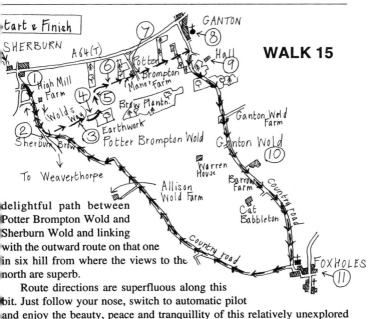

delightful path between
Potter Brompton Wold and
Sherburn Wold and linking
with the outward route on that one
in six hill from where the views to the
north are superb.

Route directions are superfluous along this
bit. Just follow your nose, switch to automatic pilot
and enjoy the beauty, peace and tranquillity of this relatively unexplored
corner of the Wolds. You'll love it.

Things Seen On The Way

(1) High Mill. Soon after forking left along the road signposted to
Weaverthorpe the lane end to nearby High Mill is passed on the left. The
main building was built in 1843 and a small stream from a spring rising at
the foot of the Wold was dammed to make a mill-pond. Today this long pond
is edged with fine mature poplars that can be seen from the road. Some of the
old mill machinery is still there but nowadays the machinery used in the
making of animal feed at the mill is driven by electricity. The pond is a
favourite place for wildfowl and swans.

(2) Lucerne. The crop in this large field was lucerne or alfalfa. It is one of the
world's very important fodder crops but is not popular in Britain where,
outside the dry, sandy areas of the Brecklands of Norfolk and Suffolk, it is
seldom cultivated. It thrives in hot, dry countries because it is extremely deep
rooted; but is easily choked with weeds. It's bluish, purple flowers made a
rare sight.

(3) Ganton Church. The lovely fourteenth-century spire of St Nicholas church stands on a tower with battlements below which some little stone faces stare, in springtime, onto a carpet of snowdrops, crocuses and a stream. Most of the church dates from the fifteenth century but parts of two windows in the chancel are much older than that. The south porch, with its ribbed roof, shelters a doorway decorated with medieval faces and the shield of Acklams. The door swings on ancient C-shaped hinges.

(4) Ganton Hall. Hiding in a beautiful park that climbs the hillside, Ganton Hall is built in the style of a Victorian French chateau.

(5) Ganton Wold. Man first began to colonise the Wolds 5,000 years ago, since when almost every Wold and dale has been used for agriculture, first the grazing of stock on the sweet, chalk pastures, by the Parisii, then, as this tribe became assimilated into the Roman system of farming, by tilling the light soils.

Today the grassed over scars of early man are scattered around the Wolds like pock-marks on a face. A system of earthworks runs east to west along the rim of Ganton Wold's northern scarp and north to south between Ganton and Foxholes. There are tumulae on many of the higher, drier parts of Ganton Wold.

When you take a look at the large system of earthworks and the scattered tumuli on Ganton Wold, surrounded by acres of waving barley you don't just see 5,000 years of evolution. At a glance you have both the seed and the fruit of the Wolds themselves.

(6) Foxholes hamlet and Wolds' Newton village. Four miles south of Staxton the B1249 neatly cuts through the middle of Foxholes, a quiet hamlet, very much involved with farming. It is dry, the nearest pub being at Wold Newton, two miles to the east.

Some of the houses in Wold Newton are built of chalk quarried locally. There is a large pond near the crossroads and the Gypsy Race nudges the southern end of the village. This interesting water course is one of the few streams on the Wolds chalkland. It flows from Duggleby to Bridlington, much of the time underground; and we are to see it again later on. The local name for these streams or races is "bourne".

A monument standing on high ground ³/₄ mile south-west of Wolds Newton marks the spot where, in 1795, a meteorite weighing half a hundredweight fell. The meteorite is now in the National History Museum in South Kensington.

WALK 16. GANTON - STAXTON WOLD - LANG DALE - FORDON - WILLERBY WOLD FARM - GANTON

From Ganton[1] crossroads on the A64(T) go south, briefly and turn left, as directed by Centenary Way and Wolds Way signs, through the village. Where the road curves left, go straight ahead, following a Wolds Way sign.

Cross a beck and continue between a wood on your right and the vicarage. Where the path splits, go left, skirting the vicarage garden, to a stile, which cross. Turn right, edging a large field close to a hedge on your right, crossing a clear farm road and continue along a narrow path, waymarked at intervals, to the end of the field to cross a waymarked stile into a narrow copse.

Cross it to exit into another field, where turn right. Keeping close to the hedge on your right, continue to a waymarked stile and cross it[2].

Now go left, along the bottom of a field, close to a hedge on your left. This field contained ripening barley when we walked it and had a bronze sheen. On reaching the fields edge turn right, along a signposted lane and enter the field ahead. Climb it, following the arrows, close to a hedge on your right, along a way that becomes a sunken track. Cross a stile at a facing gate and keep going straight ahead. On reaching another facing gate turn left as directed by a Wolds Way sign.

The farm seen distantly beyond this gate is Binnington Wold Farm.

Cross the field close to the hedge on your right and exit right, over a waymarked stile. Go along the left side of the field ahead and, just past a large tree that overhangs the route, go left over a waymarked stile and cross the field ahead, keeping close to the hedge on your right to exit onto a road[3].

Cross the road and continue along the one facing you, signposted R.A.F. Staxton Wold[4], passing Willerby Grange Wold Farm on your right. Within a mile of steady, uphill walking along a surfaced road the radar station with its spinning scanners is reached. On reaching the perimeter fence turn right, past the entrance of R.A.F. Staxton Wold, and continue, passing a farm building on your right, along a lane that descends into Cotton Dale, passing a waymarker that confirms your route.

At the bottom of the hill turn left at a Wolds Way sign, cross a stile and climb steeply through scrub to a stile at the dale's rim[5]. Continue up the side of a field, keeping close to a fence on your left, to a ladder stile ahead, which cross.

Continue along the edge of a vast field, close to a hedge on your left[6] and at the end of it turn right at a Wolds Way sign and continue along the field's edge. Where a hedge coming from the left meets the one on your left at right angles, turn left over a stile and continue close to the hedge on your

WALK 16

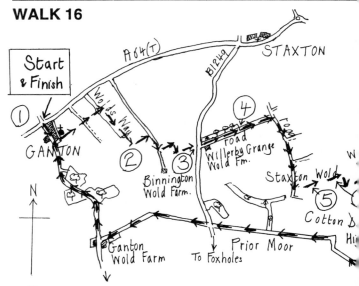

left[7]. Exit the field over a ladder stile, descend into a dry valley and go straight up the far side of it to descend into another and immediately climb out of that one to another ladder stile. Climb this stile and continue still with the fence on your left. Descend into yet another dry valley, Lang Dale, where turn right and say au revoir to both the Centenary Way and the Wolds Way.

Go down the dale, keeping to the left of a small fenced field and aim for a hawthorn tree at the end of a facing hedge. On reaching it turn right, over a gate. Continue, keeping close to the hedge on your right, towards a farm track leading to some sheep pens and cross it.

Cotton Dale is on your right but the way ahead is along the left-hand side of North Dale, to your left. Continue to a waymarked stile in a facing fence and cross it. Now walk diagonally right, out of a wooded area, to a gateway in a facing hedge on the far side of the field ahead from where cross the next field to a waymarked but broken stile near a gate.

Keeping to the dale bottom, following a rough, green track, passing a concrete pond and going through thickening undergrowth to reach a farm. Go past the farmhouse on your right and, passing a footpath sign on your left, enter Fordon[8], a small village where live some of the friendliest of Wolds folk.

Turn right, uphill, along a quiet road that crosses Prior Moor for a three mile hike through more lovely countryside, passing a crossroads to a T-junction where turn right, northwards, along the side of Staxton Wold to make an impressive descent to Ganton and enjoy a well earned pint.

Things Seen On The Way

(1) Ganton Village. Pretty white cottages line Main Street, the lane leading through Ganton to the church, standing among trees at its eastern side alongside a large vicarage with a huge garden.

(2) Binnington Brow. At the time of the last Ice Age the view to the north from Binnington Brow was across Lake Pickering, which at that time was 25 miles (40km) long and 8 miles (12.8km) wide. Today it is known as The Carrs, that part of the coastal plain reaching to Filey Bay which swallows the Vale of Pickering.

The red roofs seen in the middle distance to the north-east are part of Scanner and the outskirts of Scarborough.

(3) Grange Farm. Sited on the B1249 at the turn off to R.A.F. Staxton Wold, Grange Farm is less than half a mile south of Staxton Brow picnic site with its panoramic views.

(4) R.A.F. Staxton Wold. Perched 600ft above sea level and nine miles from Scarborough, R.A.F. Staxton Wold stands on the site of a Roman signal station. The world's oldest operational radar station and one of ten similar stations throughout Britain, it was opened on 1st April, 1939.

During the Second World War it made a large contribution to the country's defences by monitoring movements of Luftwaffe aircraft, picking out "hostiles" heading towards England across the North Sea.

(5) High Wolds Country. With elephant-high corn rolling into the distance this landscape is straight out of Oklahoma. This is an area of intense, arable farming where modern trends favour specialist farming in which only one crop is grown.

(6) Coursing. The wide open spaces of the High Wolds were most popular in the early days of coursing. Some of the best greyhounds of those times were bred from indigenous stock, originally used for hunting wolves. They "resembled more the shaggy wolf-dog of former times than any sporting dog

of the present day".

Major Edward Topham, (1750-1820), of Wold Cottage, Thwing, was primarily responsible for popularising greyhounds and coursing on the High Wolds.

(7) Wold-Deep Dales. Cotton Dale, which is edged and Lang Dale and North Dale, along the dry bottoms of which the route passes, are beautiful, steep sided valleys with splendid long views. North Yorkshire inherited this splendid heart-of-the-Wolds countryside from the East Riding in the Local Government reorganisation in 1974.

(8) Fordon. The hamlet surrounding the church, St James', was previously known as Fordune and was under the control of the church at Hunmanby.

The church was built between 1086 and 1115, when it was included in a grant of lands made by Walter-de-Gant to Bardney Abbey Lincolnshire. It was small, oblong, built of stone found locally, probably with a wood and thatch roof and a floor of crushed chalk and earth. A few rough seats would have been placed inside for the aged but most of the congregation stood.

Situated in a wild and lonely place in what for centuries were the desolate, unfenced Wolds of East Yorkshire it was violated many times and, more recently, was used to shelter sheep.

Today the church is fully restored and very beautiful. It has a Norman floor and there are Norman shafts with scalloped capitals in the chancel. The font appears to be a Norman bowl set on part of a thirteenth-century pillar carved with foliage.

The interior of the church has been replastered and redecorated. Electricity has been installed both for light and heating. Two very beautiful oak-framed windows with leaded lights have been installed. The east window is also completely restored with new leaded lights and repairs have been made to the walls and the roof. This has all been accomplished with money raised by the sparse population of Fordon and friends of the little church of St James.

The church has no churchyard; but it has the love and support of worshippers with hearts as big as any in the Wolds. It is the smallest church in the Wolds.

CHAPTER IX
FORDON TO FILEY

Length of section: linear 11¾ miles (18.8km)

Distance covered walking clockwise from Hessle: 103¾ miles (166km)

Walk 17: Circular: Fordon - Camp Dale - Hunmanby - South Dale - Fordon. 11 miles (17.6km)

Walk 18: Circular: Hunmanby - Stockendale Farm - Muston - Filey - North Moor Farm - Hunmanby. 8½ miles (13.6km)

Map Ref: Landranger 101

Parking: Roadside parking in Fordon and Hunmanby.

Handy hostelries: Hotels, pubs and cafes in Hunmanby and Filey. The Ship, Muston.

WALK 17. FORDON - CAMP DALE - HUNMANBY - SOUTH DALE - FORDON.

From the middle of Fordon[1] go westwards and, on leaving the village, go right, past a farm, as indicated by a waymarker, and through a facing gate. Continue along the bottom of this dry valley, North Dale, keeping close to a hedge on your left. The track becomes a rough farm road which passes a concrete pond.

Soon a gate in a facing hedge is reached, which go through, avoiding a nearby stile which is in a dangerous condition. Continue up the dale alongside a wire fence on your left, guided by a marker on a telegraph post, and beyond this field cross a stile in a facing fence. Continue over the next field to a clearly seen gate in a facing row of tall trees and cross the next field, aiming for its right-hand corner. There, partly hidden by trees, is a waymarked stile which cross.

Proceed along the right-hand side of the valley and where it splits keep on the right fork, Lang Dale, avoiding Cotton Dale on your left, beyond which an early warning station mast is seen.

Keep to the right of a waymarked gate ahead and continue close to a fence on your left, go over a stile to the right of some sheep pens, cross a farm road and go along the right of first a hedge, then a fence, as waymarked. Cross

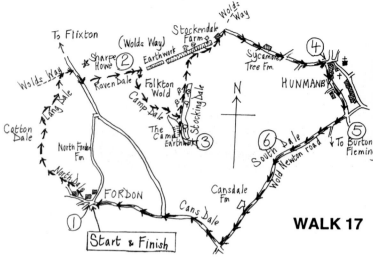

WALK 17

Start & Finish

a stile in a facing hedge which also marks the end of the fence on your left.

Here, where the valley splits again, take the left fork, aiming for a wire fence edging a small field. There is a yellow marker on the right-hand corner post of this field. Go past the field to join the Wolds Way at a facing gate and turn right, uphill, along it, crossing another gated stile near the top and reaching a road.

Turn right, along the road, as signposted, for about $^{1}/_{4}$ mile and at a left-hand side passing place turn left at a Wolds Way/Centenary Way sign. The signpost implies that the walk continues close to a fence on your right but the way is along a farm road close to the fence on your left. Where the farm road curves right, away from the fence, continue ahead as waymarked, still keeping close to the fence on your left. Cross a facing fence at a waymarked stile and edge the huge field ahead, close to a fence on your left and with the land falling away to a dry valley bottom on your right.

Every so often along this fence wooden steps have been placed for use as emergency exits should an unwanted encounter with an unfriendly bull seem likely!

We encountered lots of inquisitive bullocks but not one bull. No matter: it's the thought that counts, so full marks to a kind Wolds farmer.

Soon the way drops into a dry valley where a waymarker directs you up the other side[2].

Where a facing fence meets the one on your left, turn right and, keeping close to the fence, skirt the dale on your right, Camp Dale, the main feature of which is a waterhole where beasts were standing knee deep in muddy water when we saw it.

Yellow markers, Wolds Way and Centenary Way signs mark every bend in this fence so you can't go wrong. Where a corner with a facing fence is reached[3], descend, right, into the valley, close to a fence on your left, cross a waymarked stile in a facing wire fence and continue along the left-hand side of a corn field that is guarded by Wurzel Gummidge's relatives.

Soon a gate with a stile is reached on your left beyond which go diagonally right along a somewhat overgrown track, entering another dry valley bottom. The way is a little clearer now and follows the middle of it. This is Stocking Dale.

At a bifurcation of valleys turn along the left-hand side one and soon a waymarker will confirm that this is the right one. Here scrub mantles the left hillside while bigger trees cover the other. As you progress the taller trees begin to predominate on both sides and the path enters a shady glade, mottled with sunshine.

Soon, on your left, a field containing an orange marker is edged; and where the path leaves the wood into a cornfield, there is another marker. On entering a wood at the end of the cornfield follow the sign, using a clear path which soon bears right and emerges from the wood to continue alongside and to the right of it, edging a vast arable field. As you proceed, the path becomes even clearer and a waymarker shows that you are spot on course.

Soon the path turns left, Stockendale Farm is passed and a minor road is reached. Turn right, along it, to Hunmanby[4] where go over the crossroads, then turn right, passing, on your left, a church.

Continue through this pleasant little town and on leaving it, turn right, uphill, along the Wold Newton road.

Go straight ahead at the hilltop crossroads and ignoring the Burton Fleming[5] turning on your left, cross South Dale[6] along a quiet road from where sweeping views ever please the eye. After two miles of easy walking, turn right at a crossroads along Cans Dale, back to Fordon, so ending an exhilarating encounter with the Wolds countryside.

Things Seen On The Way

(1) Fordon. Only six miles from Filey as the crow flies, lovely Fordon fits snugly into a crease in the Wolds where West Dale and North Dale meet.

(2) Camp Dale. The field edging the northern rim of Camp Dale, when we saw it, was blue with Linum, the plant which produces flax.

An earthwork, almost a mile long, runs eastwards from the Flixton to Wold Newton road to Stockendale Farm. Your route follows it along Raven Dale and, having skirted Folkton Wold, rejoins it on entering Long Plantation, which leads almost to Stockendale Farm.

In Camp Dale bulls are often run with cattle which are being reared for beef. They are usually docile breeds like Hereford and Charolais, but bulls, like humans, can have their off days, so take care and if you see one keep close to the boundary fence where, at intervals, steps have been placed for use in an emergency. Some bulls are mercenary: they may charge. And, please, please, if a dog is with you keep it under strict control.

Although the geology of Camp Dale is permeable chalk, the steep sided valley contains a dewpond near its head where water is trapped in a saucer of clay. We watched cattle standing knee deep in it like beasts at an African water hole.

(3) Folkton Wold. (Southern tip). Camp Dale is named after the Camp, the site of a deserted settlement on the southern tip of Folkton Wold of which only a few mounds remain. Robert Knox wrote in 1855 that the settlement was lived in until the middle of the eighteenth century when it was abandoned. He noticed "at this deserted village, Camp, certain blue stones which had stood at the doors of the cottages and were used formerly to beat upon, instead of washing linen garments etc. when lotium or urine supplied the place of soap".

(4) Hunmanby. Hall Park, which runs almost the full length of the western side of Hunmanby is entered through an imposing arch, which looks positively medieval. It was, in fact built in the early 1800s of stones that were cut from the rocks of Filey Brigg. The hall, now a school, was the home of the Osbaldeston family for some 200 years; and it was the Osbaldestons who built the arch.

This one-time market town looks from the Wolds to the two miles distant sea. It is a most pleasing blend of inns, modern houses, white cottages with red roofs, a church and part of an old market cross, all set about with old world tranquillity.

The churchyard is entered through a stone archway decorated with a shield and tracery built to the memory of Admiral Mitford, a benefactor. The church tower is part Norman and part fifteenth century. The south wall and the chancel arch are also Norman. Fragments of coffin lids and the head of a cross, probably Saxon, are built into the walls. A marble monument showing a woman beside an urn commemorates many of the Osbaldestons.

The vicarage, set in a garden and almost hidden by trees, is close to the church. It was built in 1675 and later Francis Wrangham, one of Hunmanby's most amazing vicars, added a wing. He had it built to house some of his books. He travelled throughout England buying books and when his library and every other room in the vicarage was filled with them a new wing was deemed to be essential. Following his death in 1842 his library was sold by auction and the sale lasted three weeks.

The grave of a British charioteer was found at Hunmanby in 1907. Along with his bones were those of his horses, fragments of the chariot wheels and a piece of metal which was thought to have been fixed to the front of the chariot as a sort of wing mirror.

(5) Burton Fleming. Since Tudor times thirteenth century Burton Fleming has also been known as North Burton. It is an open village built around a crossroads in a shallow dip of the Wolds. The church, originally all stone, has had alterations done to it in brick and this hasn't done much for its appearance. Still, some Norman and medieval work remains. The tower is mainly thirteenth century and a west window is fourteenth century. A thirteenth century doorway is sheltered by a medieval porch. Two round arches, all that remains of a Norman arcade, are built into the south wall of the nave. There is a timber framed window under each arch.

Queen Henrietta Maria spent a night at the old manor house, now a farm, on her way to join Charles I at York.

Close to the farm road to Willy Howe Farm, between the village and Wold Newton, is the grave of an ancient British chieftain known as Willy Howe.

(6) South Dale. This quiet road along South Dale crosses a landscape of large fields, mainly winter wheat and spring and winter barley. Here dramatic changes have taken place to accommodate the demands of modern agriculture. Many plantations that have been cut down have not been replaced, countless hedgerows have been grubbed out to create a prairie landscape suited to the needs of giant combines and the like. As the large farms have developed, swallowing smaller ones, so buildings that had survived from the seventeenth and eighteenth centuries have vanished. Here the big farmer is, indeed, King. And since his wealth comes from large estates, the hiker and the tourist is not always encouraged. Because the need is not there, neither is the want.

Wolds farming is intensive and the quality of the soil has a lot to do with it. It is very good at the northern end and gets better further south. It is a medium to heavy loam, lightened and well drained by stones, most of which are chalk. Dry valleys, like South Dale, are characteristic of the Wolds. The slopes have soil that is not so good because much of it has been eroded into the dale bottoms where it lies deep.

Ninety-five per cent of farming in the Wolds is arable and between 60 and 65 per cent of that is cereal crops, winter wheat, spring and winter barley predominating. The remainder is mainly oil-seed rape, vining peas and pasture. This is typical of low rainfall, east coast areas.

Production of oil-seed rape, which increased dramatically in the late 1970s and 1980s, has fallen because of cuts in subsidies. But it is still grown in quantities sufficient enough for its distinctive yellow flowers to add a touch of surrealism to the rolling Wolds landscape in springtime. Oil-seed rape is a very important crop because as well as supplying animal feed it is a central ingredient in a whole range of processed foods, in particular cooking oils and margarine.

WALK 18. HUNMANBY - STOCKENDALE FARM - MUSTON - FILEY - NORTH MOOR FARM - HUNMANBY.

From the crossroads at the north end of Hunmanby go left, north-westwards, along the minor road that joins the A1039 east of Folkton and after just over a mile, near Stockendale Farm on your left where a lane crosses the road, turn right, through a wide waymarked gate and go straight ahead. The lane[1] runs down from the higher ground towards the plain between it and the one mile distant sea.

As you descend from the Wold and the lane curves right there is a signposted stile with an acorn and a yellow marker directing the Wolds Way across an arable field. Because the track you are on is so clear, this stile could easily be missed, so begin looking for it as a line of electricity wires crosses your line of walk. The stile is on your right.

The path through the cornfield is clear and leads to a stile in the facing hedge. Follow it and turn left along the left-hand side of the field ahead, close to a hedge on your left and exit over a facing stile alongside a gate. Continue as directed by a Wolds Way sign, close to a hedge on your left, and at the end of the field cross a stile at a field gate and continue down the next field on a clear path.

As you proceed a road is seen curving towards you at a tangent on your left. Soon a stile is seen in the hedge on your left leading to this road. Cross this stile, then go right, along the road, the A1039, into Muston[2] and continue through the village following the road sign to Filey.

Where the road bears right, past a triangular green on your left, turn left along a side road and go right up a bank fronting a terrace of houses that faces the green and turn left to a clearly seen signpost. The way is through a garden and over another stile, waymarked, into a field where continue close to the hedge on your left.

WALK 18

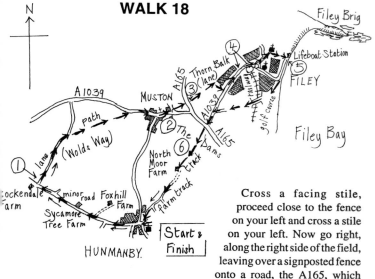

Cross a facing stile, proceed close to the fence on your left and cross a stile on your left. Now go right, along the right side of the field, leaving over a signposted fence onto a road, the A165, which cross to a signposted stile beyond which continue over the short field ahead to a waymarked gate. Continue close to a fence on your right.

Just ahead is your first really good view of Filey[3].

Cross a stile leading into a narrow lane that edges a playing field on your right and proceed along it to exit over a stream on a little bridge. Turn right along a long, narrow field, edging some dwellings on your left, and when a road is reached go left, along it.

Continue through a pleasant residential area of Filey[4], cross a railway crossing and go forward towards the clock seen ahead. On reaching a Methodist church at a corner on your left, turn left to a T-junction, where turn right and continue for a few yards to another T-junction with a facing fish restaurant.

There turn left, along another street at the end of which turn right, along a street that will take you straight to the sea. At the sea-front end of the street, descend some steps to the lifeboat station.

Turn right, either along the beach or the sea front, as far as the south end of Filey where, just past a cafe, a tarmac road comes down a side valley. Climb a flight of steps on the left-hand, southern, side of this valley[5] and at the top turn left, along a path edging a golf course and follow it round to the cliff top.

After about 100 yards, where the path splits, take the right-hand fork, away from the sea, passing to the right of the club house. Cross the road ahead and go along a lane that bridges the railway. At a crossing of lanes go straight ahead to a surfaced road and continue along it. When the main road is reached turn left, along it, for 200 yards to a road junction where you go straight across the A165. Continue through a gap between two gates and through a silage area to a stile near a gate and cross it.

Go over the field ahead on a clear track close to a hedge[6] on your left to exit over a gated stile. Cross another field, still near the hedge on your left, and go over another stile which is waymarked Centenary Way. Walk over another field and leave through a kissing gate. Go over the field ahead to North Moor Farm seen ahead, reaching it over a signposted stile.

Bear left along a very clear farm track leading to Hunmanby, where continue along the street ahead back to the crossroads where the circular began.

Things Seen On The Way

(1) The lane near Stockendale Farm. This delightful lane and many others like it are being discovered by people seeking pastures new. I have talked to many people who, having seen something of the Yorkshire Dales, the North York Moors and other leisure areas, have turned to the Wolds as an escape from the madding crowds and in search of solitude and pulchritude and been pleasantly surprised. Don't you agree? Look around.

(2) Muston. Most of Muston is built along the A1039 where the Wolds end. Its houses are a mixture of eighteenth century and Victorian. Willows and other fine trees adorn Muston Hall. The Ship Inn has dormers and curved gables. Ships are painted on its walls and the inn sign. Facing it are the steps of an ancient cross topped by a finger post.

The tiny church, rebuilt circa 1863, has a clock on its bellcote. Retained from the original church are a medieval altar stone, a cheese-shaped font, a shaft piscina and a square stoup or holy water drinking vessel. The heads of a knight and a bishop are in the porch, while outside there is a pleasant tree-lined walk.

(3) Approach to Filey. Although the North Sea has been in view for some time, it is not until Filey is seen ahead that its influence is felt. So far the walk has been through a landscape populated by people, most of whom are pre-eminently tied to the land; people with all the conservative, hard bargaining,

rough hewn, paucity-of-words characteristics traditionally associated with farming. But, with Filey just ahead, the strong influence of the sea on those living within sight and sound of it is much in evidence. Its lode stone, though confined to a thin sea-shore strip, is powerful and fishermen have at least one affinity with farmers: pessimism. Where fishermen complain of the scarcity of fish and bad weather farmers complain of the scarcity of money and bad weather.

(4) Filey. Now a popular holiday town, Filey has been involved with fishing for over a thousand years. It is a charming place, well sited on the edge of a superb sweep of bay. Filey Brigg marks its northern end with Bempton Cliffs six miles to southwards as the crow flies marking its southern limit.

Ptolemy's map of Britain was made a century before Julius Caesar came and saw and conquered; and Filey Bay is shown on it. There is ample proof that Roman ships anchored in the bay. Until a few years ago the remains of a Roman pier could be seen and some carved stones are the remains of what is thought to have been a Roman lighthouse.

There were 505 people recorded as living in Old Filey village in 1801. The single village street was dominated by the activities of fishermen. Then, in the 1830s, a Birmingham solicitor, Mr Unett, began to develop it. The coming of the railway in 1846-7 encouraged population growth as many who had spent a holiday there, seeking peace and tranquillity, decided to live there permanently.

St Oswald's, the Parish Church, stands at the head of Church Ravine on land given by Walter de Grant to the Prior of Bridlington. Building began about 1180 and was completed in 1230. It is shaped like a cross and is enriched with fifteenth century battlements. Its tower rises like a castle keep and rests on four splendid arches. Like the chancel and the transepts it is thirteenth century. The floor of the chancel is two steps lower than the nave.

(5) Martin Ravine. From the cliff-side path at the top of the steps leading from this valley there are fine views over Filey Bay with the Brigg to the north and southwards along the coastline towards Flamborough Head. To many people, Filey is the most idyllic spot on the whole of the north-east coast. With views like these it is easy to understand why.

(6) Hawthorn And Blackthorn Hedges. Many hawthorns and blackthorns are used in hedges hereabouts. Hawthorn has been a popular hedging material since Anglo Saxon times. Its thorny tangle makes it ideally suited for this role. For the first four years of its life it makes rapid growth, after which further growth is very slow. Blackthorn is also frequently used and since it blossoms in March, white bloom on black leafless spikes, it is regarded as a herald of spring. Many of these hedges were put down in the eighteenth century and are rich in wild plants and animals.

113

CHAPTER X
FILEY TO BUCKTON

Length of section (including a there and back linear detour to Filey Brigg and the northern end of the Wolds Way): 15¾ miles (25.2km)

Distance covered walking clockwise from Hessle: 119½ miles (191.2km)

Walk 19:	Filey to Filey Brigg and northern end of Wolds Way and back linear. Then Circular Filey - Reighton - Hunmanby - Filey. 14 miles (22.4km)
Walk 20:	Circular: Buckton - Grindale - Reighton - Buckton Cliffs - Buckton. 13 miles (20.8km)
Map Ref:	Landranger 101
Parking:	North end of foreshore, Filey.
Handy hostelries:	Hotels, pubs and cafes in Filey and Hunmanby.

WALK 19. (a) FILEY TO FILEY BRIGG AND NORTHERN END OF WOLDS WAY AND BACK, LINEAR. THEN (b) FILEY - REIGHTON - HUNMANBY - FILEY CIRCULAR.

(a) From the car park at the north end of Filey go inland, briefly, to a Wolds Way sign opposite toilets on your left. Here take a little path, right, that climbs steeply to join a clearer one near two seats in an open space.

Continue climbing behind the seats along a clear path, stepped in parts, bearing left, and leading to the cliff top. Proceed northwards along the cliff top path which incorporates the Wolds Way and the Cleveland Way. When a V-shaped nick appears ahead, Church Ravine, either skirt it or cross it down a flight of steps and climb another flight on the far side. Here the cliff blushes with a superfluity of great willow herb.

Follow the path to the end of Carr Nase[1] and go down its sloping point. It is steepish, so care is needed, but if the tide is out Brigg rocks[2] are well worth a visit. Cross the rocks along what looks like a concrete path but, in fact, the concrete was laid to seal a sewage pipe. The further along it you go, the more wide spread the seaweed, which is very slippery, so care is needed. Seabirds gather where Brigg End is swallowed by the waves[3].

On returning to the Brigg, continue along its southern side for a little way to some steps leading up the cliff face and, using them regain the top of Filey

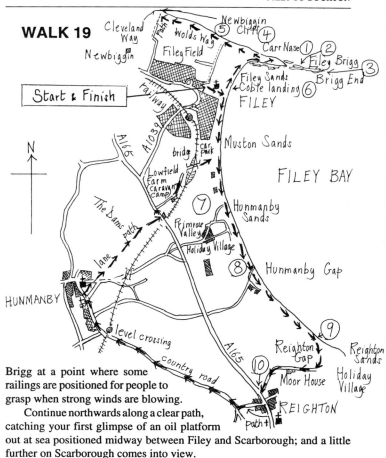

Brigg at a point where some railings are positioned for people to grasp when strong winds are blowing.

Continue northwards along a clear path, catching your first glimpse of an oil platform out at sea positioned midway between Filey and Scarborough; and a little further on Scarborough comes into view.

At this point[4], when we passed, the field on our left was linseed. The flowers are blue and linseed oil is made from the seeds. The next field contained more familiar wheat and we could detect, in the heat of the day, the warm bouquet of the corn, the sweet smell of summer and, oh, it was good!

On Newbiggin cliff the path edges a field signposted "Newbiggin: The National Trust" and it is hereabouts that the Wolds Way ends, although

115

View of Filey Brigg from Muston Sands

exactly where is not evident. Its official end is the old East Riding County Boundary, which was marked with a line of fence posts, all of which have gone. Somewhere about the middle of this signposted field the Wolds Way quietly ends and the Cleveland Way continues alone.

[You can return to Filey by continuing towards Scarborough for a short distance, along the cliff top to where the coast turns north. At this change of direction go left along a signposted footpath, over fields, past Newbiggin Farm and on to reach the A1039 where, by turning left you will reach, in a mile, Cobble Landing at the north end of Filey from where you set out.

But it is much better to retrace your steps to the start because not only are the views over the one-time German Ocean superb, the route directions are easier to follow.]

(b) From Cobble Landing go along the full length of the promenade and turn right along Martin Drive for 60 yards or so to cross a concrete bridge and climb a flight of steps. Turn left at the top, edge a golf course on your right and turn left, along a path, cross a little wooden bridge and continue along the cliff top. When the path splits take the left-hand fork, the great sandy sweep of Filey Bay is on the left and the golf course is on your right. Soon the path descends into a ravine down steps onto Hunmanby Sands.

Cross a stream and walk towards the beach where, on the corner of the cliff turn right, up a broad path that climbs to the cliff top on the ravine's south side. Turn left, along the cliff top, keeping close to a fence put there to stop people going too close to the edge, which is beginning to erode. Soon a World War II pill box is reached. Skirt it, either side, and continue on the land side of some markers because to seawards the cliffs are a bit dodgy. Play safe.

Soon Primrose Valley Holiday Camp is reached on the right. On coming to a surfaced road that leads down hill towards the beach, turn left, along it and when it levels out at the bottom and a fork in it is reached, go left to Lower Flat Cliff, which brings you almost to the beach and slightly above it. At the road end, ignore a "private" sign if it is still there because this section can now be used by the public, and continue straight ahead. As the path comes almost to the end of some flats on your right, turn left, down some steps and just before reaching the beach turn right, along a rough track which climbs up the shore line. At the end of a long, uphill climb, where the path bifurcates, take the left one. On reaching a road that goes through the Holiday Camp, bear slightly right to pass close to a telephone kiosk and continue straight ahead, along a surfaced road, parallel to the cliff. Go along the left-hand side of the camp and almost at its end, go between some hawthorns. Once past them, bear left to join a clear path, keeping well to the left of some fencing, which marks the boundary of Butlin's now derelict Holiday Camp[5].

When a surfaced road crosses your path, close to the tall metal railings which here carry a "keep out" notice, turn left, along it, down to the beach because the path straight ahead soon becomes so overgrown through lack of use, it is really a toil of a pleasure to use.

On reaching the beach turn right, along it, staying close to the edge of the foreshore. It is quite safe to walk along the beach at this point because even at high tide there is still enough of it remaining above sea level. However, should the tide be exceptionally high, several paths lead inland and uphill from the beach so you are quite safe even then.

On reaching a surfaced road near a lifebuoy, a telephone, a seat on the right, and a danger warning to bathers, either turn right, along a clear path through some very rough terrain or go across the sand. The climbing path soon drops into a little ravine where the sandy alternative is rejoined.

Cross the ravine bottom and climb another rough track on its other side, soon to descend into another little ravine, Hunmanby Gap, from where again climb up the shoreline to the cliff top on a clear path. Here there is a field on the landward side and some bungalows.

Continue along the cliff top, slightly inland, towards a wooden hut where turn left past a metal barrier onto a surfaced road. Go left, down hill, passing Four Oaks Farm cafe.

Continue down some steps to the beach, where turn right for 100 yards and go up a little valley to the right, almost as far as a small building on the right, where turn left, along a stepped path towards a small, brick building. Continue along a very clear path, through shrubs that arch to form a tunnel. No problems are met and the path leads you to the cliff top. Now you have open countryside to landward.

This is superb high cliff-top walking, with big cliffs ahead, the sea to your left, Wolds to your right.

On approaching a bungalow[6] slightly to the right leave the field you have been edging and bear left onto an unsurfaced road. Turn right, along it, away from the sea. On reaching a surfaced road near a telephone kiosk turn right and where the road reaches a junction go right, inland. After passing Moor House on the left continue, turning left with the road, to reach the A165 at the north end of Reighton[7].

Turn left into the village and just below the church turn right, cross a stile near a gate and go over the field ahead, close to a hedge on your left to reach a fence in the top left-hand corner, which, cross. Continue straight ahead across the next field, aiming for a telegraph post in the middle of the field. It carries a yellow waymarker. From it continue straight ahead to its bottom right-hand corner and continue close to the hedge on the right. Turn right over a stile, waymarked, and go down a lane that soon bears right. At the lane end turn left, along a minor road, briefly, to a crossroads where turn right, using a very broad road verge. From this elevated road the view through the trees of Filey, Filey Brigg and the sea is excellent.

On reaching an industrial estate, keep straight ahead, cross a railway level crossing at Hunmanby station and go through the town, ignoring all side streets, and bear right, along a footpath just before the church, going left, then right, briefly, to turn right at a public footpath sign along a very pleasant road. Continue past some concrete bollards along a footpath that edges the road and bear left, directed by a footpath sign along a flagged lane. At the lane end cross the road ahead and go along a broad, green lane, directed by another footpath sign. When the lane goes into a field continue along the left-hand fork of the same lane to exit at a lane end kissing gate. Keep straight ahead, through a gate, cross a small stream, and go directly across the next field, leaving at a waymarked stile near a gate. This area is known as The Dams.

Cross the next field directed by a yellow arrow, leaving through a gate in a hawthorn hedge. Directed by another waymarker, continue in the same direction, on rising ground, to cross another waymarked stile. Continue over the next field, exit through a gateway and go along the left-hand side of the next one to its top left-hand corner where the path goes through the hedge onto a road at a waymarked post.

Cross it and turn left along a roadside footpath. Just past a Royal Oak sign on the left, turn right, along a surfaced road, directed by a footpath sign to reach Low Field Farm Caravan Camp. Go through the farmyard and leave through a gate into the Caravan Camp itself. Go through it, along an avenue of trees and with caravans on your right. Just past some buildings on the left, bear right, then left. Where the path deteriorates into a rough one, go through a gate with a notice "To The Beach And Filey". At a T-junction bear right, bridge the railway and enter a car park. Cross it and the road beyond and following a signposted direction, descend Martin Drive to rejoin the outward route at the bottom and retrace your steps along the foreshore to Cobble Landing.

Things Seen On The Way

(1) Carr Nase. The narrow headland that stretches out to Filey Brigg proper is called Carr Nase. Once a Roman signal station stood at the outward end of this cliff of boulder-clay which today is a coastguard look out point.

(2) Filey Brigg. Pointing a finger in a more or less south easterly direction from the higher boulder-clay cliffs of Carr Nase towards Flamborough Head, Filey Brigg is a small but conspicuous promontory composed of the calcareous grit of the Corallion series.

A superb, sandy beach has accumulated in the shelter of the Brigg and this stretches away past Primrose Valley to Reighton where it gives way to stones and boulders and eventually to the dramatic cliffs of Speeton and Bempton. The complex system of rocky pools and ledges coupled with the relatively shallow, sandy bay makes the area one of the most important feeding areas for seabirds and waders along the Yorkshire coast.

(3) Brigg End. Seabirds gather where Brigg End is swallowed by the waves. Reptilian looking cormorants, the only web-footed birds not to put out waterproofing oil for their feathers, stand on these rocks between dives for fish, wings outspread to dry while well-oiled gulls bob on the sea and gloat.

(4) North Cliff. From here, in the middle distance, looking inland, are the rooftops of Filey with, more distant, a fine panoramic view of the north-eastern end of the Wolds.

(5) Butlins. Founded by Billy, later Sir Billy, Butlin, these famous holiday camps provided cheap, carefree holidays for the masses during the drab years of post-World War II. There, holiday makers were called campers, housed in gaily painted chalets, given three meals a day and the use of the camp's many facilities, including chalet patrol for families with babies and live shows, often with star names, all for one inclusive price. People were looking for a brief escape from the daily grind of a Britain in the doldrums, and

Butlins provided it.

Butlins, Filey, had its own railway station to where each weekly intake was brought: it was a big camp with two of everything, but what it gained in mass appeal it lost in intimacy.

Cheap overseas holidays brought about the decline of the Butlin holiday empire and although it has adapted to modern tastes, Butlins, Filey, lives no more, except in the memories of the thousands of happy campers who were there during its hey day.

(6) Reighton Gap. From Reighton Gap, southwards, the cliffs begin to rise to the impressive chalky heights of Speeton, Buckton and Bempton, long famous for the seabirds which nest there in their thousands.

(7) Reighton. The Dotterel Inn at Reighton was built by the Strickland family for the use of gamekeepers and "Sportsmen" who gathered from all over the north to shoot migrating dotterels in the spring during the end of the nineteenth century.

Reighton church is much older than it looks, some parts being twelfth century. The chancel arch is Norman, as is the richly carved font. Some pebbles from the beach are set in the floor at the west end of the nave, a reminder that at one time the whole of the church was paved this way.

WALK 20. BUCKTON - GRINDALE - REIGHTON - BUCKTON CLIFFS - BUCKTON.

From the duck pond[1] at the eastern end of Buckton go left, briefly, along the B1229 into the hamlet and take the first turn right, along a quiet road. Go over a level crossing and immediately turn right along the road for about 1³/₄ miles to reach a crossroads with the A165, which cross. Continue along the quiet road for a further 1¹/₂ miles to a T-junction where turn right into nearby Grindale[2].

Go through the hamlet and take the first turning on the right. Continue along the road for a mile, recrossing the railway en route, to a T-junction where turn right, briefly, then left, along the A165 into Reighton.

Go through the village and at its far end turn right, along a minor road that first goes north, then bears right before making a sharp right turn to pass Moor House Farm. On reaching a T-junction turn left, soon to reach a crossroads where continue straight ahead, towards the sea, and where the road ends at a barrier, go down a path, directly to the beach and turn right, along it.

The way is along the foreshore because there are no suitable paths along

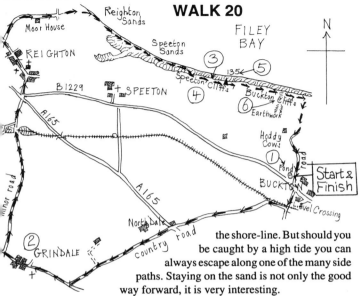

WALK 20

the shore-line. But should you be caught by a high tide you can always escape along one of the many side paths. Staying on the sand is not only the good way forward, it is very interesting.

Continue along the beach, aiming for the most distant of some giant concrete blocks, placed there to act as breakwaters in the ceaseless war on erosion.

The chalk cliffs ahead, Speeton cliffs, look magnificent.

Once past the last of the concrete blocks, bear right, over the chalky foreshore and climb some rough steps.

[Anyone so wishing can walk from Filey the full length of the bay to these steps, provided the tide is not high, without using the route detailed above. Beyond the steps there are no more escape routes from the beach and the tide comes in quickly here, so be careful.]

From the top of the steps bear right, along a clear track, aiming for the top of the steep shoreline at a point where a red telephone box can be seen.

The path meanders then climbs a series of steps at the top of which go left towards the telephone box. On reaching it turn right, over a stile, then left, along the cliff-top, directed by a sign, "Footpath to Buckton".

On reaching a signposted stile turn right, as directed, uphill, away from the cliff edge which, at this point is some 200ft above sea level. It is a diversion to avoid getting too close to the cliff edge which could be

121

dangerous. At the top of the slope turn left, into a corn field, again directed by a signpost. Soon a trig point[3], at 450ft is reached and it makes a good butty stop.

Continue along the cliff top[4] to another stile, which has a footpath sign. Here turn right, to 1¼ miles distant Buckton. Keep forward, along the edge of a field, close to a fence on your right and cross a facing stile close to a gate. Keep straight ahead to just before a sheep paddock where turn right, over a stile. Bear left, briefly, to cross a little footbridge, beyond which cross a stile. Turn right, along a farm road, which brings you neatly into Buckton, alongside the duck pond.

Things Seen On The Way

(1) Buckton Duck Pond. So many people feed the many mallards on the pond that they have become quite tame. While watching them we saw a sandpiper and some waxwings.

The black-and-white covers on many of the trees near the pond do not mark where some Darlington supporters are buried - they have been put there to protect tender boles from destructive animals!

(2) Grindale. The neat nineteenth-century church contains a tub shaped Norman font and the huge bowl of an older one. Add a cluster of houses and farms, some green mounds that are said to mark where a Roman house once stood and a pond and you have the windswept, Wolds hamlet of Grindale.

(3) Trig Point. Buckton Hall can now be seen on the right and the headland of Flamborough Head is visible across the next bay.

(4) Sea Birds. Buckton Cliffs mark the northern extremity of chalk in Britain. Here, on the south side of Filey Bay, they plunge dramatically hundreds of feet into the North Sea; and every summer they, along with adjoining Bemptom Cliffs and the slightly lower ones on the northwest face of the small Flamborough Peninsular, become a teeming city for upwards of 100,000 pairs of sea birds.

Flamborough Head

CHAPTER XI
BUCKTON TO FLAMBOROUGH VILLAGE

Length of section: linear: 9¹/₂ miles (15.2km)

Distance covered walking clockwise from Hessle: 129 miles (206.4km)

Walk 21:	Linear: Buckton - Bempton Cliffs - Thornwick Nab 9¹/₂ miles (15.2km)
Walk 22:	Circular: Flamborough village - North Cliff - Flamborough Head - South Landing - Flamborough village 8 miles (12.8km)
Map Ref:	Landranger 101
Parking:	Wayside parking in Buckton village: car park at Thornwick Nab: roadside parking at Flamborough Head and Flamborough village.
Handy hostelries:	Cafe at Thornwick Nab: Seabirds, The Ship, The Dog And Duck, Flamborough.

WALK 21. BUCKTON - BEMPTON CLIFFS - THORNWICK NAB.

From Buckton village duck pond go northwards, following a public footpath sign, along a lane which, in summer, has white convolvulus slung over its hedges like washing.

WALK 21

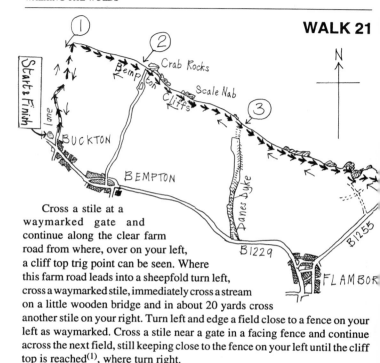

Cross a stile at a waymarked gate and continue along the clear farm road from where, over on your left, a cliff top trig point can be seen. Where this farm road leads into a sheepfold turn left, cross a waymarked stile, immediately cross a stream on a little wooden bridge and in about 20 yards cross another stile on your right. Turn left and edge a field close to a fence on your left as waymarked. Cross a stile near a gate in a facing fence and continue across the next field, still keeping close to the fence on your left until the cliff top is reached[1], where turn right.

To continue straight ahead at this point is simply asking for trouble for the cliffs are tall so the drop is a long one. From here Filey Brigg, Filey town and the full sweep of Filey Bay are clearly seen and look specious.

The way ahead continues along a cliff top footpath, crossing waymarked stiles as they are reached.

John Masefield came to mind along here as a "dirty British coaster with a salt-caked smoke stack" butted a choppy course along the curving horizon.

Soon what looks like an obsolete radar station is passed on your right and, ahead, a kissing gate is reached. Go through it and follow a lovely cliff edge fenced lane from where Flamborough Head is clearly seen ahead. The route takes you along Bempton Cliffs[2], which are an R.S.P.B. Nature Reserve and with the cliffs being spectacular and the birdlife fantastic, the walk, which has a good start, gets even better all the time.

Towards the eastern end of the high cliffs a pre-historic earthwork,

Danes Dyke[3] is crossed. Its 2¹/₂ miles course is indicated by a narrow band of trees and since the surrounding land is flat, it is always in view, complementing the scenery.

The path continues along the cliff top and soon a lighthouse is seen ahead. Where a ravine with a house on its far side sweeps down to the sea, descend some newly placed steps, cross a footbridge at the bottom and climb up the steps into the bay now on your left, to look at caves and, if you feel peckish, to have a butty stop.

North Landing
Lifeboat Station ④

FLAMBOROUGH
HEAD

Returning to the cliff top, continue along an unsurfaced road which soon curves right. Where a private road branches left from it take a footpath to the left of it and continue along the cliff top. Where the path splits, ignore the downward one and take the less obvious of the two, along the same contour. Soon some steps come up from the left to meet it and from then on it becomes much clearer. The cliffs are dangerous so take care as the notice advises.

Keep going and soon Thornwick lifeboat station[4] is seen ahead and at a lower level with, above it, a car park and toilets.

Buckton village pond

This is the apex of the linear walk. Anyone wishing to complete a circle may do so by taking the B1255 inland to Flamborough village, then the B1229 to Buckton. But with a return along some of the most exciting sea-cliffs in Britain in prospect, the road walking pales significantly. Let excellence be your guide.

On the return journey the high, chalk, Bempton Cliffs unfold in a most dramatic way. From various viewpoints above where rocky arches extend from the main cliff face like flying buttresses, resting gannets can be seen on the arch tops.

On reaching the point where, as signposted, the cliff top is left behind, make sure that you keep the fence on your right. It was on your left on the outward journey but the signpost seems to point along the other side of it. This is wrong, because there is no exit from that field. Otherwise you will have no problems because the return from the cliff to Buckton is so clearly defined you simply can't go wrong.

This linear was specially made for making many happy memories.

Things Seen On The Way

(1) The White Cliffs of the Wolds. The great sweep of Filey Bay, to your left as you reach Buckton Cliffs, is sheltered at its northern end, by the long finger of calcareous gritstone called Filey Brigg. The name is derived from the Scandinavian "bryggia" which means jetty or loading place.

Many fishermen's cobbles have struck the Brigg's jagged rocks and ferocious waves crashing over them have swept many people to their deaths. One of the ships wrecked on this promontory was a Norwegian vessel with a cargo of herrings. The mishap occurred in 1928, all the crew were saved, the cargo was washed ashore and for a while the people of Filey ate rather well!

During World War I seventeen sinkings were recorded in Filey Bay. One, a cobble, the Edith Cavell, was torpedoed by a German U-boat which picked up the crew and released them on the Farne Islands. On their return to Filey the whole town went to the station to welcome them.

When at the end of the last century a Grimsby trawler founded on the rocks at the foot of Speeton Cliffs, local gull's eggs collectors, "climmers", went down the cliffs on their ropes to save the crew. This was at a time when pressure was being put on them to stop their annual plunder of gull's nests. As a direct consequence of this rescue the "climmers" became coastguard auxiliaries specialising in cliff foot rescues. This entailed "exercises" on the cliffs and so egg collecting was legitimised.

(2) Bempton Cliffs. During the 1860s, at a time when egg collecting and the

shooting of wild birds were at their peak, Yorkshire naturalists were instrumental in promoting the very first act of legislation that protected birds for other than sporting purposes. The focus of this historical event was the large sea-bird colonies on the cliffs at Bempton and Flamborough. On these cliffs, from the 1830s, could be seen the result of commercial exploitation, appalling cruelty and sheer ignorance.

Steamships from Bridlington regularly took large parties of shooters beneath the cliffs and sounded their sirens, which caused all the birds to take flight; only to face an intense barrage of shot.

Charles Waterton, 1782-1865, a field naturalist of Walton Hall, near Wakefield, was appalled both by this senseless destruction and by the fate of the young left to starve on the nest ledges.

Thousands of kittiwakes and terns were also shot annually in Bridlington Bay and their wings and feathers sent to London to supply the demands of the milinary trade.

These atrocious activities continued for many years, but in 1868 Professor Alfred Newton, a founder member of the British Ornithologists Union, drew widespread attention to this slaughter in his address to the British Association. The resulting publicity eventually led to the formation of the East Riding Association for the Protection of Sea Birds, which soon had the support of many influential men, including two major landowners at Bempton and Flamborough, the Archbishop of York and several Yorkshire MPs. The historic Sea Birds Preservation Act became law in June, 1869, and gave protection to 36 species by a closed season from 1st April to 1st August. The eggs, however, were specifically excluded from the Act at the request of local "climmers" who for generations, had traditionally harvested the eggs and whose trade had been badly affected by the more recent shootings. These hardy folk had a long tradition of working certain sections of the cliffs on a rotational basis so as to ensure a continuous supply of eggs, which were sold for food in the markets of the West Riding and as far afield as London. This was the livelihood of several local families and, although the practice continued up to the end of Word War II, it subsequently declined and was ended in 1954 with the introduction of the Protection of Birds Act.

Bempton Cliffs are now an R.S.P.B. Nature Reserve and at a point above them at Crab Rocks an unsurfaced path leads inland, climbing to the R.S.P.B. administration centre some 400 yards away. It is closed during the late autumn and winter months, the keeper having migrated to winter at an estuary.

During the summer months these cliffs are used by 150,000 birds, each species occupying a different part of the cliff, so making the best of the limited space. The cliffs are home to herring gulls, puffins, guillemots, kittiwakes, razorbills, gannets and shags. Some 800 pairs of fulmars nest there.

Bempton Cliffs are *the* breeding place of the gannet, unique among Yorkshire breeding birds because it nests nowhere else on the British mainland. Between 400 and 500 pairs now nest there, yet it was not until 1924 that the first pair arrived and frequented "Black Shelf". The first nest was built in 1925. For most of the year these magnificent birds are silent, but in the breeding season the screeching roar of a gannet colony has few equals in nature. They fish from a height of up to 100 feet, diving sharply and folding back their wings, all six feet spread of them, to form a living arrow head. For this spectacular sight alone the walk along Bempton Cliffs is beyond compare, throughout the Wolds.

The rock doves found on Bempton Cliffs in large numbers are the original stock from which homing pigeons and those which frequent our towns and cities are descended; and thereby hangs a tale. Many years ago, when all-year-round supply of fresh meat was a rarity, rock doves were kept for food in some districts. When tame birds escaped they interbred with the rock doves and hybrids have now replaced pure rock doves in many places. Most of the "rock doves" seen on Bempton Cliffs, although very similar in appearance to the ancestral rock dove, are really descended from pigeons that have gone wild. When in flight, two black wing bars and a white rump distinguish the rock dove from the stock dove.

(3) Danes' Dyke. Towards the eastern end of Bempton Cliffs over which, in the strongest gales, salty spray is tossed higher than 300 feet to spoil any crops onto which it falls, Danes Dyke is to be found: not that it takes much finding. It stretches due south from Crab Rocks to Sewerby Sands to provide a primitive form of defence along an abrupt line where chalk ends and the boulder clay of the headland begins. Its $2^{1/2}$ miles long course is indicated by a narrow band of trees and, since the surrounding land is flat, it is always in view, complementing the scenery. The southern end of the Dyke was largely formed by a natural ravine scooped out by floodwater from melting ice towards the end of the Pleistocene period. The northern end was man made 2,000 years ago as a major defence work, at which time the natural ravine to the south was incorporated into the protecting dyke. At that time it was not known as Danes' Dyke: that came much later when it was repaired by some immigrant Danes.

Apart from the cliff top path, which crosses it, Danes' Dyke's northern end is privately owned. The southern end belongs to the East Yorkshire Borough Council and the general public have free access to the delightful

The gatehouse at Burton Agnes Hall *(Ron Dodsworth)*

town centre with a difference - Nafferton Mere (Walk 28) *(Ron Dodsworth)*

The village pond at Hutton Cranswick (Walk 30) *(Ron Dodsworth)*
Beverley Minster (Walk 34) *(Ron Dodsworth)*

woodland walks and can picnic in places with fine views of the sea.

Wild life abounds within this copious mix of mainly deciduous trees.
(4) Thornwick Bay. Here, where a huge chalk buttress holds the North Sea in an imposing frame, we sat on the shingle eating sandwiches and watched cormorants dry off after diving. They held their wings like Dracula's cape to dry in the breeze and the warming sunlight because they are less waterproofed than other water fowl. They do not have the oil sac that ducks and geese use to keep their feathers drip-dry. This apparent disadvantage is the cormorant's best fishing asset. Such easily waterlogged feathers allow him to sink and dive effectively. Air sacs let him spend as long as a minute or more under water. And all the while, the rocks on which they stood were pounded by the same restless waves that sucked and pulled at the pebbles at our feet. Wonderfully marbled with sea foam, the white veiny effect was heightened by the luminous blue-green water that was flat and gleaming and held the essence of timelessness.

WALK 22. FLAMBOROUGH VILLAGE - NORTH CLIFF - FLAMBOROUGH HEAD - SOUTH LANDING - FLAMBOROUGH VILLAGE.

From Flamborough church[1] turn right, along the B1255 and, where it goes left, do likewise. Do not go along Lighthouse Road. The remains of an old, chalk castle[2] are passed to the left of the road. Go straight through the village[3], walking northwards, and where the road bends to the right, cross it and go straight ahead to cross a waymarked stile in the fence ahead. Go forward, briefly, to turn left, through a waymarked gate, then right, over a stile, and follow a clear path to the cliff top[4] where turn right along it. In about half a mile the car park above Thornwick Nab lifeboat station is passed; beyond which follow an easy-to-follow cliff top path that edges Flamborough Head Golf Course on the right. Continue past the club house and climb to the B1259, close to its end at Flamborough Head.

Here a small detour right will reward you with a close up view of the old beacon tower[5], sited on the right, just inside the golf course.

Retrace your steps and, passing to the south of the lighthouse[6], continue to the coastguard's iron-fog station at the Head's most easterly point[7]. From here, follow the clearly defined cliff-top path[8] south-easterly for almost a mile, ignoring any paths leading inland, to descend some steps to South Landing[9] with its lifeboat station. Cross a surfaced road and climb a flight of steps up the other side of the valley to regain the cliff top.

WALK 22

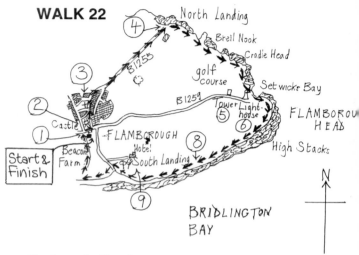

Flamborough village is now in view to the right.

Continue along the cliff top to reach a footpath that shoots off inland and turn right, along it, directed by a yellow waymarker, close to a fence on your right. Where the path curves, stay with it, following yellow markers, soon to cross a stile into a farmyard on the outskirts of Flamborough. This is Beacon Farm. Keep straight ahead to reach a surfaced road, turn right at a facing house, along West Street, towards the church seen ahead. At a T-junction turn right, then left, through the churchyard at the far side of which the start is reached.

Things Seen On The Way

(1) Flamborough Church has been largely rebuilt. Most of the remaining old parts are fifteenth century, with some thirteenth century work in the arcades. A beautiful fifteenth-century oak screen hides the rich moulding of the Norman chancel-arch. There are only two roodlofts surviving in Yorkshire and this is one of them. The Norman font is carved with herringbone and diamonds.

A fine parchment hangs in the nave. It is a pardon for Walter Strickland of Boynton, who supported Cromwell in the Civil War and was a regicide. At the restoration in 1660 he received a pardon and this document with its long list of Strickland's offences, is it. Walter Strickland died in 1671.

(2) The Fighting Constables. Some grass fringed walls, about 20 feet high, are about all that remain of a chalk castle that sits in a field to the west of Flamborough's main street. It is a place with a past, having once been the home of the fighting Constables. For half a millennium they were the creme de la creme of Flamborough society. One of the earlier members of this redoubtable family was nicknamed Little Sir Marmaduke, which was a bit unfair because he was a valiant fighter, serving in France for Edward IV and, as a swords man, at Flodden Field when he was seventy years old. He died circa 1518, having lived through six reigns. There were Constables living at Flamborough in the thirteenth century and Little Sir Marmaduke used to say that his family had lived there for so long that, although he could not be certain, they thought that the person to whom their rent should be paid was the King of Denmark. So every year he would go to the cliffs and shoot an arrow with a gold coin tied to it far out to sea, calling out that, if anyone cared to come for it, he was ready to pay his rent to the King of the Danes.

Sir Marmaduke's son, Robert, also fought at Flodden Field. He was knighted at Blackheath for bravery in the Cornish Rising, joined the ill fated Pilgrimage of Grace, was found guilty of treason and was dragged, in chains, through Yorkshire. He was killed at Hull and his body was hung over the highest gate.

Perhaps the most famous of the Constables was Sir William. Having escaped execution for treason, he was imprisoned by Charles I for objecting to the Ship Tax. He fought for the Parliamentarians at Edge Hill, commanded the siege of Scarborough, distinguished himself at Marston Moor and was one of the judges who signed the King's death warrant while the King was in his charge at Carisbrooke Castle. He was buried in Westminster Abbey but following the Restoration his remains were removed and scattered.

(3) Flamborough Village. Because of Flamborough Head's very strong links with the Vikings, Flamborough, one of Yorkshire's best known villages, is referred to as the capital of Little Denmark. Many of its houses, built of either chalk, brick or stone, remain, although much of the place is new.

(4) North Cliff. A continuation of Speeton, Buckton and Bempton Cliffs, but not as high, North Cliff attracts thousands of guillemots, razorbills, kittiwakes and puffins, all of which find shelter on the narrow ledges. Ceaseless pounding by relentless seas has sculpted this north-facing coast into many strange shapes. Of the many caves gouged from the cliff face the most spectacular three are St George's Hole, Smuggler's Cave, and Robin Lythe's Hole, the roof of which is 50 feet high.

In early summer the peninsular is aflame with gorse.

(5) The Old Beacon Tower. Beacon Tower still stands where the first coal fire

beacon was lit in 1674. The Flamborough look-out watched Bridlington and as soon as they saw a flare, that was the signal for them to fire their beacon and so on to Rudston Parva, Bainton, Wilton and Holme to York.

The Old Beacon Tower continued to be used until 1806 when a new lighthouse, built nearer the cliff's edge came into use. The tower, restored in 1978, is still used as a navigation aid. It is 52 metres above sea level and stands alongside a trig point.

(6) Flamborough Lighthouse. John Matson built this lighthouse to replace the old beacon, which had been built by Sir John Clayton. It was completed the year after Trafalgar and every night since then, apart from the war years, the Flamborough light flashes 20 miles out to sea.

(7) Flamborough Head is famous for its association with the American pirate John Paul Jones, who engaged two English ships off this famous headland one September evening in 1779. The ensuing fight took place by moonlight, watched by Flamborough folk from the cliff top. At one point in the battle, following an explosion on the pirate's ship, the master gunner, thinking that Jones had been killed, hauled down the flag; but Jones, very much alive, had it hoisted again and the fighting continued until the commander of the convoy surrendered. It was a pyrrhic victory because soon after the surrender his ship *Le Bonhomme Richard* sank.

A commemorative plaque at Flamborough acknowledges John Paul Jones as the father of the U.S. Navy.

(8) Flamborough Head Heritage Coast. One of the first projects of its type to be established, the Flamborough Head Heritage Coast is designed to give extra protection to the natural beauty of the area and to improve its facilities for visitors. Its emblem is a gannet set against a lighthouse backed by a green headland, edged by a sea of blue.

(9) South Landing. The cliff-tops hereabouts are uncluttered with developments and all that remains of the fishing community of South Landing is an old lifeboat house which was used as such until 1938. It is now used for storing fishing tackle.

Unlike the chalk cliffs around Dover, which have lost most of their bird life because of pollution, those of the Yorkshire Wolds still support tens of thousands of nesting sea birds; and for this much credit must go to the R.S.P.B., Heritage Coast project and similar enlightened organisations and dedicated individuals.

Sewerby Hall

CHAPTER XII
FLAMBOROUGH VILLAGE TO CARNABY

Length of section: linear: 8³⁄₄ miles (13.5km)

Distance covered walking clockwise from Hessle: 137³⁄₄ miles (220.4km)

Walk 23: Circular: Flamborough village - Sewerby Rocks - Bridlington - Flamborough village 8¹⁄₂ miles (13.6km)

Walk 24: Circular: Bridlington - Wilsthorpe - Carnaby - Roman Road between Carnaby and Boynton - Bridlington. 8¹⁄₂ miles (13.6km)

Map Ref: Landranger 101

Parking: Roadside parking in Flamborough village: Danes Dyke car park: roadside in Bridlington.

Handy hostelries: Seabirds, The Ship, The Dog And Duck, Flamborough; hotels, pubs and cafes in Bridlington.

WALK 23. FLAMBOROUGH VILLAGE - SEWERBY ROCKS - BRIDLINGTON - FLAMBOROUGH VILLAGE.

Leave Flamborough village[1] along Tower Street and turn right into Church Street. On reaching the parish church turn right, through the church yard where a notice informs that "Surely the Lord is in this place". Exit through a white kissing gate and cross the road, bearing slightly left. Go down Church Lane and turn left at its far end. Follow a finger post, "Footpath to Beacon Hill", pass some farm buildings and continue straight ahead to cross a waymarked stile to the left of a facing gate. Cross the field ahead along a very clear, unsurfaced farm track, climb a stile between two gates and cross the field ahead close to a hedge to your left. On reaching a facing gate, turn right, as indicated by a yellow arrow, close to a wire fence on your left and with the sea ahead. It was turquoise when we saw it and blended rather well with the sky.

On reaching the cliff top[2], Bridlington is spread along the shore-line[3] to your right with, to the left, Flamborough Head lighthouse. Ahead is the sea[4].

Turn right along the cliff top and continue towards Bridlington. On reaching a shallow ravine descend some steps to its bottom and climb some more up its southern side. The effort calls for deep breaths and with every one you can smell the ozone.

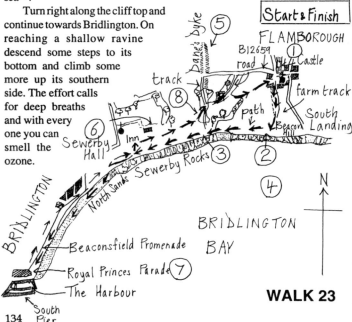

WALK 23

Still follow the cliff top and soon a shallow depression is reached, which cross, using steps down and up.

Ahead, the line of trees coming from the right follows the line of Danes Dyke[5]. They edge a deep ravine into which the path descends, becoming stepped. A third of the way down there is a recessed viewing point with a seat. From the bottom of the ravine continue along the path which climbs for a while before becoming stepped. At the top of the slope there is a welcome seat. There is also a bifurcation of paths, and here turn left to the cliff top where the walking is excellent.

The path passes in front of Sewerby Hall[6], beautifully sited behind fine trees over to the right. The wall in front of it, when we passed, was smothered in white, yellow and blue flowers. A cricket field lies between the path and the hall and alongside it are two adjoining enclosures in which are large goats, red deer, fallow deer and llamas.

On reaching the Ship Inn, beyond which the path becomes surfaced you have the choice of either continuing along the promenade or walking along the beach. By taking the latter and using the promenade on your return there is more variety.

Leave the sands on approaching the sea wall and climb steps onto Royal Princes Parade[7] from where continue southwards, briefly, into Crane Wharf, the apex of this walk.

From Crane Wharf return to Royal Princes Parade, continue northwards along it and keep straight ahead, along Beaconsfield Promenade, climbing the rim of the clay cliffs that extend as far as Sewerby before becoming chalk. On reaching a "Ship Inn" sign, bear left alongside the enclosures passed on the outward leg, along a surfaced path, which soon goes left, towards Sewerby Hall. Bear right, directed by a finger post, along a clear path, moving away from the sea towards Danes Dyke. The path edges a ha-ha on the left, goes through a facing broken fence and cuts through a long narrow copse and continues straight across a new golf course. On reaching a facing fence with two gateways, go through the right-hand side one and continue along a green track, close to a hawthorn hedge. The track descends a slope and continues to a stile in a facing fence, which cross.

When the path ahead splits three ways take the left-hand one which climbs some steps. Follow it, gradually descending into Danes Dyke[8], clearly defined and lovely to follow. Soon a bridge over a stream is reached, which cross to climb a long flight of steps just ahead to bring you clear of the wood.

At the rim of the Dyke go straight ahead, along a surfaced path, close to a fine wall on your right, to reach a tarmac road. Continue along it, straight ahead, soon to pass a farm building on the left. Just past the second sleeping policeman, where the road curves left, go right at a finger post set on the bend. Go along a clear, unsurfaced farm track, through a shallow wood, and on, edging a field close to a hawthorn hedge on the right. Soon the clear path curves to the right, straight towards Flamborough village. On reaching a stile in a facing fence, waymarked, cross it and continue over the next field along a clear path. Leave through a kissing gate into Flamborough.

Three cheers to Humberside County Council for the admirable way in which they are keeping the stiles and route directions in good condition.

Turn right, then left, into Church Street.

Things Seen On The Way

(1) Flamborough Village. Sited half way between the two inlets of North and South Landings, is the ancient village of Flamborough. It's name originates from the Anglo-Saxon word FLAEN, meaning arrow point. The name is a good description of the headland east of Danes Dyke.

The old village is centred around Dog and Duck Square, with the Dog and Duck Hotel on one side of it. The village green is just off the High Street with the Women's Institute nearby. Post Office Street runs into Chapel Street where, at the corner, a new Methodist Chapel has been opened to replace an older one. At the junction of Chapel Street there are gardens and seats and there is also a red granite memorial to six local fishermen who died in February, 1909, trying to rescue the crew of another coble, in the teeth of a severe gale. Brave men, all. The Parish Church is dedicated to St Oswald and a fish is depicted on the weathervane atop its massive tower, which is apt because St Oswald is the patron saint of fishermen. The church's chancel arch and font are Norman.

The ladies of Flamborough used to wear black bonnets, made by themselves from cashmere and tied at the back with a satin ribbon bow. They also used to wear long skirts, and when they were collecting limpets for their men folk in baskets strapped to their backs, it was customary for them to hitch up these long skirts and tie them in that position to keep them dry. Some, gathering bait, were lowered down the sea-cliffs so that they could reach a good bait ground. Formidable females, these Flamborough fisherwomen, who also knitted jerseys and, some of them at any rate, were not above dabbling in a little smuggling. The jerseys the Flamborough fisherwomen knitted had a distinctive pattern and on several occasions the body of a shipwrecked fisherman has been identified through the pattern on the jersey, or at least the village from which he came.

For many years sword dancing has been popular in the village. The dance involves eight men, dressed in blue jerseys and white trousers, with a melodian and, at times a tambourine, providing the music.

As with many other villages involved with fishing, superstition played a big part in Flamborough life. A fisherman meeting a woman on his way to his coble would turn back unless he had first met a man or unless the woman's name was Mary or Ann.

(2) Flamborough Head And The Danes. The jutting "arrow head" that is the headland of Flamborough protects Bridlington Bay from the northerly dales. Many ships have foundered beneath its chalky cliffs and countless thousands of sea-birds have found shelter on its ledges. Its two tiny inlets, North and South Landings, have been a haven for fishermen since the days of the Vikings.

The Danes were active on the headland and eventually settled there. Danish words still linger in the local dialect and can still be heard occasionally among older folk. In fact the most distinguishing mark the Danes left at Flamborough was the dialect of the people. So firmly entrenched were the Danish words among the inhabitants of the headland that in 1846 the Danish King sent scholars to Flamborough to pick up any Danish words that had survived there, even though they had fallen into disuse in Denmark.

(3) The Shore-line. At both North and South Landings the nearby beaches and cliff slopes are composed entirely of sea shells.

(4) Famous Flamborough Cod. A cod, caught in 1893, had at least 59 hooks in its belly, baited with whelks. Another, unbelievably, had swallowed a six-inch wooden doll in a woollen dress, a pair of unbroken spectacles and a coral necklace.

(5) Danes' Dyke. The $2^{1}/_{2}$ miles long fosse and vallum dug across the base of the Flamborough headland to defend it against all comers is much older than the Danes who later made the land to the east of it "Little Denmark". In 1879 General Pitt Rivers excavated part of it and found 800 worked flints and the chips that had been struck while working them. It is thought that this giant fortification is Early Bronze Age. The Danes, who knew how to use bronze and iron would never have worked with implements as primitive as flint. In fact the name Danes is derived from Dinas, which is Welsh for fort, and it covers 146,295 acres. Its southern end, from where the Bridlington road cuts through it to the sea, is mostly a natural ravine but the northern section was dug out and is about 60 feet wide and 18 feet deep, the earth being thrown up on the Flamborough side to form a vallum 18 feet high. In its day Danes' Dyke was a very effective defence against marauding tribesmen.

(6) Sewerby Hall. The chalk cliffs of Flamborough Head, where the Wolds meet the sea, which are met at Speeton Cliffs, end in front of Sewerby Hall,

giving way to clay. Their compostion is complex, as a look at the geology of the area shows.

The 400ft high Speeton Cliffs are comprised of Lower Chalk which is sub-divided into three bands, the highest being "Black Chalk" or Belemnitella Plena with Grey Chalk below it. The Grey Chalk contains lots of manganese but no flints. Both these bands are set on a base of chalk marl which contains pink bands of Holaster Subglobosus. This is the northern scarp of the chalk.

Under the landslip near Speeton Gap is Red Chalk or Hunstanton Limestone with Belemnites Minimus and Terebratula Biplicata.

Now come the Lower Cretaceous with some of the fossils it contains. Inoceramus Mytiloides are found around Thornwick Nab. The Middle Cretaceous, which contains flints and Awanchytes Ovatus begins at the High Stacks and continues northwards.

The Upper Cretaceous which is clearly seen between Sewerby and Danes' Dyke is soft and contains no flints. Numerous sponges and marsupites are found in it, along with Belemnitella Mucronata and bands of Fuller's Earth.

At Sewerby the East Coast is transformed. All the way from Marshall Meadows on the Scottish border the shore has been rock; but at Sewerby the chalk cliff retreats inland behind a mass of boulder clay and, except at Hunstanton, no more real rock is seen again until the white cliffs of Dover are reached.

In an old gravel beach below the boulder clay at Sewerby have been found the remains of the Straight Tusked Elephant, Leptorhine Rhinoceros, Hippo and many molluscs.

Sewerby Park, which is open to the public, is a delight. There are beautiful grounds, plantations, a cricket field, putting greens, a golf course, croquet lawns, a bowling green, archery butts and a small zoo.

The Hall itself is a museum with a small archaeological collection and, joy of joys, it houses the Amy Johnson Collection.

"Amy, wonderful Amy" was born in Hull in 1904. In 1930 she was the first woman to fly alone from England to Australia ($19^1/_2$ days) and later made record flights to India (6 days), Japan and back (1931) and Cape Town and back (1932). She married James Mollison in 1932 and flew the Atlantic with him in 1933 (39 hours). Her greatest achievement was the record - making solo flight to Cape Town and back in 1936. She was drowned in the Thames after an air crash in 1941.

(7) Bridlington. It used to be called Burlington and its name is derived from an Angle called Bretel who settled in the Old Town and called it Bretelston. The town is situated in the eastern part of the Dickering Wapentake, known

less romantically today as the Borough of East Yorkshire. The county was divided into Wapentakes in 1166 in the Danelaw, and Dickering most probably derives from the Old English words "dica-hring", meaning dyke circle, one of which was Paddock Hill, Thwing, where a court meeting place is thought to have been.

The town used to be in two separate sections, the old market town, a mile inland, built around the Priory and now called the Old Town and Bridlington Quay, the harbour at the mouth of the Gypsey Race, a meandering stream which winds its way through many Wolds villages and supplies water and power to many areas.

The cliffs of boulder clay and sand erode very quickly. It has been estimated that south of the harbour the cliffs receded 230 yards between 1805 and 1885, but north of the harbour they receded only 30 yards between 1771 and 1852 as the cliffs become chalk about Sewerby. The twentieth-century sea walls have prevented further erosion.

(8) Danes' Dyke (Again) Nature Trail. Danes' Dyke is a haven for ornithologists with a Nature Trail embracing $1^{1/4}$ miles of it. Myriad birds can be seen from it, including yellow hammers, corn buntings, blackbirds and chaffinches. House sparrows, fed by visitors, are attracted to the car park while pied flycatchers favour the ravine bottom and long eared owls keep to the margins.

WALK 24. BRIDLINGTON - WILSTHORPE - CARNABY - ROMAN ROAD BETWEEN CARNABY AND BOYNTON - BRIDLINGTON.

From Bridlington's Crane Wharf[1] go southwards, edging the harbour, soon to cross it along the harbour bridgeway to reach the landward end of South Pier. Continue southwards, past the lifeboat station[2] and where the concrete marine walk ends[3] continue along a tarmac path leading to a fairly low cliff top. Go straight along it, passing a large parking area, beyond which there is a large caravan site. In front of the parking area there is a hotel, "The Bay Inn". Once a boatyard is passed, the path becomes unsurfaced and sandy. Where it dips into a hollow, turn right, away from the sea[4], and go into a lane, soon to pass the remains of a stile. Keep ahead, along a surfaced road that comes in from the left, passing, after 125 yards, a farm house on the right. The road has a wooden fence on its left-hand side. On passing a boarded-up cottage, where the road bifurcates, turn right, around the side of a large midden and continue along a tarmac road with no fences on either side, which is a bridleway. On reaching a T-junction turn left, alongside a road towards

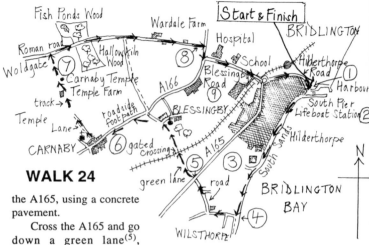

WALK 24

the A165, using a concrete
pavement.

Cross the A165 and go
down a green lane[5],
following yellow arrows and a finger post. It is a lovely lane and you have
a hedge on your right and a field on your left. It meanders, keeping to the edge
of the field, and is so clear you simply can't go wrong. Where the hedge ends,
you have a ditch on your right, and the track leads to a stile to the left of a gate,
beyond which a railway line is crossed. Go over a stile to the left of another
gate and continue along another clear track, close to a ditch on your right.

When the track reaches the field corner do not go through a gap in the
facing hedge. Go left for a few yards, then right, over a stile in a facing wire
fence into a lane. Immediately turn left, along the lane, guided by yellow
arrows. Soon the lane turns sharp right; and you simply continue along it and
at its end turn left, towards a road, which cross, close to a house on the left
to reach a signpost. Now go diagonally right, across a field, on a very clear
path to join the A166 over a stile with a finger post. Cross the road to take
advantage of a tarmac footpath and turn left along it.

On reaching Carnaby[6] go along Main Street and take the first turn right,
Temple Lane, uphill, past where another road joins it from the left out of the
village. At the hill top go through a gate, directed by a Bridleway sign and
continue, still on the surfaced road, towards Temple Farm. On passing the
farm on the left follow the blue bridleway sign and go straight ahead, passing
Carnaby Temple[7] on your right. The track, though no longer surfaced, is
wide and easy to follow. It descends gently along a line of telegraph wires,
towards the village of Boynton, seen ahead, and ends at a facing Roman road.

140

Turn right along it as it dips down the side of a shallow, partly wooded valley, soon to cut between Fishpond Wood on the left and Hallow Kiln Wood on the right. As the road climbs before bearing right a caravan and camping site is passed and, a little further on, as it descends, Bridlington is seen ahead.

On reaching a T-junction turn right, along a roadside footpath and cross the busy road when you get the chance. Continue to where a major road goes left, signposted "Town Centre[8] 1 1/2 miles" and turn left, along it, passing, on the left, first Bridlington Hospital, then Bridlington School, to cross a railway bridge. At a roundabout just beyond it, keep straight ahead, as signposted to the town centre and the north beach. This will bring you to the harbour and completes the circle.

Things Seen On The Way

(1) Bridlington Quay. Once the Quay and the Old Town were two separate sections. The Quay area became popular after 1750 and grew rapidly in the 1880s. The coming of the railway in 1846 made it possible for many more people to come, and by 1850 the Quay and the Old Town began to join along Quay Road, with the railway station about half way between the two communities.

Crane Wharf was used as a fish market until 1915 and, when it became too small, larger ships began to use the South Pier. The Crane Wharf development of shops was given the Civic Society Award in 1986.

Whenever the tide is very low it is possible to see, at the seaward end of the North Pier, stone from the Priory in the Old Town, most of which was demolished at the Dissolution of the monasteries.

The Gypsey Race runs below buildings into the harbour at Clough Hole. Clough is an old name for a ravine and there used to be lock gates at Clough Hole to assist the shipping sailing up the river.

On Gummers Landing at the landward end of South Pier there are some workshops where Lawrence of Arabia worked as a marine craft mechanic and designer when he was an airman with the R.A.F. marine craft until 1934. He had taken the name T.E.Shaw so that no one would recognise him. He retired and left Bridlington only three months before being killed in a motor cycle accident in 1935. The R.A.F. continued to use these workshops for Air Sea Rescue craft until 1978 when they were superseded by helicopters. Lawrence, as Shaw, stayed in the tower room of the Ozone Hotel at the junction of Windsor Crescent and West Street, now the Royal Yorkshire Yacht Club. A sundial was erected in memory of him in South Cliff Gardens.

The harbour was once used by the Romans. From early times the bay was a centre for shipping and fishing, with Irish gold crossing the Pennines to be shipped to the continent. Herring has long been an important industry with herring houses at the harbour as far back as 1530; and fishing is still important.

For centuries shipping was also an important part of Bridlington's livelihood. The Priory exported wool in the 1300s, and by the 1500's regular shipments of coal were brought in. In the 1700's London and the Continent were big markets for the malt grain and vegetables grown in the area. There was a ship building yard on the seafront and the last locally built ship was launched in 1834.

There were two timber framed piers in 1554 and to help with the maintenance of these a toll was collected on goods shipped or landed. New stone piers were built between 1816 and 1848.

(2) The Lifeboat Station. Sited at the northern end of South Marine Drive, the lifeboat house was built in 1904. If called out, the lifeboat has to be towed by tractor down the slipway to the sea. Between the lifeboat station and the sea is the Spa building complex. It was built, together with the sea wall, in 1896 by Whitaker Brothers of Horsforth and is used for many functions throughout the year.

(3) Queen Henrietta Maria. North of where the marine walk ends and set back from the harbour, is Queen Street, named after Queen Henrietta Maria who stayed there in 1643 after selling her jewels in Holland in exchange for arms to be used by Charles I in the Civil War.

Parliament ships, under the command of Admiral Batton, stormed the town, looking for her. She sheltered in what was to become known as Queen's House.

Later, with arms loaded on carts she followed the Gypsey Race to Boynton Hall. There she stole the gold plate, leaving a portrait of herself in its place and continued to York where her husband, Charles I, was fighting the Parliamentarians.

(4) Lost Villages. South of Bridlington the geology is boulder clay with rather muddy sand between the coastline and the sea; and the sea eats into it at an average rate of two yards a year. At least two and a half miles of land have gone right along the coastline since the Romans left and, as a consequence, almost a score of towns and villages have vanished under the waves.

The chalk escarpment of the Wolds, which becomes lost beneath the boulder clay around Sewerby, runs south westwards as a low ridge of hills that forms the eastern face of the Wolds. In glacial times the whole of the area was cluttered with boulder clay brought into the area from Scandinavia and the North of England. It is this soft clay that is being washed away by the sea.

The route passes between Bilderthorpe and Wilsthrope villages with, a little further south, Auburn village, all of which, although still above the waves, have died.

(5) Carnaby Airfield. To the south of your line of walk can be seen some of the hangars that were part of the old Carnaby airfield, which was one of only two airfields built in Britain specially to help damaged aircraft returning from missions over Germany.

(6) Carnaby. The village church is perched on a steep hillside overlooking the houses, cottages and farms spread along the Bridlington to Great Driffield road that are Carnaby. The church has a fifteenth-century tower, a coffin lid built into the south wall, a Norman font and a good view. It is dedicated to John the Baptist.

(7) Carnaby Temple. This octagonal building, which was once a lookout place is now a cottage.

(8) Bridlington Old Town. The Old Town was made a conservation area in 1969.

Narrow Bayle Gate, leading to the Priory, was lined with houses until the early 1900s. The Bayle was built in 1388 as the gate house to the Priory, and after the Dissolution of the Monasteries was virtually the only building left intact, apart from the church, as nearly all the rest of the Priory was pulled down. The National School was started in the Bayle in 1818, and the building has also served as a prison or kidcote as it was known locally. It is now a museum and a meeting place of the Lords Feoffees: a body of 13 men, formed in 1630, who governed the town and administered the Manor on behalf of the inhabitants under a deed of 1636. They still administer some manorial property in the town.

Just past the Bayle, on the right, is Applegarth Lane which was part of the Priory orchard. Mid-way along it, hidden behind iron railings, is a tiny chapel. Built in 1699 by Robert Prudom, who lived in Bayle Gate, it was the first Baptist chapel in Bridlington.

At the bottom of Applegarth Lane and a few yards to the left, in the playing fields of the College of Further Education are two mounds. These are the remains of the archery butts, used in the days when men had to practice archery in case they were conscripted to fight. The grounds also contained fish ponds that were used by the Priors.

Nearby Church Walk, now edged with allotments, was once covered with Priory buildings. Only the nave remains of the original Priory church which is now the Parish Church of St Mary the Virgin. It's towers, designed by Sir Gilbert Scott, were completed in 1875. The Priory was founded by Walter de Gant in 1113 and was important enough for Henry V to visit it in 1421. The last Prior was William Wood, who was accused of treason and executed in 1537. After this the Priory and the Manor of Bridlington was forfeit to the crown and much of it was demolished and used to build surrounding houses.

Church Green, in front of the Priory, was used for sheep fairs and other village activities. High Green, adjacent to Pinfold Street, was used for cattle and horse fairs. Once there was a pinfold for stray animals at the top end of Pinfold Street. Farmsteads and barns surrounded the green and the great barn, used for storage by the Priors was at its top end. The annual Charter Fair was held on the green until 1973 when a new site was found. Until 1910 people brought their produce from the villages to be sold in the markets. The market bell was fixed on the pillory next to the stocks and these have been rebuilt to show where wrong doers were shackled and pelted with rotten food and mud.

Westgate was the site of a development of large houses built by wealthy families in the 1600's. Numbers 6-7 Westgate mark the former home of the Hebblethwaite family, large local landowners in the 1600's. The initials W.H. can be seen on the rainwater heads. The building is in rich dark red brick and has eight mullioned bay windows with coved cornices and acanthus leaf decoration above the bedroom windows.

Ye Old Star Inn, an old, timbered building, parts of which go back to the 1600's, has a horse mounting block in the yard.

Many of the houses in High Street were built in the 1500's but were altered to Bow fronted shops in the early 1800's by the Bridlington architect John Matson, known for building Flamborough lighthouse without the aid of scaffolding.

The chemist's shop at number 64a, still with the original interior fittings, was opened in 1813 by Mr and Mrs Gatenby. She was well known for her remedies and they had moved from further along the street to be next door to the doctor. The interior was purpose built with labelled drawers and shelves lined with balloon topped jars and central heating coming through carved grills under the counters. The original scale balance is still in use. The cellars are lined with stone from the Priory, as are others in the street.

The Dominican convent is the largest house in the street. It has nine bay windows, many dating from the early 1700's. The Tuscan door was added in 1825.

There were once twelve clockmakers in the area and Craven House, number 16, is said to be named after one of them. The house is late 1600's was remodelled in 1806 and later restored.

William Kent, the architect and designer, was born in the Old Town of Burlington in 1684. He designed the interiors of 10 Downing Street, the Prime Minister's residence.

CHAPTER XIII
BOYNTON TO LOWTHORPE (outskirts of)

Length of section: linear: 6¹/₄ miles (10km)

Distance covered walking clockwise from Hessle: 144 miles (230.4km)

Walk 25:   Circular: Boynton - Roman Road between Carnaby and
                   Boynton - Burton Agnes - Rudston - Boynton 11¹/₂
                   miles (18.4km)

Walk 26:   Circular: Burton Agnes - Harpham - Kilham - Burton
                   Agnes 7 miles (11.2km)

Map Ref: Landranger 101

Parking: Roadside in Boynton, Burton Agnes, Harpham and
                   Rudston; but first check with the local inhabitants.

Handy hostelries: The Blue Bell, Burton Agnes, Kilham.

WALK 25. BOYNTON - ROMAN ROAD - BURTON AGNES - RUDSTON - BOYNTON.

From St Andrews' church, Boynton[1], go right for a few yards and turn left
at a bridleway signpost. Where the road bifurcates keep straight ahead, along
the bridleway ignoring the footpath on the right. The way is along a broad
unsurfaced road which soon crosses a dry stream, Gypsey Race[2], which
hereabouts flows underground. Boynton Hall[3] is on the left and from this
road there is a good view of its side. The road goes past the right-hand end
of some farm buildings and round the back of them, passing a building on the
left, then on the right. Turn right, past this latter building, going behind it
along a track to reach a waymarked stile on your left leading into a field.

Climb a bank and from the top of it go directly across the field to leave
at a facing stile, beyond which turn left along the field's edge. On reaching
the field corner turn right and continue straight up the field on a clear path.

Exit the field onto a Roman road at a point where the previous walk
reached it from Carnaby via Carnaby Temple seen on the near horizon, so
linking this circle with the previous one. Turn right, along the road, on rising
ground, soon to edge Sands Wood on the right. When a crossroads is reached
go straight ahead. As the road follows the ridge top the view to the east opens

WALK 25

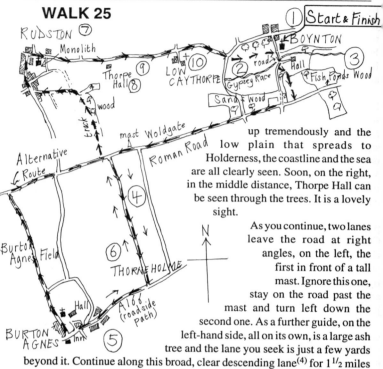

up tremendously and the low plain that spreads to Holderness, the coastline and the sea are all clearly seen. Soon, on the right, in the middle distance, Thorpe Hall can be seen through the trees. It is a lovely sight.

As you continue, two lanes leave the road at right angles, on the left, the first in front of a tall mast. Ignore this one, stay on the road past the mast and turn left down the second one. As a further guide, on the left-hand side, all on its own, is a large ash tree and the lane you seek is just a few yards beyond it. Continue along this broad, clear descending lane[4] for 1 1/2 miles to reach Thornholme where, at the lane end, turn right, along the A166, soon to reach Burton Agnes[5], seen ahead. The road is busy but there is a footpath alongside it. On the right, with few hedges to obstruct the view, the countryside is displayed in all its beauty and Burton Agnes Hall can be seen through the trees. Continue through the village, passing, on the right, the imposing entrance to Burton Agnes Hall and on the left, a duck pond. Keep straight ahead to the Bluebell Inn, the apex of this section.

From the inn, having first possibly sampled the fine fare inside, retrace your steps along the A166 to Thornholme and turn left along the 1 1/2 miles long lane used earlier. It will bring you to the Roman Road, where turn left, along it, for a short distance, then right along an unsurfaced track, just past the ruins of a building.

[Alternatively, on leaving the inn, cross the road and turn right along it, briefly, to turn left along a quiet road through the village. At the first road junction on the right, outside the village, turn right, along a quiet road, soon to turn left along another quiet road that climbs steadily across Burton Agnes Field for almost a mile to reach the Roman Road, where turn right, along it, for a short distance to turn left at the same unsurfaced track reached by the alternative route.]

Continue alongside a hawthorn hedge on your right on a track that becomes green and marvellous to walk along. At the end of a day, with the sun sinking to westwards the whole landscape has about it a dream like quality that stirs the blood. As the track descends, Rudston[6] is seen lying snugly in the valley bottom a little to the left. It is a most delightful sight. The descent, alongside a wood on your right, is the steepest part of this section. When a facing path is reached, turn left, along it. As it curves to the right and descends to a footpath sign, turn left because the way directly ahead, through a gate, is private. The path leads into Rudston.

On entering the village turn right at a signpost, cross an open space and pass in front of a building fronted by a covered loading area, to your right. Cross a facing stile into a narrow field, leaving it at another stile. Continue along a little passage which turns left, past a house and leads to a tarmac road at a cul-de-sac. Turn right, out of the cul-de-sac and on reaching the road turn right, along it, soon to cross a bridge over a stream. Turn left, along a footpath edging a stream. On reaching a road continue along it and turn right at a road junction.

As you come out of the village a detour, left, to see the church is well worth the effort, for there is much to see.

On reaching a road junction turn right, past the war memorial on the left to continue along the road for $1\frac{1}{2}$ miles, at first using a footpath that is raised above the road. Where it ends cross the road and continue along the verge, facing the traffic. Soon Thorpe Hall[7] is seen through the trees on the right. A little beyond the wooded grounds of Thorpe Hall[8] Low Caythorpe Farm is passed on the right and a little way past the farm entrance is the site of a capped wellhead[9].

Where the road makes a sharp left turn on approaching an area of afforestation turn right very briefly, down a minor road and almost at once turn left, as directed by a footpath sign and yellow waymarker. Continue along an unsurfaced farm track to the left of a field, close to the woodland on your left. Climb a stile at a facing fence and keep straight ahead, close to the wood on your left. Cross a stile alongside a facing gateway and go slightly right, directed by yellow arrows. On reaching a facing gate, fronting a large sycamore in a step in the fence, cross a stile alongside it. Continue close to a fence on the right, following a yellow waymarker. As Boynton village is approached bear slightly away from the fence and aim for a facing stile, which cross. Go along a short, grassy lane between conifers to reach a road that leads past dwellings back to the front of St Andrew's church.

Things Seen On The Way

(1) St Andrew's Church, Boynton. A country churchyard often holds surprising information about a place and its inhabitants; and a good example of this can be seen in St Andrew's churchyard. Sited close to the boundary wall to the right of the church tower as approached up the entrance steps, one of the tombstones has this to say about the grave's occupant.

> George Stevens, shepherd for nearly fifty years to Sir George and William Strickland, died on 7th day of April, 1812, in the 69th year of his age and is here buried. To record and to hold up as an example to others his assiduity and fertility as a servant, his care, affection and prudence as the father of numerous family and his honesty and uprightness towards all men this stone is erected by Sir William Strickland.

Two tall yews shade the church's fifteenth-century tower and its buttresses, one of which is much older than the tower and has a cross carved into it. A more modern figure of St Andrew is in an old niche. Much of the church was rebuilt by John Carr of York in 1768. The chancel was rebuilt in the eighteenth century and the predominant colour of the interior is green. A gallery at the western end is reached from the nave by a flight of stairs. Four columns and fine ironwork mark what used to be the chancel but the altar has now been set back in the Strickland chapel at the east end.

It was the distinguished Stricklands of Boynton Hall who rebuilt St Andrew's church. Time and again members of this remarkable family have shone in the chronicles of England. An early Strickland fought at the Battle of Hastings and another carried the banner of St George at Agincourt.

When Henrietta Maria of France landed at Bridlington en route to join her husband, Charles I, at York, she found shelter, if not friendship, at Boynton Hall, home, at that time, of William Strickland. At the Restoration he was knighted by Charles I.

Another Strickland, Walter, was an ardent Roundhead. The Long Parliament chose him to go to Holland to complain about the help given to Henrietta Maria. He sat in several of Cromwell's Parliaments and narrowly escaped death at the Hague, where he was trying to arrange an alliance between England and Holland. At the Restoration he got a pardon.

Perhaps the most famous of the Stricklands was William who, as a youth, sailed to the New World from Bristol with Sebastian Cabot, (1483-1557), in search of a north-east passage to India, which resulted in trade with Russia. While on this venture they discovered the turkey, which had been domesticated by the Indians. Young Strickland was appointed turkey boy to the expedition. He was entrusted with the care of these birds on voyage and had to tend them on reaching land.

As befits Boynton's association, through William Strickland, with the first turkeys to come to England from America, there is a turkey lectern inside St Andrew's church. William Strickland, having grown rich from the profits of his voyages, applied for a coat of arms showing a turkey cock as the family crest; and he drew a crude picture of a turkey to show how it looked. This drawing is at the College of Arms, entitled "A turkey in his pride" and is unique as the first known picture of a turkey anywhere.

Sir George Strickland wrote a review of agriculture and published a map of Yorkshire.

Sir Charles Strickland is said to have been the original Martin in *"Tom Brown's Schooldays"*.

Hugh Strickland, the naturalist, was another distinguished son.

(2) Gypsey Race. The only constant thing about this stream is its inconstancy.

(3) Boynton Hall. The Stricklands no longer live at Boynton Hall, parts of which, through necessity, had been converted into flats, an unbecoming fate for so fine a building with such a glorious past. It now belongs to a gentleman with the means, the desire and the ability to restore it to its former glory, which he is doing. It is good to know that the future of Boynton Hall is in such good and caring hands.

(4) Arable Fields. The fields edging this broad lane are all arable: cattle are seldom seen around here, and the fields are very large indeed. In one that lies alongside the track we watched five tractors working: one was cutting stubble, one was loading manure and the other three were muck spreading. With so much manure about we expected to see herds of cattle but there were none to be seen.

(5) Burton Agnes. Take some pretty cottages, fronted by neat gardens, add a large pond, shaded by tall trees and alive with mallard and other water fowl, a tall memorial cross, a church, parts of which are Norman and a friendly inn and you have a delightful village. Wrap part of it around a green hillside that offers long views across the Plain of Holderness and the village becomes memorable. Add one of the most noble of England's stately homes and you have Burton Agnes, an absolute gem.

From its gate the church porch is reached through a tunnel of yews 27 feet wide; and inside the church the nave and the aisles give the church one of the widest interiors in the country. The north arcade is Norman but the wooden arch over the squire's pew in the church's eastern bay cannot claim such antiquity. The south arcade was made during the thirteenth century from the remains of a Norman wall. A griffin carved on a capital of the fine tower arch is thought to be the bade of the Griffith family. Although the arch between the nave and the chancel is thirteenth century the chancel itself was rebuilt in the nineteenth century.

In the middle of the aisle there is an alabaster tomb enriched with angels and 14 saints in niches. The knight and lady lying on it are believed to be Sir Walter Griffith and his first wife, Joan Nevill, said to have been a great-granddaughter of John of Gaunt.

The seventeenth-century monument to Sir Henry Griffith and his two wives is much more macabre. Part of its decoration include bones and skulls and three black coffins piled one above the other.

It was Sir Henry Griffith who rebuilt the hall during the reign of Elizabeth I.

(6) Rudston. In 1933, in a field beside the Kilham road at Rudston, a plough revealed the remains of a fine Roman house. Further excavation showed that it had central heating, beautiful rooms with tessellated floors and a wide gateway.

From the junction of this descending track with the Roman Road Rudston Beacon can be seen on the horizon to westwards.

Rudston church is built on an eminence overlooking the village and surrounded by rolling Wolds, a patchwork of fields and woods. Its chancel is 600 years old, the arch to the nave is Norman and its tall arcades are thirteenth century, although the aisles were rebuilt in 1861. Its tower is Norman, sturdy and has four feet thick walls.

In the churchyard is the grave of Winifred Holtby, author of the famous novel *South Riding* which depicted life in the 1920s and 30s in a small Yorkshire town. She died in London on 29th September, 1935, aged 37.

The tallest standing stone in England is in Rudston's churchyard. Taller than the Devil's Arrows at Boroughbridge, it is known as the Cleopatra's Needle of the Wolds. The part of it sticking out of the ground is 25 feet high and it is thought that another 25 feet lie below the surface. Deposited by a glacier, this prehistoric monument was old when the Romans lived close by in the central heated house. Today it wears a cap to protect it from the weather.

Our old friend Gypsey Race surfaces in Rudston but with little water in it.

(7) Thorpe Hall. Gypsey Race, having spent so long underground, makes not

The Rudston Monolith in the churchyard

one but two lakes in the park of Thorpe Hall.

Many generations of the Bosville family lived in beautiful Thorpe Hall which was home to Sir Alexander Macdonald of the Isles until his death in 1933. He lies in Rudston churchyard.

(8) Low Caythorpe Village. To the east of Thorpe Hall park but before Caythorpe Farm is reached is the site of long-since vanished medieval Low Caythorpe Village.

(9) Kelt-UK Ltd Wellhead. Kelt-UK Ltd is applying to the East Yorkshire Borough Council for planning permission for the development of the Caythorpe gas field. Meanwhile the well head is capped.

WALK 26. BURTON AGNES - HARPHAM - KILHAM - BURTON AGNES.

From the Bluebell Inn go left, out of the village, and where the road curves to the right, turn left at a footpath sign towards Harpham village, seen in the distance. Go diagonally right across a large field, aiming for a waymarked stile 70 yards to the left of the field corner. Once over the stile turn right, close to the fence on the right, and on reaching the field corner turn left, briefly, to a waymarked stile in a facing fence. Cross the stile, then a ditch and aim for the first of a line of telegraph poles crossing the field and from there go diagonally left towards the field corner.

Just to the left of the field corner cross a waymarked stile and turn right along the edge of the field close to a hedge on your right. As an added guide there is a tall, solitary hawthorn right in the corner.

Where there is a gap in the hedge on the right go diagonally left to an ash tree, cross a step stile to the left of it and go down the next field close to the hedge on your left. Where the hedge ends keep straight ahead, along a clear path, aiming for a stile at the far side of the field. Continue past a converted chapel on the right to another step stile leading onto a road where turn left into the village.

Cross a road and continue into the middle of Harpham[1] along a road called Cross Gates. Leave this part of the village along a lane to the right of the church, go through a wicket and continue straight ahead towards some more houses, passing a tennis court on your left. Exit the field through a wicket on your right and turn left, passing to the right of a farmhouse. Go through the farmyard and leave through a gate in the hedge on your left. Turn right along a little path back into the village.

On reaching a surfaced road turn right, then left, along it, out of the

WALK 26

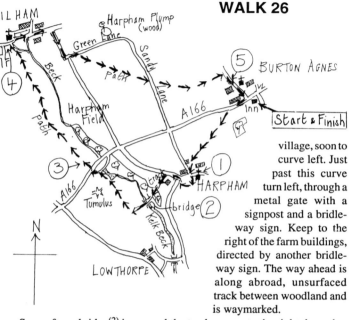

Start & Finish

village, soon to curve left. Just past this curve turn left, through a metal gate with a signpost and a bridle-way sign. Keep to the right of the farm buildings, directed by another bridle-way sign. The way ahead is along abroad, unsurfaced track between woodland and is waymarked.

Soon after a bridge[2] is crossed the track curves to the right through a metal gate. Continue straight ahead as indicated by a marker and proceed close to a fence on your right. Cross a corner stile at a facing electrified fence and go diagonally right, directed by a sign, along the field's edge, close to a wire fence. As the path goes under some power cables an arrow on one of the posts confirms your route. Another sign, on the left, opposite some farm buildings, underlines the confirmation on the post.

On reaching, at an angle, a signpost beside a farm road, go left, along it towards the A166. Very prominent on the horizon to your left there is a tumulus with some trees on it. Before the A166 is reached the original road, now a picnic area, is crossed, guided by a yellow arrow.

Cross the A166 guided by a signpost and a yellow arrow, descend the far embankment and cross a facing stile. Continue straight ahead, edging a wood on your right[3]. Cross a waymarked stile in a facing fence and cross the field ahead bearing slightly right to exit at a facing stile with the forest still on your right. Cross the next field to a clearly seen waymarked step stile.

153

From here Kilham church is clearly seen ahead.

Cross the next field, bearing slightly left, to a clearly seen waymarked stile, which cross. Go over the next field, keeping slightly to the left of two pylons seen behind the facing field hedge. Cross a waymarked step stile at the far end of the field. It is some distance in front of the two pylons but they serve a purpose as a guide.

Continue ahead, bearing slightly left, to the edge of the field and continue along the field's edge, passing underneath the electricity cables. Go through a gateway in a fence at the end of the field, cross the next one to a clearly seen waymarked stile and go over the next field bearing slightly to the left, aiming for the church tower.

As you cross the field a yellow marker can be seen at a stile in the hedge to the right of the church. Cross the next field, bearing slightly left, to a yellow marker clearly seen at a gap in the far hedge. From it go straight across the next field to another marker at a gap at the other side of the field. From here go diagonally left across the next field towards the right-hand side of some large trees. On reaching a hedge at the end of the field go through a broad gap that is not waymarked. Continue straight across the next field, aiming for an electricity pole near some beech trees at the far fence. To the left of the pole cross a waymarked stile. Continue diagonally left, over the next field, aiming for a gateway in front on the village[4]. Leave the field through this gateway and continue straight ahead, towards the church. On reaching it, turn right, along a road that curves to the left then to the right, leaving the village.

Where the road reaches a junction, turn right and where it zigzags sharp left, then sharp right, continue straight ahead at the second bend along a green lane. After 60 yards cross a stile on the right at a footpath sign and go diagonally left across the field ahead on a drunken track. As you approach a facing hedge at a tangent a post is seen ahead and it is here that you leave the field. It has a yellow footpath marker on it. Continue diagonally right across the next field, following a clear track. Cross a stile and go diagonally left over the field ahead. Soon you will see, almost at the end of the hedge ahead, where it is high, a yellow marker alongside a step stile, which cross. Go diagonally right over the next field, a fairly big one, aiming for two electricity posts close together, set a little to the right of a distant church.

On approaching the hedge ahead at a tangent you will see two very tall trees, the only tall ones along your line of vision. Although they are not in the same hedge, from a distance they look as though they are. Cross a stile midway between them and go straight across surfaced Sandy Lane to a gap alongside a metal gate, which go through.

Continue diagonally right across the next field, directed by a footpath sign. Approach the hedge ahead at a tangent and cross a step stile where the hedge has a bend in it, to the right of a clump of trees seen just beyond it. The trees are a good guide. Go diagonally left, aiming for this clump of trees, from where cross the field ahead, bearing slightly right, aiming to the left of twin telegraph poles. As the fence ahead is approached a yellow arrow in it can be seen. Go through a gap alongside it.

Cross the field ahead and when you reach the forward part of a hedge with a step in it continue straight ahead, along the stop, close to the hedge on the right to reach a road through a stile. Turn right, along the road, soon to enter Burton Agnes[5]. On reaching the A166, cross it, diagonally right, and enter the Bluebell Inn for a well deserved pint of the brown stuff.

Things Seen On The Way

(1) Harpham. St John's church tower is fifteenth century but the nave and chancel are older, being fourteenth century. When the church was restored between 1908 and 1914 the Georgian furnishings remained untouched.

William St Quintin, knight, whose fine alabaster tomb can be seen, is one of many St Quintins buried at St John's church. This prominent family held land in Holderness from the time of Edward II until the late nineteenth century.

One of two village wells, the Drummer Boy's well, has associations with the St Quintins. Tradition has it that while soldiers were practising archery a drummer boy fell into it. For centuries it was believed that whenever a St Quintin was about to die the boy could be heard beating his drum.

The other well is linked to St John of Beverley, patron saint of Harpham church, who is said to have been born in the village near Kelk Beck.

The St Quintin family home has not survived but memorials from it are treasured by the villagers.

Parts of a Roman house were found in a field near the village in 1905. Among the relics was a 1700 years old tile that showed the imprint of a dog's paw. The mosaic floor is now in Hull Museum.

(2) Bridge. To the right of this bridge, as you cross it, is a stream which flows under it, while on the left-hand side, where the trout are, is where a canal starts.

(3) Quintin Bottom. Taking its name from the St Quintin family, Quintin Bottom is planted with line upon serried line of poplars, straight as dies, like guardsmen marching as to war.

(4) Kilham. Situated on the eastern slopes of the Wolds, this restful village is nine miles from Bridlington. Its position as a halfway house between the High Wolds and the lowlands of Holderness made it an ideal site for a market.

Consequently Kilham survived as a site for a market and as an administrative centre. Indeed, when Daniel Defoe visited it in 1778 Kilham was a main regional market centre. With the cutting of the Driffield canal its importance declined and now it is no more than a large village.

Kilham is of particular interest to archaeologists. Bronze Age men lived hereabouts and Ancient British graves have been found on the surrounding hills. In 1897 a chariot burial of the early Iron Age was discovered as well as a large number of Neolithic implements.

The base of All Saints' Church is Norman and there are many Norman carvings in the walls of its massive tower. One feature of the church is the south doorway, lavishly decorated with chevron moulding.

(5) Burton Agnes Hall dates from 1173 when Roger de Stuteville built the Norman Manor House, the lower chamber of which still remains. In 1457 Sir Walter Griffith, an heir to the estates, came to live in the old Manor House. It is thought that he added the Great Hall. It was the first Sir Henry Griffith (1559-1620) who built the Elizabethan Mansion.

Frances, one of Sir Henry's daughters, married Sir Matthew Boynton, a name borne by successive owners until the death of Sir Marcus Wickham-Boynton in 1989.

In 1942 the estate passed to Marcus Wickham Boynton, who became responsible for extensive restorations to the house, the most notable of which was the restoration of the Long Gallery. He added greatly to the treasures at Burton Agnes, notably the collection of French paintings, the Epstein bronzes, the Chinese porcelain and much rare furniture.

In 1977 a registered charity was formed for the protection and future upkeep of Burton Agnes Hall and its valuable contents. This ensures that the Hall remains well-cared for and open to the public for at least six months of every year. At the same time it remains a "lived in" family home occupied by future generations of the Boynton family.

Outside, visitors are invited to wander around the lawns, explore the walled garden, the maze, the woodland garden and the woods. Susan Cunliff-Lister has transformed a paddock into a fantasy garden reflecting her own imagination and sense of humour.

Realising that when families go around houses children get bored she set about creating something that was fun but not an adventure playground; and what a good job she has made of it! There are labyrinthine paths leading through herbs and vegetables, a yew maze with a riddle to solve, a jungle garden, giant games of chess, draughts, noughts and crosses, snakes and ladders, hoop-la and hopscotch. There are statues, fountains, ponds, herbaceous borders and a children's corner with rabbits and guinea pigs.

CHAPTER XIV
LOWTHORPE TO DRIFFIELD

Length of section: linear: 6¹/₂ miles (10.4km)

Distance covered walking clockwise from Hessle: 150¹/₂ miles (240.8km)

Walk 27:   Circular: Lowthorpe - Nafferton - Carr House - Outgate
                      Farm - Lowthorpe 6³/₄ miles (10.8km)

Walk 28:   Circular: Nafferton - Driffield - Skerne - Wansford -
                      Nafferton 8³/₄ miles (14km)

Map Ref: Landranger 101 and 107

Parking: Roadside in Lowthorpe, but first check with the local
                      inhabitants. Limited street parking in Driffield and
                      Nafferton.

Handy hostelries: Hotels and pubs in Driffield and Nafferton.
                      The Trout, Wansford.

WALK 27. LOWTHORPE - NAFFERTON - CARR HOUSE - OUTGATE FARM - LOWTHORPE.

From the eastern end of Lowthorpe village[1] turn left along a lane directed by a footpath sign and a yellow waymarker, soon to pass some kennels on the right-hand side. Just past the last house on the right cross a facing stile and continue straight ahead along a farm track, crossing a small field to exit over a stile at a facing gate. Cross the next field on a broad, green track to go over a stile in a facing fence. Edge the next field, close to the hedge on your left, and at the end of it go through a gate and continue ahead, now with the hedge on your right, to a metal gate. Edge the next field, close to the hedge on your right and almost at the end of it cross a waymarked stile on the right-hand side. Immediately turn left to join the track from Harpham used on the previous section.

Turn left, along it, guided by a yellow arrow and when the track curves right to a metal gate do likewise, go through the gate and bear left. There is an arrow on the corner of a fence on your left to guide you. From this corner go diagonally right, aiming for the right-hand corner of a wood ahead and at the bottom of the field go through a gate with a bluemarker and continue along a short lane to another marker pointing straight ahead. You are now

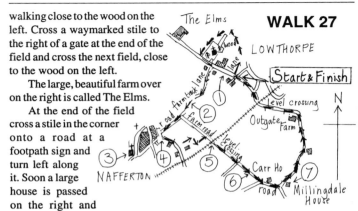

walking close to the wood on the left. Cross a waymarked stile to the right of a gate at the end of the field and cross the next field, close to the wood on the left.

The large, beautiful farm over on the right is called The Elms.

At the end of the field cross a stile in the corner onto a road at a footpath sign and turn left along it. Soon a large house is passed on the right and immediately beyond it turn right, as guided by a signpost and a waymarker, along a surfaced lane which soon continues as an unsurfaced farm track through lush, flat, arable farm land at the foot of Nafferton Wold. The farm track has waymarkers at different points along it and eventually it reaches derelict East End Farm on the left, beyond where the way becomes surfaced and continues straight ahead to Nafferton, seen ahead.

On approaching this large village a huge turkey farm[2] is passed on the left. Continue past a side road on your left to a T-junction where turn left, briefly, along How Lane and at the end of it turn right.

Ahead, on a high bank, Nafferton church[3] dominates rather splendidly while, below it, across the road, water fowl swim in a small lake.

From the middle of Nafferton[4], retrace your steps along Coppergate and continue past the entrance to Coppergate Close. Keep straight ahead, along a road that soon begins to turn sharply to the right. Here, at a waymarked gate with a footpath sign leading into a field on the left, cross an adjoining stile. Go over the field and leave through a waymarked gateway on the field's right, just short of the corner. Cross the bottom of a narrow field to a waymarked stile and turn left along a lane. Where the lane turns sharp right, before a ditch, do likewise as directed by a waymarker and follow a meandering path to a stile fronted by a ditch that is crossed on a plank bridge. Turn left, beyond the stile, as directed by a marker and in a few yards cross another ditch on a plank bridge. Cross another stile and continue up the field ahead, close to the hedge on your left. At the field corner exit through a gateway at a footpath sign and turn right, along a surfaced farm road which soon crosses a railway[5] at a level crossing and becomes unsurfaced.

Once over the level crossing continue straight ahead along this clear lane[6] for almost a mile to reach a surfaced road and turn left, along it. The road is a quiet one and it passes, in a few yards, Carr House on the left. At a T-junction turn left along a meandering road that passes, on the right, a pig farm, Millingdale House[7]. Ignoring a public footpath sign, continue along this surfaced road that is neither fenced nor hedged as it passes through lovely countryside that is flat and offers long views. It passes Outgate Farm, crosses a level crossing and before you know it you are back in Lowthorpe, the end of the circle.

Things Seen On The Way

(1) Lowthorpe, with its scattering of dwellings, Tudor stile Lodge, eighteenth-century mill and ancient church, is set among fields and trees. Primroses and bluebells carpet Church Wood, which lies beside the church after which it is named.

A seven feet high cross stands at the eastern end of the church's neglected chancel. Some think it is Kilham's old market cross. The chancel is fourteenth century and was formerly a chapel for a college founded by Sir John de Hesellarton for a rector and six priests. It is ruinous. In the nave are a brass portrait of an unknown knight, a fragment of a Saxon cross and a foot thick gravestone. The lower part of the tower is probably fifteenth century. *Tempus fugit* and the church shows it.

(2) Turkey Farm. Thousands of turkeys are kept here, housed in at least six specially designed deep litter buildings. Come Christmas most of these gobblers will have been gobbled and the awful din will be much more subdued.

(3) Nafferton Church. Perched on a high bank in the middle of Naffterton, the church gives a touch of class to the village. It is mostly medieval but the chancel arch is twelfth century and the crudely carved font is Norman. The tower is fifteenth century and the stone figure of a boy in a short tunic could be thirteenth century.

One Nafferton vicar was Rev. Francis Orpen Morris the distinguished East Riding ornithologist whose book of British birds is a standard work.

His son, Rev.C.F.Morris, made a close study of the "Waudsman" in the early years of the present century when people born "up i t' Wauds" tended not to stray far from their native "heeaf". He found that as late as the beginning of this century people in Holderness considered themselves superior to those living on the Wolds and were inclined to patronise "the Waud Wappers".

(4) Nafferton. The small lake across the road from the church gives rise to

West Beck, a stream which has flour and malting mills on its banks and flows to the canal at Wansford. The lake with its many and varied water fowl is Nafferton's most attractive feature.

(5) Railway Crossing. The crossing is on the Beverley to Bridlington line.

During the days of steam the line's embankments were occasionally set alight by falling sparks. These fires and the large numbers of rabbits populating these long, grassy banks prevented tree seedlings from growing unhindered. But once the steam trains had been replaced by diesel engines and myxomatosis had reduced the rabbit population the effect on the railway embankments was dramatic. With little to hinder the tree seedlings, they developed and today small, slim areas of woodland and scrub occur along the line.

(6) Laneside Habitats. The hedgerows alongside this long lane are fine examples of an ecosystem, providing shelter, food and nesting sites for birds. Small animals live among the grass and the herbs at the base of the hedge and the hedging trees themselves support a very varied insect population.

(7) Millingdale House. Anyone seeing the "No Through Road" sign near Millingdale House could be forgiven for thinking that the road to which it refers comes to a dead end. But this is not the case. Soon after passing Outgate Farm it crosses the Beverley to Bridlington railway and continues to Lowthorpe and places beyond. Why, then, have the road sign? It is placed there in the interest of safety. The level crossing gates are unmanned; and the British Rail, fearing that someone using the crossing will leave the gates closed against rail traffic, have restricted its use to a handful of people who live nearby. Each person authorised to use the crossing, which is kept closed and locked against road traffic, is given a key on the strict understanding that it is not lent out to anyone else. Should the key holder ignore this condition the key becomes forfeit. Perhaps someone should tell B.R. that these days most unmanned level crossings are controlled by barriers. If a barrier replaced the gates, the "No Through Road" sign would become redundant and car drivers would be able to contend with one less cause of frustration.

WALK 28. NAFFERTON - DRIFFIELD - SKERNE - WANSFORD - NAFFERTON.

From the village centre end of Coppergate turn left, in front of Nafferton church and immediately bear right along Westgate, climbing the bank the church sits on, to leave Nafferton[(1)] and continue along a straight road past Westfield Farm[(2)]. In a third of a mile, where the road goes straight towards

WALK 28

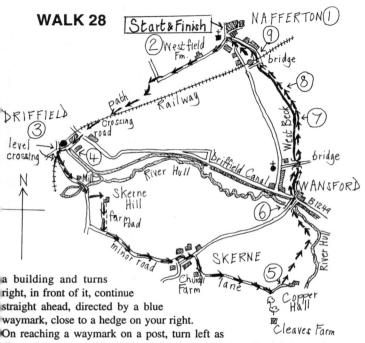

a building and turns
right, in front of it, continue
straight ahead, directed by a blue
waymark, close to a hedge on your right.
On reaching a waymark on a post, turn left as
directed, and on reaching a plant bridge over a ditch on the right just before a
few trees, cross it and continue straight ahead, directed by a waymark.

As you cross the flat land there are marker posts to guide you; and
Driffield is seen just ahead. At the end of the long field cross a stile and go
over the railway line at a waymarked crossing.

Bear right, along a surfaced road parallel to the railway line on your right.
The road leads into Driffield[3] and soon the surfaced road becomes a wider
street. Turn right at a T-junction, then left, along the A164, Beverley, road
towards the railway station, passing the end of the Driffield Navigation
canal[4]. The road crosses the railway at a level crossing close to the railway
station on the right. Once over it, immediately turn left for a short distance
and turn left again along a road signposted to Skerne and re-cross the railway
line. Continue along the road, leading out of Driffield, soon to edge the river
Hull and the canal near Bradshaw's mill on the left.

Nafferton Mere

Once past the mill the road climbs a slope near the top of which there is a footpath sign on the left. When we were there it was pointing diagonally right but this is wrong. The correct and authorised route is at right angles to the road, straight across the field, aiming for some tall trees at the far side of it. On reaching the hedge at the left-hand side of these trees go through a clear gap in it and immediately turn right. A waymarker sign on a fence is soon seen. Continue past it, close to the fence on your left and a low building behind that. Pass another building on your left and continue as directed by another yellow waymark, straight ahead, along a farm road.

On reaching a minor road turn left, along it, to the village of Skerne where the road bends sharp right, briefly then left, through it. At the eastern end of the village turn right, down a surfaced lane, passing Church Farm on the right, beyond which is the church itself.

Where the lane bifurcates, turn left, walking through a landscape that is as flat as a pancake. Soon a wood is passed on the right, behind which Cleaves Farm can be glimpsed peeping through the trees. Just past the wood, where the track makes a sharp turn left, stay on it to Copper Hall, along a line of poplars. In front of the farm house, where the track divides, take the left-hand one, passing the house on the right.

Beyond the end of the far buildings on the right, go through a waymarked metal gate and cross the field ahead, diagonally left to a waymarked gate in the hedge on the left, but don't go through it. Instead, turn right alongside a hedge on your left[5], guided by a yellow waymark. On reaching a facing
162

hedge turn right, along it, briefly, to a gate, which go through. Cross the next field to where a hedge comes along to a corner and then curves away to the right. Aim for the corner of hedge to begin with and then continue along the edge of the field close to the hedge on your left. At the field corner cross a waymarked wooden footbridge and immediately turn left. Cross a stile and follow a yellow waymark, straight ahead, close to a drain on your left and the River Hull on the right, along an easy - to - follow track. The track bends left, continuing between the drain and the river to reach a post with a waymarker sign on it, where bear right, with the river, to a bridge seen just ahead.

At the side of this five arched bridge cross a stile and turn right, over it, to cross, almost at once, the Driffield canal at Wansford[6]. Again, almost at once cross the B1249 at a crossroads, directed by a footpath sign. Continue along a road that very soon curves left and leads to the front of a beautiful mill house where go over a culvert alongside the canal, round the side of the house and over a waymarked double stile where a wooden footbridge crosses a canal overflow.

Here, on a post, are two yellow waymark arrows. Follow the one pointing right, alongside the stream, West Beck, on your right, soon to cross a waymarked stile. Continue, through rough undergrowth, along a path which leads up the bank of West Beck between it and a ditch on your left. So you can't go wrong: deviate either way from your route and you are in the water.

On reaching a facing surfaced road, turn right to bridge the stream and immediately turn left to continue up the stream's eastern bank. At the end of the field cross a stile where a bridge crosses the stream. Don't do likewise. Continue up the eastern bank to cross another stile[7] and continue edging the stream to cross yet another stile. Now follow a stream side path which is separated from the field by a fence on the right. Leave it over a stile and continue upstream, edging another field, cross another stile and continue along another strip of land. Keep alongside the stream, crossing stiled fields to join a facing road at a waymarked stile. Turn left to bridge the stream and immediately turn right, up the streamside, now on its west bank, over a short field. Exit over a stile, cross a railway line[8], descend a short lane, cross a step stile and follow the stream again, through stiled fields.

On reaching Nafferton the path curves away from the stream and enters a street through a signposted kissing gate. Go down the street into the middle of the village turn right just past the mere to return to Coppergate.

Things Seen On The Way

(1) Nafferton. Nafferton village is situated on the edge of the Wolds and 1800 people live there. The place name is derived from NATFERTON, "wanderer

by night", the earliest reference being in the Domesday Book of 1086, which indicates its Scandinavian origins. In the main street several eighteenth-century houses, some with dated stones, are overlooked by the church which is much older than they are and dominates the village centre. It overlooks the mere, which is spring fed and used to supply water power to a succession of water mills. The last water mill and malting were demolished in 1985. The mere supports a variety of water fowl.

(2) Westfield Farm Environs. Hereabouts there are a lot of Suffolk sheep, the commonest and most popular of the down breeds. It originated from a cross between the Southdown and the Norfolk Breckland sheep. It has been recognised as a breed in its own right since 1810. The Suffolk's ears, carried at right angles to the head, are black, like the head and the legs. The rest of it is white. Suffolk tups have sired most of the top quality butcher's lambs in Britain and have been successfully exported all over the world.

(3) Driffield. At about the middle of the sixth century the area from Spurn Head to Scotland was divided into the two kingdoms of Bernicia in the north and Deira, which included all the Wolds and the rest of East Yorkshire, in the south. Driffield, the capital of the Wolds, perpetuates the association with Deira. Its original name was DEIRAFJELD, meaning "the plain of Deira". DHRIFIL is a corruption of DEIRAFJELD.

Driffield, the market of the Wolds, was the centre from which almost everything radiated. In the days when travel was difficult and Wold folk were not given to "gadding about", a visit to Driffield was a spellbinding adventure into an extraneous world of well stocked shops, gaiety and bustle, far removed from the uncomplicated quiet life style of the remote Wold homesteads. The town had numerous tradesmen and famous fairs. In the days before "the wireless", news of the outside world, gathered on such visits would be retold and savoured over many subsequent days.

(4) Driffield Navigation Canal. Built in 1772, the canal joins the River Hull about one and a half miles south-east of Brigham. It is about three miles long and has a minimum depth of six feet. The river itself was made navigable for vessels of sixty tons, and joins the Humber about twenty miles from Driffield. The whole neighbourhood has been called a trout fisher's paradise.

(5) Copper Hall: Red Deer. In a large enclosure surrounded by a high wire fence to the right of your line of walk Copper Hall keeps its herd of red deer: venison on the hoof.

(6) Wansford. Here the River Hull, the Driffield Navigation canal and a minor road run side by side. The pub overlooks all three and is aptly named "The Trout".

We stood on the bridge over the Hull and watched a heron fishing while, above our heads, a succession of mallard formations flew past. On the canal a pair of whooper swans, wings spread and beating, necks stretched forward, ran on the water until sufficient momentum had been gained to give them lift off. Seen at such close quarters these magnificent birds with a five foot wing span presented the visual embodiment of unbridled power.

(7) Increased Cost Of Farming. The farmer whose land the streamside path edges was ploughing the field in a tractor, screwing five stripes out of the ground as he went. Year by year he ploughed the fields in a different direction from that used the previous year. This way all the soil remained more or less in the same place. To repeatedly plough in the same direction on this flat, deep-ditched landscape would cause the top soil to be pulled to one side of a field and eventually to fall into an irrigation ditch and become lost.

The tractor was huge, a mechanical monster, well capable of simultaneously ploughing seven furrows. The purchase price of a tractor of this size is in excess of £50,000. This makes it too expensive for most farmers to buy, especially when for most of the year there is little use for a tractor of this size. So the tractors are rented. This removes repair and maintenance expenses and the rental can be set against tax.

With just one paid hand, the farmer farmed 600 acres of prime, arable land.

(8) Nafferton Station. A little to your left, as you cross the line, is a signal box and Nafferton station.

CHAPTER XV
DRIFFIELD TO CAWKELD

Length of section: linear: 9¾ miles (15.6km)

Distance covered walking clockwise from Hessle: 160¼ miles (256.4km)

Walk 29:   Linear, Driffield - Hutton 7¼ miles (11.6km)

Walk 30:   Circular: Hutton - Hutton Cranswick - Watton - Burn
                   Butts - Hutton Cranswick - Hutton 9¾ miles (15.6km)

Map Ref: Landranger 106 and 107

Parking: Limited street parking in Driffield. Roadside in Hutton
                   and Hutton Cranswick, but check with the local
                   inhabitants first.

Handy hostelries: Hotels and pubs in Driffield.

WALK 29. DRIFFIELD - HUTTON.

From Driffield railway station turn left, passing the end of the road on your left that has just crossed the railway line and continue along Beverley Road, soon to turn left along Skerne Road to cross the railway. Continue along the road, southwards, leaving Driffield, soon to pass between the Driffield Canal[1] on your right and the River Hull[2] on your left. After passing Bradshaw's large flour mill[3] on the left continue along the road as it climbs a rise. Near the top of it turn left at a footpath sign and cross a corn field on a clear track cut through it. Leave the field over a stile in a facing hedge and turn right, directed by a yellow waymark, close to the hedge on your right. Go through a gap in a facing hedge and continue, directed by another waymark, passing some farm buildings on your left. Once past the last building continue along a clear track, guided by both a finger pole and a waymark, and at the end of it turn left along a minor road.

After passing a Skerne[4] sign post the road curves left, edging woodland. Here turn right at a signpost, into the wood, and follow a very clear track, soon to reach a facing metal gate, which go through. Go straight across the field ahead towards Skerne Grange, on a bridle way. Leave the field through a waymarked gate in a facing hedge and cross the short field ahead, exiting through another metal gate in its right-hand corner. Continue over the next field on a clear track, edging farm buildings on your left, leaving it through a white, wooden gate at a signpost.

Turn right, along a quiet road and soon after Rickle Pits Farm is passed on the left the ditch - like Skerne Beck is bridged. Immediately turn right, following a footpath sign, along the bank of the beck. Where the beck curves left, under a culvert, do not cross. Continue with the beck still on your right, cross a facing ditch at a culvert and, still with the beck on your right, keep straight ahead, aiming for Hutton village, seen ahead. Cross a footbridge over a ditch and turn right alongside a hedge on your right. Here a broad swath has been cut along the edge of the corn field to facilitate progress. Soon two Hutton Hike signs confirm the route. On reaching a railway at the field's right-hand corner turn left, edging the field as waymarked, going parallel to the railway on your right. On reaching the field

corner turn right, over a stile and, taking care because of passing trains, cross the line to another stile, which cross into a field.

Now go diagonally left, aiming at first for a clearly seen gate at its left-hand corner, backed by farm buildings. The gate is, in fact, sited midway along a step in the facing fence. On approaching it, go to the fence corner to its left and continue close to the fence on your right, skirting the farmyard area. At the field corner turn right over a waymarked stile into the farmyard area, go forward briefly and exit left, through a gateway into Hutton.

Because rights of way immediately south of Driffield are thin on the ground this short but very pleasant section is linear. However there are two alternative means of returning to Driffield: retracing your steps through very pleasant countryside as we did or going southwards, through Hutton to adjacent Hutton Cranswick, which has a railway station, and returning by train. There is a frequent service.

Best of all, using the route directions for Walk 30, a circular, explore more of this fascinating area, then retrace your steps. The total mileage for this "balloon on a string" walk is 17 and with so much to see the distance is hardly noticed.

Things Seen On The Way

(1) Driffield Navigation Canal, opened in 1772, brought considerable trade to Driffield, its northern terminus. The trade increased dramatically during the 1790s when more dredging was done and a further two warehouses were built at Driffield on the site of a coal wharf which was demolished to make room for them.

In 1817 a steam packet, the Express, was advertised to run three times a week between Driffield and Hull but the journey took too long and the venture failed. In 1825 a new, quicker service was advertised. This venture was also short lived and the service was not advertised the following year.

In 1845 the Hull and Bridlington Railway came to Driffield and the commissioners who controlled the navigation welcomed it.

During the 1850s and 60s coal coming onto the navigation from the Aire and Calder remained constant but grain going towards the Aire and Calder dropped from 31,898 tons in 1852 to none at all in 1862, although later a small amount of grain traffic did return. An average boat load was 60 tons with a maximum of about 75 tons.

The real value of the Driffield Navigation, however, was simply that its very existence kept down railway rates.

The last commercial craft to enter Driffield was the Caroline in 1944; and the last one to enter Brigham was the Ellen in 1948. Soon afterwards the canal became unnavigable north of Struncheonhill.

Bargees working to and from the mills at Driffield frequently moored to the bank about a mile to the south-east of the town to wet their whistles at the Ship Inn. Today this ancient hostelry, now a very comfortable farm house with an attached restaurant called Paddock Lodge, is one of the very few B and B establishments around Driffield and I can vouch for its comfort and hospitality.

(2) River Hull. The gently flowing River Hull is renowned as one of the best trout streams in England.

(3) Bradshaw's Flour Mill. This towering building, beautifully sited alongside the Driffield navigation and the River Hull on the southern outskirts of Driffield, looks large enough to accommodate an army of workmen. But appearances can mislead. Discounting management and office staff, the whole production side of the mill is run by just three men.

(4) Skerne. Our intended route out of Driffield was to have been a circular via Skerne, Wansford and Brigham but a missing footbridge over the River Hull at its confluence with navigable Frodingham Beck at Emmotland put paid to that exit. A detour eastwards through North Frodingham to bridge that gap also proved abortive. We headed south, following a series of large

ponds, the remains of Frodingham Beck's original course, re-crossed the main stream below the missing footbridge over the River Hull and, assured by locals on their crafts, that by following the Hull upstream to Corps Landing the circular could be achieved. What they failed to point out was that at this point the River Hull flowed through a nature reserve that was strictly private. The landowner was understanding and allowed us to complete the circle but, of course, it cannot be used by the public at large.

I contacted the Director of Technical Services, Beverley, regarding waymark from north and south leading to the missing bridge and was told that this is not a proven right of way, despite the waymarks! Furthermore, because of navigation rights the provision of an opening bridge, which is what the craft owners demand, would be so costly it could not be justified in the current financial climate. Other circulars out of Driffield to the south and west were equally impractical. The problem was solved by making the section to Hutton a linear and it has worked well.

However had we not attempted the original circular we would have missed Skerne, which is a lovely, quiet village, with a charming church containing a mostly fifteenth-century tower and a little chancel in which are two fourteenth century and one Norman window.

Wansford with its delightful water mill and aptly named Trout Inn would have remained unseen and ancient North Frodingham, the ancestral home of the Frodings, descendants of Froda who is woven into the saga of Beowulf, would have undeservedly slept unsung.

WALK 30. HUTTON - HUTTON CRANSWICK - WATTON - BURN BUTTS - HUTTON.

From the entrance to Low Green Farm at the north-east corner of Hutton go along Orchard Road and turn left at a T-junction along a road signposted Skerne and Wansford. Just before an automatic barrier for a railway crossing is reached turn right at a finger post and a Hutton Hike sign[1] and go along a narrow lane between bungalows. At the lane end cross a facing metal stile, go over a lane and exit over another metal stile into another lane. Where this lane ends, cross first a stile, then a ditch on a footbridge and another stile into the field ahead, guided by a waymarker. Continue close to the field's right edge and at the end of the field turn left, alongside a wire fence on your right. When almost at the field corner turn right, over a waymarked stile to go down a broad lane bordered with beautiful hedges in tentative blossom. Soon the lane becomes surfaced and, in a short distance reaches a T-junction with a minor road in Hutton Cranswick[2].

Start & Finish

HUTTON

WALK 30

Bustard Nest Fm.

Little Bustard Fm.

HUTTON CRANSWICK

lane

①
②
③
④

N

Burn Butts Farm

track

level crossing

Cheap Man Lane

moat

foot Path

Crossing

Stream

A164

track

⑥

CAWKELD

Watton Grange

path

farm road

Abbey Farm.

⑤

WATTON

Watton Abbey

Marrbottom Planta.

stream

footbridge

KILNWICK

Turn left, along the road, towards the railway crossing, alongside the railway station, go over it and continue out of the village. Take the first turning right, along Cheap Man Lane, which turns left, then right, soon to pass Spring Cottages; where it begins to lose its surface. Soon it becomes grassy and where it begins to curve left, turn right at a footpath sign, over a waymarked stile into a field.

Go forward, following the hedge on your right on a clear path, and where the hedge ends continue straight across the field still on a fairly clear path. On reaching a ditch the path turns sharp right, edging the field and is easy to follow. Soon it turns left to cross a ditch on a plank bridge. Immediately turn right, directed by a yellow waymark, to edge the next field; and the direction is westward. On reaching a stile, cross it to re-cross the railway line, which leave over another stile and continue straight ahead on a clear path, crossing a field close to a hedge on the right. Where the hedge ends, ignore the footpath sign diagonally right and keep ahead on a clear path which edges a ditch. The path enters a beautiful little lane parallel to Hutton Cranswick on the right. It leads onto the front of a delightful cottage where turn left directed by a waymark and a footpath sign that says "Humberside County Council:

Public Right of Way". The path is easy to follow and leads between fields of corn: absolutely lovely! The path crosses a ditch and goes over a broad track to continue straight ahead close to a ditch on the right, as before. Where both path and stream start to curve, descend to cross the stream on a concrete footbridge and immediately turn left over a waymarked stile. Now keep straight ahead, close to the hedge on your left, soon to cross a small stream. Immediately, turn left, through a waymarked gateway and go right, directed by a yellow arrow, close to a hawthorn hedge on your right, soon to cross a facing stile and bridge a ditch. Continue close to the ditch on your right. Leave the field over a waymarked stile and edge the next one, still close to the ditch on your right. At the end of the next field cross a waymarked stile, edge the next field and exit over a waymarked stile onto the farm road serving Abbey Farm on your left. Cross it, leaving over another stile into a field and continue straight ahead, close to a fence on your right, to a waymarked stile in the right-hand corner of a facing fence. Keep in the same direction, close to a fence on your right. At the far end of the field, where there is a derelict building[3], turn right at a waymarked stile. Immediately bridge a ditch, cross another stile and continue ahead, edging the ruin on your left, and keep in the same direction to a stile, seen in a facing fence, which cross. Immediately bridge a ditch and go along a very lovely, shaded lane, edged on one side with tall limes. At the lane end cross the A164 on the outskirts of Watton and turn left along a roadside footpath.

Immediately after the road crosses a bridge with a metal balustrade turn right, over a waymarked stile. Continue along a green path that edges a field (yellow with oil seed rape when we passed) soon to pass a beautiful house, and continue alongside a ditch on your right to cross a facing stile. You are now on an embankment raised above the ditch on your right and the arable field on your left. The path enters a wood at a waymarker and continues, clearly defined, through it. Where the watercourse on the right is bridged do not cross it. Instead, keep straight ahead to a second footbridge, which cross to turn left and continue close to the watercourse now on your left. On reaching a waymarked stile in the left-hand corner of a facing fence, cross it and keep in the same direction to a footbridge over the watercourse which cross at a waymarked stile. Now turn right, briefly, to another stile, which cross. Continue, diagonally left to a fence on your left and continue along it.

The village of Kilnwick is on your left, its church prominent on the horizon.

On reaching a "Minster Way" footpath sign turn right, across the field, aiming for a waymark on an electricity pole, beyond which, at a signpost with another "Minster Way" sign, turn left alongside a fence on your right. Where the fence turns right go diagonally right, directed by another waymark, aiming for a stile at a gate in the field corner. Cross this stile, go over a plank bridge and follow a clear path, bearing left, through woodland, to a facing, waymarked stile, which cross. Go diagonally right guided by another "Minster Way" sign, and at the field corner cross a cattle grid onto a surfaced road, passing the drive entrance to Cawkeld House.

Mallard are depicted on this house sign, which is very attractive.

Just past this entrance leave the road, left, along a track that edges a hedge on your left. Where it curves left, into a field, continue straight ahead along a fainter track, with the hedge still on your left. Where the hedge ends continue ahead on a clear path towards Burn Butts Farm, seen ahead. On reaching a waymarked gap in a facing hedge go through it and go diagonally left along a public footpath that slices, straight as an 18 inch wide die, though a cornfield and continues alongside it. A waymark confirms your route which is close to a fence on your left. At the end of the field turn right, guided by a yellow arrow, keeping off the drive as a sign requests. In other words keep on the grass on the field side of a very low hedge.

On reaching a minor road turn right, along it, and after about $1/4$ mile turn left at the first road junction. Go along this road towards Bustard Nest Farm ahead and turn right at the first road junction. Where the road turns sharp left, continue straight ahead, over a waymarked stile and keep ahead, close to the left-hand side of a field (when we passed, oil seed rape).

Where the field ends go through a gap in a facing hedge and continue in the same direction on a clear path. Soon another waymarker directs you straight ahead along a broad track. Where it curves right at a facing fence keep straight ahead to cross a waymarked stile in the left-hand corner of it. Go ahead, close to a hedge on your left, through a parking area for heavy vehicles at the far end of which continue along a waymarked, narrow passage leading to the A164, which cross to turn left along a roadside footpath. After 135 yards turn right along the road to Hutton Cranswick.

The road leads into the middle of this beautiful village, all set about the village green and the duck pond; and shades of Franz Lehar, the friendly village pub is the White Horse Inn.

Go up an alley to the left of it and cross the inn's car park. Continue over some open ground beyond, through a facing narrow band of trees and over a stile into a field which cross, bearing slightly right, exiting at another facing stile. Cross the next field, close to a hedge on your left, to a stile in its left-hand corner. Cross the stile and go left, directed by a yellow arrow, and at the far end of the field turn right, again directed by a yellow arrow. On reaching the end of this field cross a corner stile in the hedge to your left and cross the field ahead, exiting over stile to the right of a gate into Hutton.

Turn right, into the village as far as the church at Church Lane where go through the churchyard at a footpath sign and along a green path leading to a kissing gate, which go through. Turn left, cross a stile and go straight ahead, close to a hedge on your left. Leave the field along a very narrow lane onto a road where turn right through more of the village and as the road goes right at Low Green Farm turn left into the farmyard to complete this very pleasant circular.

Things Seen On The Way

(1) Hutton Hike And Other Waymarks. Humberside's Footpath's Officer, the local branch of the Ramblers' Association, local farmers and others responsible for establishing well-sited waymarks throughout this part of the Wolds are to be congratulated. What a difference it makes when the way ahead is clearly signposted and well defined! Paths that cut through fields of corn, oil seed rape, barley and the like, leaving not a shadow of doubt about the right of way, are a boon to walker and farmer alike. Where we had expected to encounter route finding difficulties we were delighted to find the way ahead clearly defined; and, oh, what a pleasant surprise it was! So heartiest congratulations to all concerned.

(2) Hutton Cranswick. The church is in Hutton and serves both villages. Its tower is fifteenth century as are some of the windows. Zigzag carvings adorn the doorway, which is Norman.

During World War II the R.A.F. had an airfield on the southern edge of this very pleasant village.

(3) Watton Abbey. The Tudor house that comes into view as you move westwards from this derelict building was once the prior's lodging. Between it and nearby Watton church, which is partly thirteenth century and has a tower built of Tudor brick, are some grassy mounds. They mark the site of Watton Priory which was founded by the Normans on what was probably the site of an eighth-century nunnery that was destroyed by the Danes. The priory was said to have been the largest Gilbertine house in England and both monks and nuns lived there.

CHAPTER XVI
KILNWICK TO LECONFIELD

Length of section: linear: 8¼ miles (13.2km)

Distance covered walking clockwise from Hessle: 168½ miles (269.6km)

Walk 31: Kilnwick - Cawkeld - Lund - Lockington - Kilnwick
7½ miles (12km)

Walk 32: Lockington - Leconfield - Thorpe - Lockington
6¾ miles (10.8km)

Map Ref: Landranger 106

Parking: Roadside in Kilnwick, but check with the local
inhabitants first. Near the church at Leconfield and
roadside at Lockington but, again, check with the locals
first.

Handy hostelries: There is a pub in Lockington, The Rockingham Arms.

WALK 31. KILNWICK - CAWKELD - LUND - LOCKINGTON - KILNWICK.

From the front of Kilnwick church[1] turn left, along the road, and where it
turns right go straight ahead along a path signposted "Minster Way"[2]. At
the end of a short lane go through the right-hand side one of two facing gates.
Continue down the field ahead, close to a hedge on your left, and leave
through a facing gate in the left-hand corner. Bridge a stream and go straight
ahead, directed by a "Minster Way" sign across a corn field, leaving over first
a plank bridge, then a stile to link up with the previous walk.

Immediately turn left down the field's edge, and, at the corner of it, turn
right, cross a waymarked stile and take the path that curves left, through
woodland, leaving over a stile to the left of a waymarked metal gate. Go
diagonally right, alongside the boundary fence and, on reaching a surfaced
road at the field's top right-hand corner, turn left, guided by a "Minster Way"
sign, along a surfaced road. Where it curves left, keep straight ahead,
alongside the hedge on your right. Cross a facing waymarked stile near the
right-hand corner of a fence, turn left alongside a hedge on your left and on
reaching the field corner turn right along the field's edge.

The route shown on the O/S map is diagonally left, through corn, and

174

there is no path. So rather than trample the crop, simply edge the field as directed above.

Ignore a stile on the left towards the end of the wood on your left and continue straight ahead to Kilnwick New Farm, keeping to the right of the farm buildings to join a farm track. Turn left, along it. The road is surfaced and edged with verges, all set between hedges interspersed with tall trees. Soon a crossroads is reached, which cross, and continue straight ahead along the road, which now climbs steadily. It is signposted to Beverley.

WALK 31

As the hill is climbed, ignore the footpath on the left at the end of a wood and continue along the road, past the wood on your left.

In Maytime this very lovely countryside is particularly inviting.

Soon after passing Moor Farm on the left turn right at a footpath signpost and go alongside the wood on the left, edging a large field. From the field corner go diagonally left, through a corn field, on a broad clear track. On reaching the hedge on your left, cross it at a waymark and continue diagonally left across the next field along a well-defined path.

At a diversion sign turn right, briefly, to the end of a hedge where turn left and continue, briefly, with the hedge now on your right to a plank bridge and a stile on your right. Cross them both and go diagonally left, through the corn along a beautiful neatly cut path that is an absolute joy to walk. On reaching the field corner, cross a waymarked stile onto a quiet road on the edge of Lund[3] on the right.

Turn left, along the road, from which the unfolding view is alive with harmonizing colours. After roughly half a mile turn right at a footpath sign and edge a field close to a hedge on your left. On reaching a broad, waymarked gap in the hedge, go through it and immediately turn right alongside the hedge for some twenty yards where turn left, alongside a hedge

175

on your right, guided by a yellow waymark. At the far end of the field exit through a white gate onto a minor road and turn right along it.

Ignore the left-hand turning to Lockington and continue along the road signposted to Beverley. Soon after passing a Dutch barn on the right, turn left at a signpost and continue along the field ahead, close to a hedge on your right, exiting through a gap in a facing hedge. Edge the next field, still close to the hedge on your right, and at the end of it turn right, bridge a ditch and immediately cross a stile. Go straight up the pasture ahead, converging on the hedge to your right, aiming for Lockington, straight ahead. Go through a waymarked gate in a facing fence and continue diagonally left, directed by a waymarker. Leave the field through a facing gate and turn left, along a lane, into the village[4]. At the lane end either ford the stream that flows down this linear village or cross it on a footbridge. This is the apex of the walk.

Turn left, down the village, past the post office and turn right at a signpost to Kilnwick along Kilnwick Lane, which has a broad verge so there is no need to use hard tarmac. On reaching a T-junction turn left, along the road, towards Lund. After about a third of a mile turn right at a public bridleway sign and edge a wide field, close to a hedge on your right, aiming for a shallow band of trees ahead. On reaching these trees, tall beeches, it will be seen that they hide a softwood plantation, recently felled. The path leads into the demolished wood, turns sharp right, then left, and cuts across the cleared out bit, where dark stumps protrude like rotting teeth.

Leave the felled wood through its outer ring of lovely beech trees, turn left, briefly, to a corner, and then right, down the edge of a field close to a hedge on your left. At the bottom of the field turn right, along a green track, directed by a footpath sign, leaving the field over a waymarked stile to the left of a gate.

Cross a facing road and keep straight ahead, along a surfaced lane, met end on, directed by a footpath sign. The road leads to Kilnwick House Farm and where it curves right, cross a facing stile and continue over the field ahead, bearing slightly to the right. Cross a facing waymarked stile, go over a footbridge and in a few yards go through a gate in a facing fence and immediately turn right, alongside a hedge on your right. Ignore the waymarked path going off to the left and continue ahead on a clear path, which bears left, close to a stream on the right. The path hugs the stream, going though a waymarked gap in a facing hedge, and bear to the right, edging a field to reach a waymarked signpost.

At this point the outward route is rejoined. Turn right, crossing the stream on a little bridge, and retrace your steps to Kilnwick, right in front of you. That's where you started; and hasn't it been a super walk!

Things Seen On The Way.

(1) Kilnwick Church. Stands at the west end of this very pretty village of neat cottages, gardens and orchards on the eastern edge of the low Wolds where they slide into Holderness. Much of the church is new but the arcade leading to the north aisle is thirteenth century. The north doorway has a Norman arch and the shallow font on its eight sided stem is Norman.

(2) Minister Way. This super walk links Beverley with York.

(3) Lund. The tower of Lund church is mainly fifteenth century; and there is a panelled arch in the north wall of the fourteenth century chancel. The font is Norman but its stem and base are modern.

An old pantile forge stands near the village green with its old market cross.

(4) Lockington. Pleasantly situated on the banks of a shallow stream that runs alongside the main road through the village, Lockington, which reputedly means "the enclosure of the family of Loca", derives its name from a brand of Anglo-Saxons who settled there in the fifth century.

St Mary's church, to the south of the village and hidden by trees, is reached along a narrow winding lane that ends at the church gate. It was built on the site of an Anglo-Saxon burial ground. It is thought that an Anglo-Saxon church occupied the site in the latter part of the seventh century. During excavations carried out on the site in 1893 a brooch and some beads belonging to that period were discovered. The present church dates from the twelfth century.

The fourteenth-century south chancel has a distinctive feature in its heraldic panelled walls. They were commissioned by John Estoft in 1634 and restored and repaired in 1851. There are 173 coats of arms and they trace the complete pedigree of the Estoft family.

Rectory House, which is sometimes called Lockington House, was built in the 1790s and is a grade II listed building. Other buildings of note are the Methodist Primitive Chapel, on Front Street (1862), the Wesleyan Chapel in Chapel Street (re-built 1879) and the National School, built in 1844 and enlarged by the addition of a classroom in 1875.

According to the Parish Registers the Remington family were connected with Lockington for almost 200 years, from the sixteenth to the eighteenth century. The family left for America in the eighteenth century where they founded the internationally known Remington Corporation; famous for their small arms rifle, revolvers and typewriters.

The Hothams have owned land in Lockington since the thirteenth century. The present Lord Hotham is still the major landowner in the village, the Family Seat being at Dalton Hall a short distance to the west.

WALK 32. LOCKINGTON - LECONFIELD - THORPE - LOCKINGTON.

From the main road through Lockington, where it passes a ford go right alongside the steam on your right, passing the Rockingham Arms on the left. Just beyond it turn right, directed by a "Minster Way" sign, along a green lane. Go through a waymarked kissing gate and continue diagonally left on a clear path across a pasture, walking roughly parallel to the stream on your right. The path goes through a kissing gate in a facing fence and continues across the next field. It is easy to follow and exits through another kissing gate beyond which go diagonally left, following a "Minster Way" direction to enter a narrow copse where, at a crossing of paths, go straight ahead and almost at once bear left to a waymarked stile, which cross. Go ahead, crossing the next field close to the stream on the right, passing Hall Garth Farm[1] beyond it, over on the right. As you cross the field a waymark confirms your course. Where the stream on your right curves left across your line of walk, cross a facing stile, bridge the stream and cross another stile at the far end of it, still on the "Minster Way".

Continue close to the hedge on your right and, in a few yards, where the hedge shoots off to the right, continue straight across the field and on reaching a facing wire fence look for a yellow waymark. From that point continue across a footbridge, beyond which, at a "Minster Way" sign, leave the "Minster Way" and go diagonally right across the field to its right-hand corner where cross a waymarked stile. Immediately go right, along the edge of the field ahead. It is a long field and at the end of it a wood is reached. Here the path curves to the left, alongside the wood, briefly, to a facing stile. Immediately turn right, along a clear path that edges the wood on the right for about 100 yards then turn left, clearly defined, and is waymarked. When a plantation of young trees is reached, at the end of the field that continues left, go right, over a long footbridge, directed by a footbridge sign, to cross a stile into a field. Now go left, along its edge, directed by a footbridge sign. Continue past a gap in the hedge and keep straight ahead, close to the hedge on your left. On reaching a waymarker when a surfaced road on your left curves left continue, bearing slightly right, close to a hedge on your left. When this hedge ends turn left, directed by a waymarker, over a ditch on a wooden footbridge, and continue straight ahead, close to the hedge on your left to a signpost at the end of the hedge at a junction of minor roads.

Continue straight ahead along the tarmac road. The farm to the left is Gommeryhall Farm and Woodhouse Farm is to the right. The slender spire, about a mile away on the left is that of St Leonard's, Scorborough[2] [3].

WALK 32

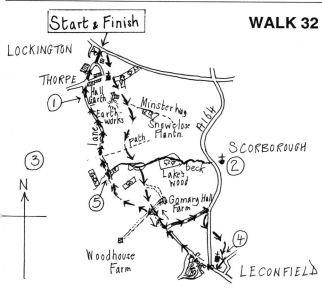

As you walk along the road the Leconfield airfield buildings can be seen over on the left.

On reaching a T-junction turn left, along the minor road, and just short of a junction with the A164 turn right, over a stile at a footpath sign. Continue along a huge field, close to the hedge on your left. On reaching a footpath sign at a gateway in the hedge cross the gate, (which will not open but should do because this is a right of way), cross the A164, diagonally right, to a waymarked stile, which cross to enter a cornfield. Go through it, along a clearly cut path, which at first zigzags a bit. The path is about 2½ft wide and so is a doddle to follow. Soon it appears to find its bearings and across the field, straight as a die. At the far end of the field, where a farm track crosses your line of walk, turn right, along it. Soon it curves left and goes through a gateway into what looks like a rather rundown farmyard. Here turn right and go through a gateway on your right, along a path through a rough pasture that leads behind the church[4] through an area of nettles, over a ditch and alongside the churchyard to reach a signpost at the right-hand corner of Leconfield church.

From the signpost turn right, along a passage, and at its end cross the A164 and turn right, along it, to a junction where take the left fork signposted to Cherry Burton.

On leaving Leconfield do not turn left, along Mill Lane. Instead keep straight ahead and where the road curves sharp right turn left along the same surfaced farm road used, on the outward leg. It is signposted "Public Footpath".

On returning to the road junction reached on the outward leg turn left, along the unsurfaced road towards Woodhouse Farm directed by a footpath sign. On reaching the first telegraph pole, which has a yellow marker on it, turn right, along a clear, green track, close to a hedge on your left. The track meanders very pleasantly through the countryside. Eventually a broad lane is reached and this will take you all the way to Thorpe.

At one point along it a very pleasant ford crosses Moor Beck, with a footbridge nearby to use when the ford is too deep to cross dryshod on foot. It is timeless, the sort of scene that would have made Constable feel at ease. At times this lone lane to Thorpe is so wide it resembles a long narrow field with an unsurfaced track right down the middle of it. The further you walk along this lane the more improved it becomes and eventually its surface is tarmac.

On reaching the lane end turn right, along a road, into Thorpe. Follow the main road through this very pretty village to return to Lockington, turning left where the road splits, along Dead Lane to cross the ford and complete the circle. Should you prefer to return right where the road out of Thorpe splits, cross the stream, on a footbridge and turn left along the main road through Lockington, briefly, to where the walk began.

Things Seen On The Way

(1) Hall Garth Manor House. The wooded eminence on the south side of Hall Garth Manor House is the site of a medieval earth works, now an ancient monument scheduled as a low motte (hill), with indications of a "bailey" or wooden enclosure. Soon after the Conquest, the Normans built a great many motte and bailey castles, from which they controlled the local inhabitants. This motte was a man-made mound surrounded by a wooden keep. The every day life of the settlement was conducted within the bailey where the domestic buildings were situated. The whole site was surrounded with a ditch, a bank and a stockade fence or palisade.

(2) St Leonard, Scorborough. In the early part of the Saxon period Scorborough, which is Norse for "the hut in the woods", belonged to Earl Addi who erected a chapel there that was later transformed into the parish church. The name of the village is recorded in the Domesday survey as SCOGERBUD. It subsequently came into the possession of the Hothams

who built a castle there. The BUD became BURGH and Camden's "Britannia" records that "at a place called SCHORBURGH is the habitation of a truly famous and ancient family, the Hothams". The Hothams lived there for several centuries before moving to South Dalton.

In the seventeenth century the moated hall which stood close by St Leonard's church was occupied by Sir John Hotham, the first baronet, renowned as the Governor of Hull who closed the city gates on Charles I, refusing to admit the Royalists even when the King appeared in person.

Later, when it was discovered that he had been secretly plotting with the Royalists to surrender Hull, he tried to escape to Scorborough. He was apprehended at Beverley by his nephew, Captain Boynton, and was sent to the Tower of London, together with his eldest son, tried for treason and beheaded on Tower Hill in 1645. He had, however, lived a very full life: as well as his successful political career he had enjoyed the benefits, and the dowries, of no less than five wives.

His son followed him to the block the next day.

His fortified manor house, which had been garrisoned by Parliamentary troops, was ravaged by the Roundheads and subsequently destroyed, although traces of the moat are still visible, though dry.

Not much of the medieval village remains, although some earthworks can still be seen.

Near the site of the original razed, mansion is a modern one in the cottage style, known as Scorborough Hall which, for many years, was the residence of James Hall Esq., master of the Holderness foxhounds.

St Leonard, Scorborough, is an estate church rebuilt in the nineteenth century by John Loghborough Pearson. It took two years to complete and the rebuilding cost was borne by James Hall of Scorborough Hall "as a thank offering for many blessings". The church has a five pinnacled tower and a splendid spire that soars above surrounding trees. It is a particularly ornate building, its walls and windows being richly carved. There is a surfeit of arches for so small a church. The floor is paved with coloured tiles, double columns of serpentine marble separate the chancel from the nave and the carved, oak roof has arched beams and traceried gables. Finely carved stonework is everywhere. Four fathers of the early church are depicted, in stone, on the pulpit panels, the Norman font is carved with biblical images and even the clock face is carved in stone.

(3) South Dalton Church. From Scorborough, the high spire seen on the western horizon belongs to South Dalton church. It greatly resembles the Scorborough church spire but is taller.

(4) St Catherine's Church, Leconfield. The present church, which is built of

stone, chalk rubble and brick, was remodelled in the thirteenth century, but fragments of the original eleventh-century church remain. It is thought that its two bells, dated 1662 and 1667, were made by Samuel Smith of York.

Many airmen are buried in the churchyard, including many foreign nationals, especially Canadians, Poles and New Zealanders who flew from Leconfield.

(4) The Village. The original centre of Leconfield was probably around the church, the first manor house being sited on the Arram road nearby. When, in 1308 Henry de Percy was licenced to crenellate his house at Leconfield, the manor house had already been moved out of the village.

A second group of dwellings subsequently grew up along the main road; and in 1811 there were still several houses of mud, plaster and thatch remaining in the village. There was little further change until the late 1930's when R.A.F. houses were built on the aerodrome to the south-east of the main village. Further Air Force development took place in the 1950's followed by the building of private houses to the west of the Driffield road.

North Bar Without, Beverley

CHAPTER XVII
LECONFIELD TO BEVERLEY PARKS CROSSING

Length of section: linear: 8¹/₂ miles (13.6km)

Distance covered walking clockwise from Hessle: 177 miles (283.2km)

Walk 33:	Circular: Leconfield - Raventhorpe Village - Beverley - Leconfield 7¹/₂ miles (12km)
Walk 34:	Circular: Beverley - Beverley Parks Crossing - Beverley 7¹/₂ miles (12km)
Map Ref:	Landranger 106 and 107
Parking:	Near Leconfield church, but check with the locals first. Car parks in Beverley.
Handy hostelries:	Pubs and cafes in Beverley.

WALK 33. LECONFIELD - RAVENTHORPE VILLAGE - BEVERLEY - LECONFIELD.

From the front of Leconfield church go straight ahead, down the road, to a T-junction where go diagonally left over the facing road to cross a waymarked stile. Continue, directed by a footpath sign, along a broad, green lane, passing a bungalow on either side. Cross a waymarked stile to the side of a facing gate and edge the field ahead, close to a hawthorn hedge on the right, leaving over a waymarked corner stile alongside a gate. Keep straight ahead, cross the next field close to the hedge on your right, following a green track, cross a waymarked stile in the field's right-hand corner and go diagonally left to cross the next field, leaving at a waymarked stile close to a dried up moat[1] on the right. Edge the field ahead close to the hedge on your right, beyond which the moat lies. In a short distance a post with a waymarker on it confirms your route. Continue straight ahead, across the next field, full of barley when we passed, along a green track. Soon, where the track curves right, a waymarker again confirms your route. The track goes through a broad gap in a facing hedge, crosses a ditch and bears slightly right to a

WALK 33

184

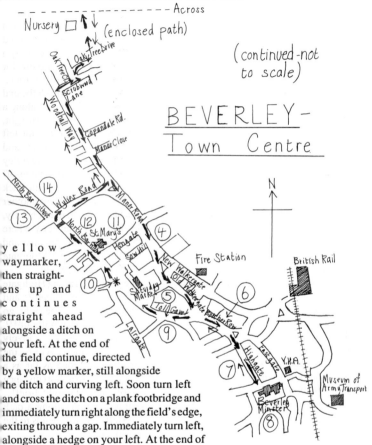

yellow waymarker, then straightens up and continues straight ahead alongside a ditch on your left. At the end of the field continue, directed by a yellow marker, still alongside the ditch and curving left. Soon turn left and cross the ditch on a plank footbridge and immediately turn right along the field's edge, exiting through a gap. Immediately turn left, alongside a hedge on your left. At the end of the field turn right, alongside a fence on your right. When a fence is reached on your left, continue straight ahead, edging a farm, Rose Cottage Farm. On passing the last building on the left continue along a surfaced farm road[2].

On reaching the main road turn left, along it. In a short distance the road curves gently to the right and crosses a disused railway line. Immediately over the bridge turn right, directed by a public footpath sign, and descend a flight of steps to the old trackway. Turn right, under the bridge and simply stay on this disused railway line all the way to Beverley.

On reaching a crossing with a cottage and a sign which says "Hudson Way: End Of Recreational Route To Beverley", go straight across the road and continue along the disused line for about 150 yards, turn right, directed by a yellow waymark and cross a cornfield on a very clear path, aiming for Beverley. A waymarker on a pole mid-way across the field confirms the route. Leave the field over a stile and continue down a narrow lane to reach the end of a cul-de-sac, which cross, directed by a yellow arrow, to continue along a narrow lane, now with houses on the right. Leave it over a stile and turn right, along a road, through residential Oak Tree Drive. The road curves to the left to another facing road. Turn right, along it, to a T-junction, where turn left; and Beverley Minster is seen ahead. Follow the road into the middle of Beverley and, just past the traffic lights, go down Walkergate[3], a street that shoots off at a tangent on the right from the main road. Walkergate is a quiet, little back street, a no-through road, that ends at a pedestrianised area. Where another thoroughfare, Toil Gavel, comes in from the right at a tangent, join it briefly, [4] continuing left, along Butcher Row which leads into an area where Wednesday markets are held[5]. Edge the right-hand side of this area and continue along very pleasant Highgate[6] to cross facing Minster Moorgate and enter Beverley Minster (as described on p.195), a real highlight.

On leaving this glorious house of God, retrace your steps along Highgate and Butcher Row. At a bifurcation of streets, go left, along Toll Gavel[7], and continue past the Market Cross[8]. Pass St Mary's church[9] on the right, go along North Bar Within[10], under the Bar and into North Bar Without[11]. Take the first turning right, into Wylies Road and, on reaching a lovely roundabout which sports a huge chestnut tree, turn left, along the A1174, the road used on the way into Beverley. Continue along the road as far as a telephone kiosk where turn right along Scrub Wood Lane. In a short distance turn left, along Oak Tree Drive. When the road bifurcates bear right, briefly, and go left, over a stile with a Minster Way sign. Continue along a path between a hedge on your right and a fence on the left. The path leads to the cornfield used earlier. Cross it on the same clear path.

On reaching the disused railway go straight across it, entering the field ahead over a stile, directed by a Minster Way signpost. Edge the field, close to the hedge on your right and at the end of it turn right, through a gap in the hedge, and immediately turn left to continue with the hedge now on your left. Leave over a facing stile, close to the field's left-hand corner. Turn left along a very pleasant country lane. Soon after passing a farm on the right, turn right at a T-junction and follow a broad, farm road directed by a waymarker and a Minster Way finger post. The farm road leads to Leconfield Low Parks where, at the farm gate, turn right directed by a waymarker. Soon an arrow on a telegraph pole confirms your route. The path edges the field to a railway where, in the field's left-hand corner, cross a ditch on a plank, then a stile, directed by a footpath sign. Edge the next field, close to a hedge on your right, to its top right-hand corner where cross a waymarked stile. Keep straight ahead, along a green track, parallel to the railway on your right. The path keeps between the railway and a deep ditch on the left, beyond which is Leonfield airfield[12] with the runways very close to the line of walk.

On reaching a facing fence cross a waymarked stile to the left of it near the very deep ditch on the left. Continue along the top of an embankment with this deep ditch still to your left. When almost at the far end of the embankment, just short of a tall tower on the left, beyond the ditch, turn right a Minster Way footpath sign, and go over a stile. Cross the field ahead, leaving over a step-stile onto the railway. Cross the line with care, leaving over another step-stile and cross the next field, (yellow with oil seed rape over five feet tall when we did it), along a clear path, leaving over a waymarked stile in its left-hand corner. Cross the next field, close to a fence on your left, leaving over another corner stile onto a surfaced road.

Turn left, along it, through Arram village[13]. Soon the road bridges a water course, beyond which, in New Arram, where it bifurcates, keep left and cross the railway. Continue along the road signposted to Leconfield to return to Leconfield church and complete the circle.

Things Seen On The Way

(1) Leconfield Manor. Leconfield was one of the chief residences of the house of Percy who also owned Wressle Castle and held lands at Seamer, Hunmanby, Catton and Pocklington. Although styled "Leconfield Manour" it was, in fact, a crenellated and moated castle and occupied a four acre site some 400 yards south-west of the village.

In 1570 it was described as the Earl's largest and most stately house in Yorkshire, though it was "in great decay and needful to be repaired". In 1577 it consisted of a courtyard surrounded by four ranges of buildings, each 324 feet long. The southern range was of brick and the rest were half-timbered. The castle walls were of brick and had battlements, with a thirty-foot tower at each corner. The gatehouse, centrally placed in the north-east wall, had a drawbridge.

By the early seventeenth century, the manor house had been abandoned and the better fittings sold in London. Other material was removed to Wressle to repair the castle there and some of the panelling went to Kilnwick Hall. When it was demolished, the panelling was moved to Burton Agnes

187

Hall where it remains. By the mid eighteenth century the last of the buildings had completely disappeared.

(2) Raventhorpe Village. Edging the south side of the drive to Rose Cottage Farm is the site of an ancient village, Raventhorpe.

(3) Walkergate House. Built circa 1770, it was the home of William Crosskill, "the father of mechanised farming in East Yorkshire," who invented the Clod Crusher and other important farming implements in the nineteenth century.

(4) Ann Routh's House. No.65 Toll Gravel, built circa 1703, was the residence of the benefactress, Ann Routh. Window tax caused the reduction in the number of ground floor windows. In the nineteenth century the house was used as a Church Institute and as Liberal headquarters. Voters went in at the front door to be bribed and out through the back door into the Walkergate where a cab awaited to take them to the poll.

(5) Wednesday Market Place, is older than the larger Saturday Market Place at the north end of Toll Gavel. It was important in the Middle Ages when the area to the north of the Minster was a flourishing community. It had a pit for cockfighting. A market cross, in the form of an obelisk, was erected in 1762 and removed in 1881. Originally the area was more enclosed. Railway Street was not built until circa 1846 and Lord Roberts Road wasn't built until 1909. Mary Wollstonecraft, the eighteenth-century writer, spent part of her childhood with her family in a house in Wednesday Market Place.

(6) 38 Highgate. At right angles to the street and to the new Vicarage is the Bluecoat School, founded in 1710, which moved here circa 1808 and closed in 1890. The Minster, never a cathedral, has no "close", but Highgate provides a very attractive route to and from the fine north porch; an important entrance. It contains some dignified Georgian houses. At the rear of "The Monk's Walk", formerly the George and Dragon, is the surviving part of a former Warton residence.

(7) 44 Toll Gavel. This building is a former chemist's; the snakes are the symbol of RESCULAPIUS, God of Medicine. "Gafol" means "tribute" or "rent" and tolls were collected in the area. In the passage to the left of Wigfall's is the blocked up entrance to an early post office, described as one of the most inconvenient in the country.

(8) Saturday Market Place. Corn Exchange. Built in 1889, it has reflected social change, later becoming a cinema, the Picture Playhouse, then a bingo hall. It replaced a building that served as a combined meat, corn and butter market.

The Market Cross. Designed by Shelton of Wakefield, it was built between 1711 and 14 to replace an earlier one reputedly big enough for carriages to drive through. The town's M.P.s, Sir Charles Hotham and Sir Michael Warton, contributed to the cost and their arms and those of Queen Anne and Beverley are displayed.

Saturday Market Place overtook Wednesday Market Place as the town developed northwards. There is an attractive variety of roof levels on its east side and one building, now an optician's, was formerly the Pack Horse Inn where "a mysterious man in a hairy cap" bribed voters in the 1860 election.

Sir John Hotham, the Governor of Hull, who refused admission there to Charles I in 1642, was captured near the Market Place in 1643 after his conversion to the Royalist cause. He was later executed.

(9) St Mary's Church. Often mistaken for the Minster, this magnificent church began as a chapel-of-ease, circa 1120, for people living in this part of the town, which at that time was developing. Transepts and aisles were added later and the chancel extended. The superb west front is very similar to that of King's College Chapel, Cambridge, but is earlier. The perfectly proportioned tower replaces one that collapsed in 1520. The nave was also rebuilt. Minstrel's Pillar indicates the importance of Beverley as a centre for the Northern Guild of Minstrels. The vaulted south porch is fifteenth century. The War Memorial Door was carved by Robert Thompson, the "mouse" man. The White Rabbit carving is reputed to be the model for Tenniel's illustration in "Alice In Wonderland". The fifteenth century choir stalls are from Ripon school and the Kings of England are illustrated on the chancel ceiling.

(10) North Bar Within. St Mary's Manor, on North Bar Within, is early nineteenth century. Because good quality local stone is rare, the North Bar was rebuilt in 1409-10 at a cost of £96.17.4$^{1/2}$. The arms are those of Michael Warton and his wife Susannah daughter of Lord Powlett. A leper house and a pond with a ducking stool stood outside the Bar. In 1867 the unsavoury Bar Dyke was filled in. Local double decker buses no longer use the Bar but when they did they were built with specially rounded tops to enable drivers to negotiate this tricky entrance.

The fine Georgian terrace adjacent stands on the site of what was probably Lade Gee's house. In 1642 Charles I and his sons, the future Charles II and James II stayed there.

(11) North Bar Without. James Elwell, father of the artist, F.W.Elwell R.A., ran a thriving woodcarving business at No.6 North Bar Without in the nineteenth century. His work can be seen in many local buildings. All the timbering and carving on this attractive range of buildings is Victorian. There is a cartoon of Disraeli, "the political cheapjack", above the door of No.4.

(12) Leconfield Airfield. In January, 1937, only a month after it had opened, R.A.F. Leconfield began life as part of 3 Group, Bomber Command, when Heyford biplane bombers arrived. On the night of the 3rd, 4th September, 1939, the first night of World War II, ten Whitley bombers of 51 and 58 Squadrons became the first British aircraft to penetrate German airspace, dropping propaganda leaflets over Germany as part of the "phoney war". They flew from Leconfield.

In October, 1939, it was taken over by 13 Group, Fighter Command, when the Spitfires of 72 Squadron arrived from Church Fenton - the first of many visits by the Squadron. During the Battle of Britain, the station was temporary home to many other famous squadrons of Fighter Command, which made short stays there to rest and regroup. During this period there was also a decoy airfield at Routh, a few miles to the east.

Several squadrons were formed at Leconfield, including No.302 (Polish) Squadron, flying Hurricanes and No.129 (Mysore) Squadron, so called because the Indian state of that name had subscribed to purchase the squadron's Spitfires.

By late 1941 Leconfield was closed for reconstruction as a heavy bomber base under 4 Group, Bomber Command. It re-opened for operations in December, 1942.

Twin-engined Wellington bombers of Nos.196 and 466 Squadrons mounted the first raids from the new base against a target in France. Later, the heavier, four engined Halifax bomber became a familiar sight at Leconfield throughout the rest of the war.

After the war, the airfield was used by various squadrons until in 1976, the air base finally closed. It was taken over by the School of Mechanical Transport in 1977 and renamed Normanby Barracks. The school's Bedford lorries are a familiar sight on the roads of the area. The R.A.F. maintains a connection through E Flight of 202 Squadron, whose Sea King helicopters took over from the Wessex's of D Flight, 22 Squadron in 1988.

(13) Arram Village. During the sixteenth and seventeenth centuries there were additional houses at each end of the village. These have long since disappeared but earthworks north of Lodge Farm may identify some of them. In 1797 it was noted that most of the houses were built of mud and were in decay. The houses east of the railway station were named New Arram in 1852.

WALK 34. BEVERLEY - BEVERLEY PARKS CROSSING - BEVERLEY.

From Beverley Minster[1] turn right, along Minster Moorgate[2], turn right along Eastgate, briefly, alongside the east side of the Minster, then left, along Flemingate[3] to cross the Scarborough to Hull railway. Pass the Museum of Army Transport on the left where a huge transport plane is prominent, along the B1230. Soon, at a public footpath sign[4], turn right along a lane that passes some tennis courts on the right and crosses a ditch, continuing, unsurfaced, between hedges. At a waymarked T-junction turn right, along a

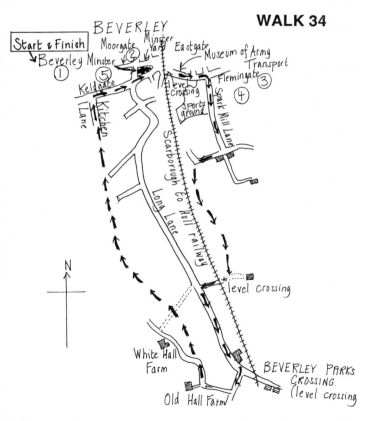

WALK 34

BEVERLEY

Start & Finish
Beverley Minster (1)

Moorgate (2) Minster Yard

Eastgate Museum of Army Transport

(5) Keldgate Level crossing Flemingate (3)

Kitchen Lane Sports ground Spark Mill Lane (4)

N

Scarborough to Hull railway

Long Lane

level crossing

White Hall Farm

Old Hall Farm

BEVERLEY PARKS CROSSING. (level crossing

191

bridleway, an unsur-faced lane, and, on passing a cottage on the left, do not turn left. Instead, continue straight ahead and where the lane curves right, turn left, directed by a footpath sign, edging a field and bearing left. The path goes left, briefly, then right, then left again, just edging the peculiarly shaped field. The land hereabouts is very flat, the ground chalky.

Where the hedge on the left ends continue straight across the field to a facing hedge, meeting it at a point where there is a post with a yellow waymarker on it. Go through a broad gap in the hedge and continue straight ahead, through a cornfield. Just short of a ditch at the far end of this field turn right, along a clear path leading directly to a gate at a railway crossing. Go through the gate, cross the railway, leaving over a concrete, ladder stile to the right of a gate and continue along a lane. At the lane end, turn left along a road and on approaching some dwellings on the left-hand side of the road just past a sub-station, turn right, along a minor road, guided by a yellow waymark. When the road bifurcates, take the right-hand, unsurfaced one. The road passes a farm on the left and continues through a field. Just after the road makes a sharp turn left, go right, directed by a footpath sign, edging, when we walked it, a field of peas on the left and a ditch on the right. Where the ditch and the field shoot off to the right, continue straight across the field, along a clear path, passing a marker post in the middle of it. Keep straight ahead and cross a ditch on a waymarked footbridge. Continue along the edge of the ditch, with the Minster now clearly seen ahead and a little to the right as you walk along. It is a lovely sight.

Leave the field, crossing a ditch and a stile in the right-hand corner. Keep straight ahead, edging the next field. The path curves to the right, parallel to the houses on the left. At a footpath sign, cross a stile and keep in the same direction, still parallel to the houses on the left. The green path you are now on eventually meets a surfaced path on the left at a tangent. Continue along it, briefly, and turn right with it to cross a stile. Keep ahead, now on an unsurfaced path, passing a Nature Reserve on the left, going down the middle of a broad lane. Cross a facing stile and continue along the same lane to a surfaced road. Turn left along it to meander back into Beverley along Long Lane at the end of which cross Keldgate. Continue alongside the Minster[5] on the right and turn right, back to the Minster Moorgate entrance.

Things Seen On The Way

(1) Beverley: A Brief History Of A Beautiful Town. Where better to contemplate Beverley's long history than from the Minster where the town itself began! The beginnings are not authenticated but the story goes that in AD 719 John, Bishop of York, a saintly man, retired and came to live in a small, wooden

monastery in a clearing in a wood, the site of the present Minster. When he died in AD 721 his bones were kept in a casket in the small monastery he had founded. Pilgrims came to worship at his shrine and in 1037 he was made a saint. Consequently, Beverley became an important religious centre and a small community developed there.

In AD 938, King Athelstan granted certain rights to the town. The Minster was given lands and the status of a collegiate church which meant that it would have regular secular priests called canons ruled by a provost. The town of Beverley was exempted from paying tax, an immunity that no longer exists. It was also granted the right of sanctuary which lasted from AD 938 until 1540.

The right of sanctuary played an important part in the affairs of the community and this is how it worked. On the outskirts of the town, a mile from the Minster, sanctuary stones were erected. Anyone believed to have committed an offence and escaping from his pursuers could claim the right of sanctuary of the Minster. If he managed to pass a sanctuary stone before being captured, the pursuers had to pay a fine of approximately £8. If captured at the Minster door, the fine was increased to £96 and this rose to £144 if the pursuers caught their man at the altar. Few, indeed, could afford to pay such a fine, on top of which there was the possibility of excommunication. Protected by the Minster, the prisoner had to promise not to wear a dagger, he had to help put out any fires in the town and crush riots and assist with mass. The canons would look after him for 30 days, during which time they would investigate the fugitive's crime. If found guilty, he would be escorted to the coast and shipped to the continent. If found innocent he would be free to go where he liked. Many innocent fugitives chose to remain in Beverley.

On three approaches to Beverley, the A164 from Hull, the B1230 from Walkington and the A1079 from York, there are sanctuary stones, each sited a mile from the Minster.

Work on the Minster we see today began in 1220 and continued almost continuously for 200 years, apart from a break of 50 years following the Black Death in 1349, and was completed in 1420. It is thought by many to be one of the finest examples of Gothic architecture in Europe.

Stone for building the Minster came from the West Riding, being carried down the Humber and up the River Hull. The stream from the River Hull to Beverley, the Beck, was widened and deepened to allow barges to come to a quay that was built a mile from the site of the Minster.

Beverley, now with direct access to the sea, could develop both as a religious centre and as a commercial centre.

In the fourteenth century a Dominican friary was built near the Minster where Edward I in 1299 and 1309, spent three days on his way north to fight the Scots.

With the whole area around the Minster supplying houses for the many wealthy church members who lived in the town, the provost became one of the richest men in Yorkshire. The Woolpack Inn, in westwood Road, is a reminder of the days when cloth was a principal product, as are some of the street names. Old Walkergate derives its name from those who "walked" the cloth to wash it in the Walker Beck along whose banks the street developed. Nearby Dyer Lane was also connected with cloth making and Flemingate is a reminder of the cloth trade's strong links with the continent.

A Poll Tax taken in 1377 showed that the population was about 5,000, making Beverley the eleventh largest town in England, twice as big as Hull and half the size of York. Thirty eight guilds flourished there, covering a wide variety of occupations, six of them entirely devoted to cloth production.

The town developed northwards from the Minster and a ditch was dug around it with five gates or Bars; Newbegin, Norwood, South, Keldgate and North. Only North Bar survives. The town was never walled, probably because good quality local stone was not available; and, anyway, the land was flat so digging a ditch presented few problems. Outside the ditch, pastures of about 1,200 acres, Swinemoor, Figham, Westwood and Hurn were essential to the town's economy. The 600 acres of Westwood, given to the town by the Archbishop of York in 1380 at an annual rent of £5, provided chalk, clay, bricks, wood and lime apart from pasturage. At that time Beverley's buildings were timbered. Few visible examples remain but ancient timbers are often hidden behind Georgian facades.

The wool trade declined in the fifteenth century and with it the wealth of the town. Many houses fell into disrepair and Beverley's importance became centred around its religious, rather than its commercial activities.

On Sunday, 8th October, 1536, following similar uprisings in Lincolnshire, the town bell was rung in Beverley's Saturday Market, summoning the town's inhabitants to protest at the threatened dissolution of monasteries by Henry VIII. The rebellion, which became known as the Pilgrimage of Grace, spread to other parts of Northern England. It was soon crushed by the King's troops and many people were hanged.

In Beverley, the majority of buildings associated with the church were confiscated and destroyed and four years later, in 1540, Beverley lost its right of sanctuary. The Minster remained intact because it was a parish church.

Undefended Beverley also did badly during the Civil War: much of the town was plundered.

Towards the end of the seventeenth century Beverley's fortunes began to improve, heralding a new Golden Age. The principal trades of the town, now a mile long, were making malt, oatmeal and tanned leather. School children were encouraged to work lace, a growing home industry that supported many families.

Grand new brick buildings were built and roofed with pantiles, first brought over as ballast in ships from Holland and later manufactured locally.

In the late seventeenth century Beverley became the administrative centre of the East Riding of Yorkshire. (In 1892 it became the County Town of the East Riding.)

During the eighteenth and nineteenth centuries many improvements were made and Beverley became a fashionable town, justifiably proud of its achievements. Commerce and trade were improving, wealth was increasing and the pursuit of leisure activities was being developed. In 1788 a theatre, now demolished, was built in Wood Lane. New Assembly Rooms, also now demolished, were built at Norwood and became the venue for many grand gatherings and dances. The race course was moved to its present site on the Westwood in 1769. Civic pride swelled and, in 1762, the Guild House was improved. In the next century a pillared porch was added.

During the nineteenth century many new schools were opened, as was a dispensary for the sick. Alms houses were built for the old and infirm. In 1824 Beverley was lit by gas and in 1846 the railway came, further strengthening its role as a residential, country, market town. In 1861 a new workhouse, now the Westwood Hospital, was built. Several Methodist chapels were built and John Wesley preached there seventeen times.

Humberside County Council, which moved into Beverley from Hull in 1984 and the Borough Council are the town's main employers. Tourism is an important industry and many jobs in the town are concerned with serving tourists, today's pilgrims, in cafes, shops and restaurants.

Beverley, now with a population approaching 21,000, remains a popular place in which to live. Many occupants are professional, skilled people, many of whom commute to work in other areas.

(2) Friary Gateway, Old Vicarage. In 1964 a sixteenth-century gateway from the Friary on the opposite side of Eastgate was moved across the road and incorporated in the garden wall of the Old Vicarage, once the home of the Rev. Joseph Coltman, said to have been the largest man then living in England.

(3) Sun Inn. This neat, timbered building containing sixteenth-century work is a reminder of what Beverley looked like before its Georgian "face lift".

(4) No.58 Flemingate. Not far from the footpath sign stands 58 Flemingate, traditionally the birth place of Sir John Fisher, Bishop of Rochester, who was executed in 1535 for his opposition to Henry VIII's religious policy. The house, however, dates only from the seventeenth century. John Fisher's home may have stood on the same site.

(5) Beverley Minster. Begun in 1220 and completed in 1420, the Minster is dedicated to St John the Evangelist although St John of Beverley is the traditional founder. It was built in three stages, the chancel, transepts and part of the nave are Early English, built between 1220 and 1275. Work began on the nave in 1308 and is of Gothic Decorated style. The west front, the towers and the east window were constructed between 1390 and 1420 and are of Perpendicular style. The different styles blend harmoniously. The Minster is largely built of Tadcaster area limestone with some Purbeck marble.

The Percy Shrine is of particular interest. It is believed to be the tomb of Eleanor Percy who died in 1328. The shrine has a beautifully carved Gothic canopy. The Archbishop of York owned Beverley so the town had neither its own castle or protector. So the Percy family, whose castle was at Leconfield, some 2½ miles from the town, was considered to be the town's protector.

The carvings under the seats of the choirstalls are sixteenth-century misericords and show many scenes from medieval life.

The Frith stool is older than the Minster.

The Norman font is huge.

Skidby Mill

CHAPTER XVIII
BEVERLEY PARKS CROSSING TO TURTLE HILL

Length of section: linear: 8 miles (12.8km)

Distance covered walking clockwise from Hessle: 185 miles (300km)

Walk 35:	Beverley Parks Crossing - Skidby - Bentley - Beverley Parks Crossing 7¾ miles (12.4km)
Walk 36:	Skidby - Turtle Hill - Little Weighton - Skidby 8½ miles (13.6km)
Map Ref:	Landranger 106 and 107
Parking:	Roadside at Beverley Parks Crossing, but check with the residents first. Roadside parking in Skidby but, again, check with residents first.
Handy hostelries:	The Half Moon, Skidby. The Black Horse Inn, Little Weighton.

WALK 35. BEVERLEY PARKS CROSSING - SKIDBY - BENTLEY - BEVERLEY PARKS CROSSING.

From Beverley Parks Crossing turn right, briefly, to a road junction where turn left along a surfaced road, guided by footpath and bridleway signs. Where the surfaced road curves right, continue straight ahead along an unsurfaced road, passing a sign which says "Private Road: Model Farm And Poplar Farm Only". Continue along the road, which is a right of way, passing a signpost that points left. Keep straight ahead, along the road to the farm in front of you. Pass the buildings on the left, still on the road which continues with a hedge on the right and a fence on the left. Go through a facing gateway and immediately turn left, directed by a yellow waymark, still on the unsurfaced road, close to a hedge now on your left. On approaching a bridge over the A1079(T) the road becomes surfaced. Once over the bridge, keep straight ahead, towards the next farm, seen ahead, still on the road which soon becomes unsurfaced again as it cuts between huge fields. On reaching the farm continue past the buildings on your left and, on approaching the farm house, turn left and leave the farm along a narrow lane that curves left.

The high rise flats over on the left are in Cottingham.

On reaching a post with a

WALK 35

yellow waymark on it, go left, edging a field, close to a high hedge on your right. Go through a facing gateway and continue still close to a hedge on your right, edging the field.

The farm beyond this field is Burn Park. On reaching it turn left, directed by a yellow waymark, passing farm buildings on the right. A short distance along the farm road turn right at a yellow waymark, cross a stile and go over a short field, keeping to the right of a group of tall beech trees. Exit over a facing stile, cross a second small field, leaving over a stile in a facing fence, cross the next field, bearing slightly left and cross a waymarked and signposted stile in the fence on your left, near the field corner. Edge the next field, close to the hedge on your right. On reaching a facing hedge at the field's right-hand corner, turn left, alongside it for a few yards, then right, through a broad, waymarked gap. Continue along the edge of the next field, close to a hedge on your right.

Although waymarked, the path edging these fields is somewhat overgrown through lack of use, which is a pity because the surrounding countryside is very lovely. Perhaps the local authority could help by cutting a swathe through the offending bits and lopping the odd branch.

On reaching the field's right-hand corner turn left, along a broad farm track that edges the field close to a hedge on the right. In about 100 yards, just past a hedge on your right that meets you end on, turn right at a yellow waymark. Immediately cross a plank bridge and continue up the right-hand edge of the field ahead, full of barley when we passed through it.

At the end of the field, continue past some caravans onto a surfaced lane and continue forward, aiming for the A164, just ahead on an embankment. At the lane end cross facing B1233 and keep straight ahead, directed by a yellow arrow. Edge a field close to a hedge on your left, climb onto the facing embankment up some steps to a signpost and cross the A164, with care, to another signpost. Turn left for a few yards and turn right to descend steps to the foot of the embankment, directed by a yellow arrow. Cross a waymarked stile in a facing fence, turn left, alongside this fence and at the field corner turn right. Edge the left-hand side of the field, leaving it through a facing metal gate near the field's left-hand corner. Turn left along a surfaced road, uphill[1], to a crossroads[2] where turn right into Skidby[3], entering this very beautiful village along a roadside footpath. Continue along the roadside as far as St Michael's church, sited on the left-hand side of the road.

From opposite the church go along Church Lane and continue straight ahead, through a gate with a bridleway marker and keep ahead along a descending green lane that goes through an avenue of overhanging hawthorn trees.

199

Where a track crosses your line of walk at an angle, ignore it and continue straight ahead to reach the lower of two facing gates. Cross a stile to the right of it and follow a pleasant, wooded path, climbing steadily. When the path splits take the clearer, left-hand one that crosses a short rise out of the wood and immediately turns right to edge a field alongside the wood on the right. Where the field curves right, a blue waymarker confirms your route. The track meanders, turning right, then sharp left at a blue waymarker. However the path is so clear you simply can't go wrong.

On reaching a surfaced road, cross it diagonally to a waymarked stile and continue along a little lane that edges a wood on the left. The wood is called Fish Pond Wood and there is a big pond in the middle of it. Where the lane ends, keep on the path which now edges the left-hand side of a field of peas, still alongside the wood on the left. Where the thick, older part of the wood ends, continue ahead, directed by a yellow waymark, descending into a fold of the land. On reaching a waymark at the bottom of the dip, keep straight ahead, still with the wood on your left, climbing steadily through a field of wheat. Where the path bifurcates, keep straight ahead, uphill, leaving the wood on the left. Another waymark on a telegraph post confirms your route, but really the path is so broad and clear that following it presents no problems. Leave the field over a waymarked stile onto a minor road and turn right, along it. Where, at a road sign to Cottingham, the road turns sharp right, keep straight ahead along a surfaced lane to the hamlet of Bentley[4], from where the view of Beverley Minster is good.

Go through the hamlet and on reaching a junction with the busy A164 turn left, briefly, along a roadside footpath to a bus shelter at the end of it. From there, cross the A164 and continue along a public bridleway, an unsurfaced road, directed by a bridleway sign. Where the road makes a sharp right turn to edge a wood on the right, keep straight ahead, along a path between fields, directed by a footpath sign.

When the path reaches a fence at a tangent, beyond which is the A1079(T), continue right, alongside this fence on your left, now with the path becoming a lane, heading for a bridge over the motorway seen ahead. Where the lane ends continue along the left-hand side of a field to join a path that leads up to the bridge, the very one used on the outward leg. Turn left, over it, and simply retrace your steps to Beverley Parks Crossing.

Things Seen On The Way

(1) Skidby Landscape. Skidby occupies the rising ground on either side of a prominent dry valley that runs through the main part of the parish. The chalk lies close to the surface on the Wolds in the west and on the valley side close

to the village but elsewhere the parish is covered with boulder clay.

Poor drainage of the low lying ground was causing problems in the seventeenth century when local dykes and sluices were inadequate to deal with it. Flooding was sometimes severe, as in 1782, when low ground was described as being "truly deplorable having laid all this year under water." Conditions were improved under the Beverley And Skidby Drainage Act of 1785 by the cutting of a drain which came to be called the Western Drain. The Beverley and Barmston Drain was cut across the area circa 1800. Most of the Parish is now in arable use.

At one time Skidby village was surrounded by open fields which were separated from those of Cottingham by a prominent hedge bank. These open fields and commons were enclosed in 1765 and the common meadows and pastures on the low ground were enclosed in 1788. Other open fields, wold pasture and the local sheep walk were enclosed in 1795.

(2) Skidby Windmill. If, instead of turning right at the crossroads you keep straight ahead, Skidby's famous windmill will soon be reached. There has been a windmill in Skidby since 1388 and in the early seventeenth century there were two, but they were demolished after a dispute. Later, a mill stood at Hindecrafts to the west of the village and a post mill smaller than the present one, was on that site in 1764. It was replaced by the present mill in 1821. The builder was Robert Garton, a Beverley millwright and the Thompson family acquired it in 1854. It was worked by wind for a hundred years when, in 1954, electrically driven plant was installed. It ceased working commercially in 1966.

Skidby Mill is blacktarred and has four white sails, each of which weighs 1.25 tonnes. It has an elegant white-painted Lincolnshire cap and its fantail provides a graceful foil to the great sails, providing a superb hilltop landmark. There is a museum in one of the outbuildings. Until 1929 six shire horses worked at the mill, drawing three single-horse and one double-horse rulleys (four wheeled carts). Then the first lorry arrived and two of the horses became redundant.

During World War II the millowners organised a fire watch from the mill tower from 6.00pm to 7.00am. There was a direct link between the mill and Cottingham police station. The closest the mill came to being bombed was when a stick of small bombs fell into the fields behind Mount Pleasant Farm on the other side of the road from it.

(3) Skidby. Probably a Danish settlement, Skidby is Old Norse and is derived from the by-name Skyti, meaning "Sykti's settlement". Or it might have been derived from "Scite" with the Norse "sk" used in later forms, meaning "dirty farm". A third possibility is "Schite's byre". A copy of a charter dated

972 mentions the name "Scyteby" and the Domesday Book refers to "Schitebi". Between 860 and 960 the Vikings made many probing raids and eventually they settled to farm the land. Halfdan, leader of the Viking army, returned to this area in 874 and allotted land to the leaders of his host, in agreement with the ealdormen. The arrangement of the vilage, a straight track leading to a main road, is typically Danish.

The village green was originally a pond near the church which became contaminated and was filled in. Another pond, in front of the school, suffered the same fate and a third, known as Slut Hole, on the eastern side of the village was filled in recently.

The old Smithy was situated adjacent to the green but is no longer there. Two pumps stood opposite 99 and 101 Main Street, the western one being for horses, and the other for general use.

Walter de Gray, 27th Archbishop of York, gave land for a building in the village in 1227 but the earliest recorded evidence of the building of St Michael's church was in 1552. For much of its life the church in Skidby was under the control of the vicars and rectors of Cottingham. Then, in 1857, the parish of Skidby was created a separate entity.

The village pub, the Half Moon Inn, was probably built in the seventeenth century and mentioned as an inn circa 1830. Its original beams remain unaltered.

(4) Bentley. Meaning "a clearing overgrown with coarse grass", Bentley is a very small settlement of about a dozen houses, half of them dating from the eighteenth and nineteenth centuries. The earliest farm houses in the area were recorded here, one in Rigg Wood being mentioned in 1600. It is thought that West End Farm occupies the site of the manor house. The Manor was held in the twelfth century by the Trussebut family who were succeeded by the De Ros and Bentley families.

WALK 36. SKIDBY - TURTLE HILL - LITTLE WEIGHTON - SKIDBY.

From St Michael's church, Skidby, go left, westwards, through the village and where the road splits take the left-hand fork and continue out of the village, passing the cemetery on the left. Stay on the road, passing a farm on the right and the lane end to a private farm on the left. Continue along this very quiet road through an area of oil seed rape stained red with poppies. Soon a bridge carrying a disused railway is reached. Go under it and, ignoring a bridleway path to the left, keep straight ahead along what has now become

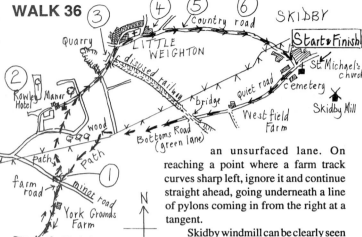

WALK 36

an unsurfaced lane. On reaching a point where a farm track curves sharp left, ignore it and continue straight ahead, going underneath a line of pylons coming in from the right at a tangent.

Skidby windmill can be clearly seen on the horizon behind.

On reaching a crossing of tracks, keep straight ahead, now on a fairly narrow path, close to a hedge on your left, aiming for a wood, seen ahead. At a broad gap in the hedge on the left marked with a blue bridleway sign, turn left, through it and go along a green lane, slightly uphill.

The line of pylons is now marching away from you on the right.

At the field corner where the green lane splits, take the right-hand path, edging a hedge on the left, skirting a field of corn.

Over on the left both supporting towers of the Humber bridge can be clearly seen.

Where the path turns left at a field corner, a waymark confirms your route. On reaching a facing road at a footpath sign turn left, along it, for 60 yards to another footpath sign and turn right along a farm road to York Grounds Farm, guided by a bridleway sign. On reaching the farm turn right at a facing building, directed by a yellow arrow on a pole, and take a climbing, clear track that curves to the left. Where it descends a slope to reach a crossing of paths it meets the Wolds Way and this is the apex of this section.

From here, there being no reasonable means of making a circular, retrace your steps to the minor road where the farm road to York Grounds Farm joins it. The surrounding countryside is so beautiful and you have stunning views of the same landscape from a different angle, so retracing your steps for about

³/₄ mile becomes a joy.

On reaching the road end to York Grounds Farm, turn left along the minor road and, ignoring the first signpost on the right, the one used on the outward leg, continue along it for a further 120 yards and turn right at a waymarked signpost. Cross the right-hand side of a field.

At the end of the field don't continue through a gap in the hedge. Instead, turn left, along the top of the field close to a hedge on your right, cutting across the line of pylons passed on the outward leg and at the field corner, go through a broad gap in the hedge. Continue, close to the right-hand side of the next field for about 45 yards to reach a post with a yellow waymark on it. Now go diagonally left, along a clear path and with Rowley Manor Hotel[1] seen ahead. Leave the field at a footpath sign, cross a surfaced, minor road and enter a field on its far side at another footpath sign. A clear path goes straight across it to a waymarked stile in a facing fence, which cross. Continue straight across the field ahead, a pasture speckled with buttercups and daisies, leaving at a waymarked stile to the left of a gate in the field's far corner. Cross the next field, a short, narrow one leaving over a stile on your right close to the field's right-hand corner. Now go diagonally left, across an area of rough pasture, approaching a road on the left at a tangent and aiming for a wicket leading into a copse close to the field's left-hand corner. Go through it and turn left for a few steps to join the Rowley Manor Hotel drive opposite Rowley Lodge. The gateway is guarded by two golden eagles. Turn right, along the drive and continue along the road, passing a watertower on your right, where a sign informs that you have arrived at Little Weighton. Keep ahead, soon to cross a bridge over a disused railway[2], pass the railway station on the left and a chalk quarry that was used a lot during World War II and is now being filled in. Bear right, through the village[3] and at the far end of it, where the road splits, take the right-hand fork, curving uphill and follow it all the way to Skidby about 1¹/₃ miles distant.

The surrounding views are panoramic and Beverley Minster is clearly seen to your left. On reaching Skidby, continue through the village to St Michael's church to complete the circle.

Things Seen On The Way

(1) Rowley. Meaning "rough hill", Rowley is famous for its depopulation, which began in 1638. Disenchanted at having to read the Book of Sports in church on the sabbath, the Rev. Ezekiel Rogers and many of the villagers set sail from Hull for life in the New World. They settled in a small township on the eastern seaboard of the United States which came to be known as Rowley

and is, today, a suburb of Ipswich, Massachusettes. The original village no longer exists but the church of St Peter's, which this walk edges, and the former rectory, now the Rowley Manor Hotel, remain.

(2) The Hull, Barnsley and West Riding Junction Railway. Opened in 1885, it was closed to passengers in 1955 and completely to the west of Little Weighton in 1964. Although the track has been lifted the large red brick station at Little Weighton still stands.

(3) Little Weighton. Set at a point where several winding rural roads converge at the bottom of a dry valley, Little Weighton is a typical Wolds linear village. Its name is thought to mean "little dwelling place". The estate, including the manor, was first mentioned in 1353 and belonged at various times to the De-Stutevilles, the Lounds, and the Waines, the Broadleys and the Wilsons. The new part of the village developed with the arrival of the railways.

There are many chalk pits in the vicinity of Little Weighton and this came about because at the time of the enclosure local people were awarded the right to extract chalk for the building of homes and roads. No.2, Little Weighton Road is a typical local chalk block dwelling.

CHAPTER XIX
TURTLE HILL TO HESSLE

Length of section: linear: 8¹/₂ miles (13.6km)

Distance covered walking clockwise from Hessle: 197 miles 315.2km)

Walk 37:	Circular: Welton - headland path - Wauldby Manor Farm - Turtle Hill - Welton Dale - Welton. 5 miles (8km)
Walk 38:	Linear: Welton - North Ferriby - Humber Bridge detour - Hessle. 9 miles, including 1¹/₂ mile each way Humber Bridge detour (14.4km)
Map Ref:	Landranger 106 and 107
Parking:	Roadside in Welton, but check with the residents first. Car park on the southern limit of North Ferriby, original start of the Wolds Way. Parking area beneath the Humber Bridge and near the Ferry Boat Inn, Hessle.
Handy hostelries:	The Green Dragon, Welton. Country Park Inn, near the Humber Bridge. The Ferry Boat Inn, Hessle.

WALK 37. WELTON - HEADLAND PATH - WAULDBY MANOR FARM - TURTLE HILL - WELTON DALE - WELTON.

Turtle Hill marks the point where the southwards route along the eastern side of the Wolds joins the northwards, Wolds Way, route. From here onward to Hessle the two routes coincide. This little gem of a circular is routed from Welton simply because it is more sensible to park in a village that is actually on the route than to use a roadside that is not.

Besides, the Green Dragon, in Welton, is conveniently sited for an end of section snifter.

From the front of Welton Hall, at the eastern end of the village, cross the end of Dale Road and leave Welton along Chapel Hill Road that climbs onto Welton Wold. At the far end of a large wood that edges the road on the left, turn right, still edging the wood and go forward to the rim of Welton Dale[1]. Turn right, along it, using a clear, grassy track, the headland path that coincides with the Beverley 20. Soon Welton Wold Plantation is edged on the left and Welton Wold Farm is passed on the right. Continue past a thin wood on the left, soon to leave it along the left-hand side of a field. There is now a plantation on the left, beyond which Wauldby Manor Farm[2] is passed. When a pond is passed on the left, leave the field and turn left, directed by a Wolds Way sign. In a short distance, on approaching a farm house, just ahead, turn right at another Wolds Way sign. Continue straight ahead, along a broad green track that meanders slightly, then turns right at a yellow waymark, soon to reach a crossing of tracks. This is Turtle Hill, meeting point of the outward and inward routes. It makes a very pleasant butty stop.

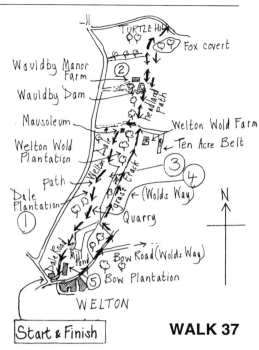

WALK 37

Retrace your steps to the south end of the field of barley where turn right at a Wolds Way sign. Edge a plantation on your left to reach another Wolds Way sign, where turn left, over a stile, cross a concrete lane and continue along a clear path through Welton Wold Plantation, exiting at a waymarked stile. Continue down the bottom of Welton Dale[3] with Dale Plantation[4] on your right and scrub on the dale's other side. Leave the grassy path through a small kissing gate to the right of the main gate and continue along Dale Road to Welton Hall at the far end of it.

Things Seen On The Way

(1) Welton Dale. This dale is one of the most secluded and unspoilt valleys in Humberside.

(2) Wauldby Manor Chapel. Glimpsed, like the manor, over the brown waters of a pond, the chapel, which dates from the nineteenth century, is no

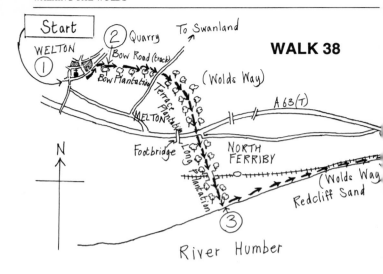

longer used.

(3) Welton Dale Track. This track was the most bitterly contested footpath in Humberside due to landowner's objection. But, thanks to the efforts of people like David Rubenstein, who contested the matter strongly, this delightful walk, along with other Wolds footpaths is now open to the public and gives much pleasure to all who walk it. This is proof, if proof be needed, that walkers, be they members of worthwhile bodies like the R.A. or not, are responsible country lovers whose interest in the wellbeing of the countryside is as strong as that of the landowners, whose fears are groundless.

(4) Dale Plantation. The trees in Welton Dale consist of ash, beech and conifers and were planted during the Victorian "age of improvement".

(5) Welton High Mill. This five storey brick and tile building, which was worked by water until 1946 and by electricity as late as 1966, had a wheel which had 120 buckets. It was a flour mill.

WALK 38. WELTON - NORTH FERRIBY - HUMBER BRIDGE DETOUR - HESSLE.

From the front of Welton Hall cross the end of the Dale Road and leave

Welton[1] along Chapel Hill Road that climbs onto Welton Wold and on leaving the village turn right, along a clear path, into woodland. Where the path splits, go left, just inside the wood's right-hand edge[2]. After a while the path curves left to exit the wood over a stile at a Wolds Way sign. Turn right, down the middle of a very wide lane that descends to a kissing gate to the right of a large gate, which go through. Immediately cross the Melton to Swanland road, going diagonally right, to enter woodland over a stile to the right of a gate. Continue into Terrace Plantation along a broad track to reach a waymarked stile at a scout's camping site, which cross to continue along this long, slender wood on a clear, descending path and exit over a stile onto the verge of the busy A63T. Cross the road with great care and turn right briefly, to go through a gate on the left into Long Plantation.

Should the A63T be really busy, and it usually is, turn right immediately on crossing the stile out of the wood, along a broad verge, to a nearby footbridge, which cross, and go left, edging the road, to reach a gate on your right leading into Long Plantation. Better to be safe than sorry; and this detour is a slight one.

Take the clear track through this long, narrow woodland, bridging the main railway line from Selby to Hull, and skirting, on the left, housing on the edge of North Ferriby to reach the Humber Estuary foreshore[3] down a flight of steps. Turn left, along the foreshore, close to a boulder barrier on your left, at the end of which climb some roughly hewn steps to a signpost. Now turn right, along the edge of the Humber Estuary, on your right, and continue along it all the way to the Country Park Inn, near the Humber Bridge.

Pass in front of this restaurant and turn left to continue past a windmill on your left to enter the Humber Bridge Country Park[4]. Go under a road, using an underpass and in a short distance go under the railway on another short underpass, beyond which turn right, along a path that climbs towards the northern end of the Humber Bridge. The path is stepped and leads to a kissing gate, which go through. Keep straight ahead on a broad level,

209

unsurfaced path, soon to join a surfaced path that curves left towards the approach road to a large car park, seen ahead, So far along the path turn right, up a narrow path that climbs to the same approach road, joining it higher up. Cross the road and go right, uphill, along the roadside footpath. Go under the Humber Bridge[5] and immediately turn left, up steps, to join a surfaced path and turn left, along it, making a spectacular crossing of the one mile long Humber Bridge[6], all the way to South Humberside.

Leave the bridge, surrounded by beautiful views, particularly of the Estuary, onto a grassy embankment overlooking Barton-Upon-Humber, where it is good to linger a while.

Retrace your steps to the north side and down, through the Humber Bridge Country Park to the riverside, where go left, under the bridge, and along the shore to the nearby inlet that is Hessle Haven, where stands The Ferry Boat Inn, where it all began many memorable adventures ago.

Having downed a celebratory couple of pints, turn right from the pub, along Livingstone Road to turn right into Hessle railway station from where there is a frequent train service to Brough. Leave the station northwards, briefly, to the nearby Buccaneer Inn, where go right to a T-junction, then left, to a crossroads in the middle of Brough, where turn right, along the main road to Welton, where you left the car.

Things Seen On The Way

(1) Welton. Welton is a picturesque and popular village with an attractive village green, a small stream, a large pond and many fine houses and cottages.

(2) Bow Plantation. From the path through this narrow wood the views over the Humber Estuary are excellent. The Romans used the Humber as a naval base and established a fort at Brough which grew into the town of "Petuvaria." It stands on the line of Ermine Street, the road from Lincoln to York.

(3) Humber Estuary Foreshore. At North Ferriby the Humber is two miles wide. Three miles down stream, at Hessle, it is only one mile wide. The Humber Bridge was built at Hessle.

The Humber Estuary, with its intertidal mud, rich in bivalve molluscs and polychaete worms, is one of the most important bird feeding grounds along the east coast. During the spring and autumn, waders that, like dunlins, redshanks and oyster catchers, are present for most of the time, are joined by large numbers of knots, curlews, bar-tailed godwits, sanderlings and grey and ringed plovers. Among the ducks, shelduck, mallard, teal and vigeons are residents for most of the year while upwards of 10,000 pink-footed geese winter annually on Blacktoft Sand, an R.S.P.B. Nature Reserve and Whitton Sand, which is a Humber wildlife refuge and, despite its name, is mostly mud.

4) Humber Bridge Country Park. A chalk quarry was recorded on this site as far back as 1317 and continued down the centuries. When, eventually, quarrying stopped, grasses, flowering plants, shrubs and trees began to over the bare, white chalk and in the deepest parts of the quarry, ponds formed. Plans were drawn up to use the quarry as a tip; but when, in 1981, the Humber Bridge was opened, the quarry's potential to attract visitors was realised and plans for the tip were abandoned in favour of a country park. In 1983 work started on this 19 hectares, (48 acres), site, using Manpower Services Commission teams who transformed it into a fascinating mixture of meadows, woodland, water areas and steep cliffs, complete with the remains of a five-sailed windmill. The park is made up of three areas, Hessle Quarry, Little Switzerland and the Foreshore, where the windmill's remains stand. Work was completed in 1986 when the park was opened.

The plants which came into the quarry were brought in when back filling of the pits occurred and as seeds blown in from neighbouring gardens and trains on the nearby railway. Today purple flowered buddleia are a major feature of the park and attract lots of butterflies. There are many sycamores and hawthorns, along with ash, holly, whitebeam, wild cherry and wild rose. Collectively, all the trees and shrubs, together with the meadows and the water areas, have encouraged many birds, insects and other animals to live in the park.

From the foreshore entrance there is wheelchair and pushchair access to all parts of the park, which has marked circular routes, a nature trail and rangers to provide help and information to visitors.

5) Humber Bridge Footpath. Two footpaths-cum-cycle ways cross the Humber Bridge, one on each side of and slightly below the main area designated for vehicles. When we crossed it, only the eastern path was open; but sometimes the situation can be reversed. So, on reaching the bridge, if the western path on to it is open, there is no need to go under the bridge before climbing onto it, as we had to do.

6) The Humber Bridge. It is a masterpiece of British design and engineering skills. Construction began on 27th July, 1972, and the bridge was officially opened on 17th July, 1981, by Her Majesty the Queen.

For the very first time, in a major suspension bridge, the main towers are of reinforced concrete instead of steel. From end to end the bridge is 7,284 feet (3,220m) or almost $1^{1}/_{2}$ miles long, the main span being 4,626 feet (1,410m), the north side span 919 feet (280m), the south side span 1,739 feet (530m) and the clearance above high water being 98 feet (30m). The bridge carries dual two-lane carriageways plus separate footpaths and the deck width is 93.5 feet (28.5m). The towers are 510 feet (155.5m) high above the piers. The Humber Bridge has the longest single span of any bridge in the world which means, in less technical language, that it is one hell of a bridge!

SELECTED BIBLIOGRAPHY

Allison,K.J.   *The East Riding Of Yorkshire Landscape*
                      Hodder and Stoughton 1976

Arnold,Sylvia M.   *Wild Flowers Of The Yorkshire Wolds*
                      Hutton Press 1985

Broadhead,Ivan A.   *Portrait of Humberside*
                      Robert Hale 1983

Eastwood,Geoff   *Walking In East Yorkshire*
                      G.Eastwood

Elliot,Stephen C.   *Bird Watching In East Yorkshire:*
                      The Humber And Teesmouth
                      Hutton Press 1989

Ratcliffe,Roger   *The Wolds Way*
                      H.M.S.O. 1982

Rubinstein,David   *The Wolds Way*
                      Dalesman Books 1979

Wallis,R.   *The Minster Way*
                      Lockington.

CICERONE GUIDES

Cicerone publish a wide range of reliable guides to walking and climbing in Britain, and other general interest books.

LAKE DISTRICT - General Books
A DREAM OF EDEN
LAKELAND VILLAGES
LAKELAND TOWNS
REFLECTIONS ON THE LAKES
OUR CUMBRIA
THE HIGH FELLS OF LAKELAND
CONISTON COPPER A History
LAKELAND - A taste to remember (Recipes)
THE LOST RESORT? (Morecambe)
CHRONICLES OF MILNTHORPE
LOST LANCASHIRE (Furness area)
THE PRIORY OF CARTMEL

LAKE DISTRICT - Guide Books
CASTLES IN CUMBRIA
THE CUMBRIA CYCLE WAY
WESTMORLAND HERITAGE WALK
IN SEARCH OF WESTMORLAND
CONISTON COPPER MINES Field Guide
SCRAMBLES IN THE LAKE DISTRICT
MORE SCRAMBLES IN THE LAKE DISTRICT
SHORT WALKS - SOUTH LAKELAND
WINTER CLIMBS IN THE LAKE DISTRICT
WALKS IN SILVERDALE/ARNSIDE
BIRDS OF MORECAMBE BAY
THE EDEN WAY
WALKING ROUND THE LAKES

NORTHERN ENGLAND (outside the Lakes
BIRDWATCHING ON MERSEYSIDE
CANAL WALKS Vol 1 North
CANOEISTS GUIDE TO THE NORTH EAST
THE CLEVELAND WAY & MISSING LINK
THE DALES WAY
DOUGLAS VALLEY WAY
HADRIANS WALL Vol 1 The Wall Walk
HERITAGE TRAILS IN NW ENGLAND
THE ISLE OF MAN COASTAL PATH
IVORY TOWERS & DRESSED STONES (Follies)
THE LANCASTER CANAL
LANCASTER CANAL WALKS
LAUGHS ALONG THE PENNINE WAY
A NORTHERN COAST-TO-COAST
NORTH YORK MOORS Walks
THE REIVERS WAY (Northumberland)
THE RIBBLE WAY
ROCK CLIMBS LANCASHIRE & NW
THE YORKSHIRE DALES A walker's guide
WALKING IN THE SOUTH PENNINES
WALKING IN THE NORTH PENNINES
WALKS IN THE YORKSHIRE DALES (3 VOL)
WALKS IN LANCASHIRE WITCH COUNTRY
WALKS IN THE NORTH YORK MOORS
WALKS TO YORKSHIRE WATERFALLS (2 vol)
WALKS ON THE WEST PENNINE MOORS
WALKING NORTHERN RAILWAYS (2 vol)
WALKING IN THE WOLDS

DERBYSHIRE & EAST MIDLANDS
WHITE PEAK WALKS - 2 Vols
HIGH PEAK WALKS
WHITE PEAK WAY
KINDER LOG
THE VIKING WAY
THE DEVIL'S MILL / WHISTLING CLOUGH (Novels)

WALES & WEST MIDLANDS
THE RIDGES OF SNOWDONIA
HILLWALKING IN SNOWDONIA
HILL WALKING IN WALES (2 Vols)
ASCENT OF SNOWDON
WELSH WINTER CLIMBS
SNOWDONIA WHITE WATER SEA & SURF
SCRAMBLES IN SNOWDONIA
SARN HELEN Walking Roman Road
ROCK CLIMBS IN WEST MIDLANDS
THE SHROPSHIRE HILLS A Walker's Guide
HEREFORD & THE WYE VALLEY A Walker's Guide
THE WYE VALLEY WALK

SOUTH & SOUTH WEST ENGLAND
COTSWOLD WAY
EXMOOR & THE QUANTOCKS
THE KENNET & AVON WALK
THE SOUTHERN-COAST-TO-COAST
SOUTH DOWNS WAY & DOWNS LINK
SOUTH WEST WAY - 2 Vol
WALKING IN THE CHILTERNS
WALKING ON DARTMOOR
WALKERS GUIDE TO DARTMOOR PUBS
WALKS IN KENT
THE WEALDWAY & VANGUARD WAY

SCOTLAND
THE BORDER COUNTRY - WALKERS GUIDE
SCRAMBLES IN LOCHABER
SCRAMBLES IN SKYE
THE ISLAND OF RHUM
CAIRNGORMS WINTER CLIMBS
THE CAIRNGORM GLENS (Mountainbike Guide)
THE ATHOLL GLENS (Mountainbike Guide)
WINTER CLIMBS BEN NEVIS & GLENCOE
SCOTTISH RAILWAY WALKS
TORRIDON A Walker's Guide
SKI TOURING IN SCOTLAND

REGIONAL BOOKS UK & IRELAND
THE MOUNTAINS OF ENGLAND & WALES
   VOL 1 WALES VOL 2 ENGLAND
THE MOUNTAINS OF IRELAND
THE ALTERNATIVE PENNINE WAY
THE PACKHORSE BRIDGES OF ENGLAND
THE RELATIVE HILLS OF BRITAIN
LIMESTONE - 100 BEST CLIMBS

Also a full range of EUROPEAN and OVERSEAS guidebooks - walking, long distance trails, scrambling, ice-climbing, rock climbing.

Other guides are constantly being added to the Cicerone List.
Available from bookshops, outdoor equipment shops or direct (send s.a.e. for price list) from
CICERONE, 2 POLICE SQUARE, MILNTHORPE, CUMBRIA, LA7 7PY

215

Printed by CARNMOR PRINT & DESIGN, 95-97 LONDON ROAD, PRESTON, LANCASHIRE, UK.